4-600. Bon-Bon Dish, bright finish, fancy handle and feet, fluted border, silver lined, as cut ... 1.50 Gold lined 1.75 Other styles ... 2.25 2.50

4-601. Pickle Cruet, bright finish, fancy feet and handle, with decorated ruby glass, n side, as cut ... 1.90 ame style, without feet, plain ass ... 1.85 ther styles, crystal glass ... and ... 2.85

read Tray, satin engraved fin d "Bread" or "Best Wishes", order, as cut ... 2.25 ame style, bright edge 2.50 Different style ... 3.50 Butter Dish, satin engraved bright base, glass drainer, as ... 3.50 r style ... 3.75

4-608. Different styles, without bale 2.25 3.25 and ... 3.50

4-609. Butter Dish, glass base, silver-plated lid ... 1.25

607. oast Rack, finish, six ous, as cut ... 2.50

Fern Pot, Filigree pattern, ex-

4-621. Nut Bowl, bright finish, floral border, gold-lined, as cut ... 4.25
4-622. Other styles ... 6.00 and ... 8.00
4-623. Biscuit Jar, dark green China, painted floral design, silver lid, as cut ... 3.25
4-624. Wave Crest ware, square ... 4.00
4-625. Silver plated Biscuit Jar ... 2.65
4-626. Cut glass pattern, silver top ... .85
4-627. Dessert Set, satin engraved finish, cream jug and bowl of spoon gold-lined, as cut ... 4.25
4-628. Cream and Sugar only, in satin lined case 2.25

4-630. Card Tray, bright edge, satin engraved centre, as cut ... 1.50
4-631. Card Receiver, on stand, round shape, silver lined ... 2.25 Gold lined ... 2.75

Set, satin engraved, fancy feet and border, spoon holder and cream jug gold lined, with tray, as cut ... 14.00 Without Tray ... 9.
4-616. Four-piece Set, bright fluted tern ... 14 With Coffee Pot 19
4-617. Same style, e handles, four piece 15.00 with Co Pot ... 22.00
4-618. Tea Set, bright finish, sterling silver ... 17.75
4-619. Round Waiters, satin engraved finish, 12 in., 3.50 15 in. ... 4.50
4-620. Square Waiters, 14 in., with handles ... 6.25 17 in. ... 8.75

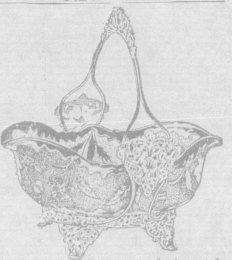

4-634. Berry Dish, ne design, ruby glass, gold decorated, as cut ... 4.65
4-635. Other styles ... 4.00 5.00

4-636. Baker or Pudding Dish, fitted with extra rim and porcelain dish ... 5.75
4-637. Plainer styles ... 3.95 5.25

4-638. Sugar Bowl, twelve spoon rests fitted with tipped pattern spoons, as cut 4.30 Cheaper quality 3.33 Fancy pattern ... 5.90
4-639. Same without spoons ... 2.90

4-642. Din Cruet, 5 ro bottles, br embossed terns, rev ing stand cut ... 2. Other sty satin eng ed finis round bot 3.35 Squ bottles 4. Low rev ing stand bossed p tern, squ bottles 5.

4-643. Din Cruet, l revolvi stand, squ bottles 5.

4-644. Child's Cup, satin engraved, gold lined, as cut ... .50 Larger ... .75 and ... 1.00

4-645. Cake Basket, satin engrav fancy feet and border, silver lir as cut ... 3. Gold lined ... 3.
4-646. Cake Basket, square sha engraved centre, burnished ed silver lined ... 4 Gold lined ... 6
4-647. Three-piece Berry Set, fit pattern, beaded border, gold lin ... 7.
4-648. Berry Bowl only ... 4
4-649. Cream and Sugar of set, pair ... 4.
4-650. Breakfast Cruet, satin finish, fitted with decorated ruby glass shakers, as cut ... 1.50
4-651. Similar style, bright finish ... 1.75
4-652. Breakfast Cruet, Wish-bone design, fitted with wave crest ware bottles ... 2.

4-653. Cr Glass Ce Holder, f pattern, fi in silver ed sta bright fin fancy bo as cut ... 2

5-002 5-003

_. Side Combs, French make, shell, amber black, per pair.................... .05

_. Heavier quality, style as above, French ke, pair.................... .10

_. Side Combs, shell color, straight or curv-pair.................... .15

5-004 5-005

_. American make, heavy top, finely finish-pair.................... .25

_. American make, extra heavy, tortoise ll color, highly polished, pair............. .50

PUFF OR BACK COMBS

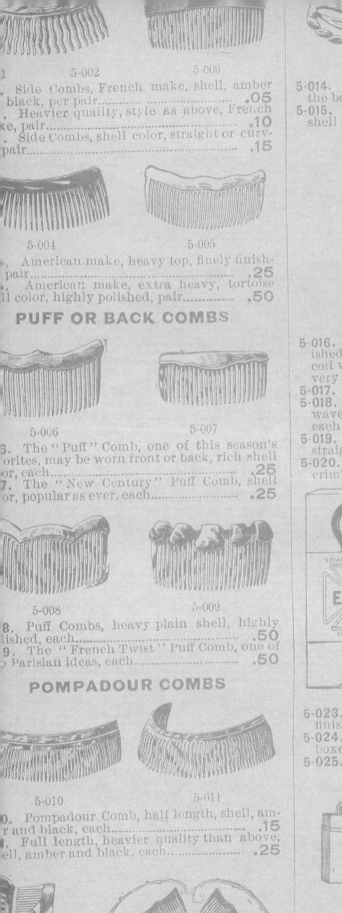

5-006 5-007

6. The "Puff" Comb, one of this season's orites, may be worn front or back, rich shell or, each.................... .25

7. The "New Century" Puff Comb, shell or, popular as ever, each.................... .25

5-008 5-009

8. Puff Combs, heavy plain shell, highly lished, each.................... .50

9. The "French Twist" Puff Comb, one of Parisian ideas, each.................... .50

POMPADOUR COMBS

5-010 5-011

0. Pompadour Comb, half length, shell, am-r and black, each.................... .15

_. Full length, heavier quality than above, ell, amber and black, each.................... .25

5-012 5-013

12. The New Pompadour Comb, (3 in one), it

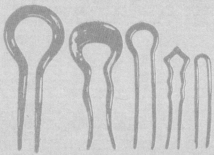

5-014 5-015

5-014. Hair Clasps, for holding the stray hairs at the back, shell color, each.................... .25

5-015. The "Miss Simplicity" Hair Retainer, shell color, each.................... .25

BONE HAIR PINS

5-016 5-017 5 018 5-019 5-020

5-016. Bone Hair Pins, extra large, highly polished, these are worn one on each side of the coil when the hair is dressed low, shell color, very popular, each.................... .25

5-017. Lighter weight, 2 for.................... .25

5-018. Bone Hair Pins, long, heavy quality, waved and crimped, shell, amber and black, each.................... .05

5-019. Bone Hair Pins, black, amber and shell, straight, per doz.................... .35

5-020. Bone Hair Pins, black, amber and shell, crimped, per doz.................... .35

5 021. "Earl Brand" Hair Pins, black, shell and amber, crimped, waved or straight, medium size, smoothly polished, put up one dozen in neat box, per box........ .25

5-021

WIRE HAIR PINS

5-022. Wire Hair Pins, best japanned, English make, crimped or straight, 2½ to 3¾ ins. long, 2 pkgs.... .05

5-023. Wire Hair Pins, light and strong, japan finish, 3 pkgs.................... .10

5-024. Invisible Hair Pins, gilt, 25 pins in box, 3 boxes.................... .10

5-025. Hair Pins, gilt, large size, crimped or plain, box containing 18 pins.................... .05

5-026. Invisible Hair Pins, best japanned, 50 in box, assorted sizes, 2 boxes.................... .05

5-027. Hair Pin Cabinet, containing 80 hair pins, assorted sizes, each .05

5-027

HAIR CURLERS

5-028. Waving Pins, for waving the hair, per doz.................... .10

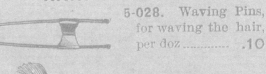

5-032. Curling Irons, double handle, pair

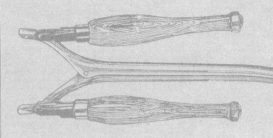

5-033. Curling Irons, oak, folding hand pair,....................

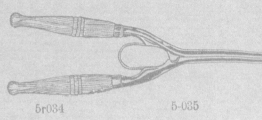

5r034 5-035

5-034. "Grace Darling" Curling Irons, steel, oak handles, medium size, pair......

5-035. As above, larger size, pair..........

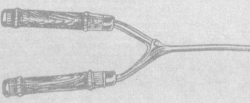

5-036. Moustache Curlers, nickel tipped h pair....................

5-037. Waving Irons, metal, highly nickeled, pair....................

POMPADOUR ROLLS

5-038. Real Hair Rolls, (state color wanted ordering)—
Length, 10 inch, each .15 14 inch, each
" 18 " " .20 22 " "

HAIR NETS

5-039. Front or Bang Nets, assorted bro black, each....................

5-040. As above, larger size, each ....

SHOULDER BRACES

5-041. "English M Brace," gives stre well as support sides, sho back, chest stomach. "Brace" do give that bu pearance so

A STORE
LIKE NO OTHER
EATON'S *of Winnipeg*

A STORE
LIKE NO OTHER
EATON'S *of Winnipeg*

Russ Gourluck

RUSS GOURLUCK

GREAT PLAINS
PUBLICATIONS

Great Plains Publications
420 – 70 Arthur Street
Winnipeg, MB R3B 1G7
www.greatplains.mb.ca

Great Plains Publications gratefully acknowledges the financial support provided for its publishing program by the Government of Canada through the Book Publishing Industry Development Program (BPIDP); the Canada Council for the Arts; as well as the Manitoba Department of Culture, Heritage and Tourism; and the Manitoba Arts Council.

Design & Typography by Relish Design Studio Inc.
Printed in Canada by Kromar Printing

CANADIAN CATALOGUING IN PUBLICATION DATA

Main entry under title:

Gourluck, Russ
  A store like no other : Eaton's of Winnipeg / Russ Gourluck.

ISBN 1-894283-48-1

1. T. Eaton Co.—Manitoba—Winnipeg—History.
2. Department stores—Manitoba—Winnipeg—History. I. Title.

HF5465.C34E325 2004   381'.141'09712743   C2004-904010-3

for Tatty

The first version of the 'Big Store' only had five storeys (left). Two extra storeys were added in 1909 because of the exceptional response of Winnipeggers to the new shopping mecca.

Contents

FOREWORD

THE STORY OF EATON'S OF WINNIPEG is, in many respects, the story of the City of Winnipeg. Very few families are without some personal connection to the "Big Store."

It was a place for Saturday and holiday employment for a host of students. It was a store with the tradition of the vision of its founder and the presence of a member of the Eaton family in Winnipeg.

Most notable in my personal experience with Eaton's was the Junior Executive Programme. Both a female and a male student were chosen each year from Winnipeg high schools, were guaranteed weekend, holiday and summer employment, and had the advantage of Saturday morning lectures from senior Eaton's executives, many of whom in later life became friends and business associates. Although we did not know each other at the time, Helen, my future wife, represented Kelvin High School while I had represented Daniel McIntyre Collegiate a year or two earlier.

Employee and customer loyalty to Eaton's was legendary. I had a cousin who worked for the company for 38 years and who is still a member of the Retirees Association. This Customer Loyalty was displayed by my mother when during the 1930 depression years and money was scarce, she would walk to Eaton's store from our family home on Banning Street in the West End and walk home again carrying her grocery purchases.

Eaton's store in the heart of downtown Winnipeg grew and prospered with the growth and prosperity of Winnipeg. However it was more than an economic impact that it had on Winnipeg. It became almost a way of life. For many years until the advent of the suburban malls it was the retailer of choice for the majority of Winnipeggers. It was also a company deeply involved in and supportive of the community. From the annual Santa Claus Parade which I participated in as a high school student to the many events in the Eaton's Assembly Hall including the annual luncheon for Boys Parliament which my father and I attended in the late 1940s, it was a gathering and meeting place for all of Winnipeg.

Russ Gourluck's *A Store Like No Other* captures many of the important and unique contributions Eaton's of Winnipeg made to our city. Founded in another era with a very special and distinctive relationship between the company and its employees and customers, it is an important component of the history of Winnipeg and most worthy of the recognition given to it.

— *Bill Norrie*

PREFACE

THIS BOOK WAS INSPIRED BY A CONVERSATION with my Aunt Betty. In late 2002, we were chatting about the fact that, after much debate, the demolition of the downtown Eaton's store was underway. The T. Eaton Company was gone, but my aunt had been a loyal Eatonian for more than forty years, and I shared her conviction that the story of Eaton's in Winnipeg needed to be told.

While writing this history, I was sometimes asked, "Can you write an entire book about one store?" That's a very understandable question. But the Big Store – as it was often called – was never just a store, or just a building. It was an icon for generations of Winnipeggers. It was a place where many had their first job; a place where people met (by the statue or under the clock); a place where first toys, or first dresses, or first grown-up fedoras were bought; and of course, a place where people just generally shopped – knowing if they changed their minds, they could always return their purchase for a full refund. Because it was such an important institution for so many years, there is more than enough to tell in one book.

One of the limitations of telling a story that involves hundreds of thousands of people is that the names of only a small percentage of them can be included. There's no doubt that for every individual whose name appears in this book there are many others who played an equally important role but aren't mentioned by name. The only consolation I can offer to those who are not specifically mentioned (and to their families) is that the people whose names do appear are representative of many others.

Similarly, there are so many interesting facts and stories associated with Eaton's of Winnipeg that only a sampling of them can be gathered together in a single book. I know that there are many more details and anecdotes that might have been included, but the limitations of time for research and the length of the finished product have proven to be blunt realities. Fortunately, many of the people who kindly agreed to be interviewed have given permission for the recordings of their interviews to be donated to the Archives of Manitoba, so information that hasn't

become part of this book will be available for others in the future who are interested in the story of Eaton's of Winnipeg.

In early 2003, I began to meet with Winnipeg Eatonians and they revealed just how remarkable the story of Eaton's of Winnipeg is. That huge red brick building on Portage Avenue was much more than a department store. It was, in many ways, a city unto itself. As I continued doing research for the book, I came to appreciate more and more the unique role that Eaton's played in the lives of Winnipeggers (and Manitobans) for so many decades. Generations of families made Eaton's their store of choice, and the company provided much more than just jobs for countless thousands of Winnipeggers. Eatonians (as they still proudly describe themselves) became part of an enormous extended family, and the bonds of friendship proved to be more enduring than the T. Eaton Company itself.

What I have chosen to present is basically a tribute to Eaton's of Winnipeg. Like any other business or individual, there were dimensions of the T. Eaton Company that can be justifiably criticized, and, in order to provide some degree of balance to the story, some of these aspects are mentioned. On the whole, however, the history of Eaton's in Winnipeg is an exceptionally positive one, and that is the focus of this book.

I want to express my heartfelt thanks to the many Winnipeg Eatonians and former Eaton's customers who took the time to share their insights and experiences and to help me to understand what Eaton's meant to them. This book could not have been written without their participation.

I appreciate the help of Alan Finnbogason, Joan and Ron Collins, and the other members of the Eaton's Retirement Club who provided so much interesting information and pointed out shortcomings in early drafts. Despite their best efforts, some errors probably still exist, and I take responsibility for them. Special thanks are due to Steve Kiz, who was instrumental in developing the chapter that helped to put the manuscript on the road to publication.

Especially helpful during the research process were Gilbert Comeault of the Archives of Manitoba, Jody Baltessen of the City of Winnipeg Archives, and Stewart Boden and Anastasia Rodgers of the Archives of Ontario. I also appreciate the willingness of Giles Bugailiskis, Lillian Vadeboncoeur, Bruce Meisner, Anne Elviss, Steve Kiz, and Walter Wright to share their photos and memorabilia with the readers of this book. Special thanks go to Guy St. Godard of Guy St. Godard Art Studio for allowing us to display his creation "Last Four Days," and to James O'Connor of Private Eye Studios for permission to include his photographs. Thanks also to Sharon Landry of Sears Canada Inc. for her assistance in obtaining permission to include copyright materials.

It's understandable that, after so many decades in the public eye, members of the Eaton family prefer to live outside the glare of the spotlight. I therefore particularly appreciate the willingness of John Craig Eaton to share his memories of Eaton's of Winnipeg, and I thank Timothy Craig Eaton for his behind-the-scenes interest in the story of the store established by his grandfather and great grandfather.

I'm very grateful for the time and thought that Gerry Mignacca (my friend of more than half a century) put into reading and critiquing chapter drafts all the way from North Carolina, and want to thank Waldi Wawrykow, Larry and Heather Borody, and Wayne Lloyd for offering advice and direction on some early drafts. And Glenn, thanks for your ongoing support and for understanding that "I'm writing" really means "Don't bother me."

Finally I want to thanks Gregg, Doug, Cheryl, Jewls (and, of course, Scout) at Great Plains , as well as the artists at Relish Design for their patience in working with a novice author.

This book is dedicated with respect and admiration to my aunt, Betty Ralph, and the thousands of other Eatonians whose loyalty and dedication truly made Eaton's of Winnipeg a store like no other.

–*Russ Gourluck*
August 2004

A Store and

The Big Store got dressed up to celebrate special occasions like the Coronation of Queen Elizabeth II in 1953.

THIS IS THE STORY of a unique and enduring relationship between a store and a city. For several decades, the T. Eaton Company Limited department store at 320 Portage Avenue in Winnipeg enjoyed a remarkable level of success that is unlikely ever to be matched. Generations of Winnipeggers did virtually all of their shopping at this one store, and many did that without even considering alternatives.

Like any successful partnership, this relationship was based on trust and mutual respect. Eaton's effectively met most of the buying needs of Winnipeg consumers, and customers reciprocated by meeting the business needs of the T. Eaton Company.

Although Eaton's in Winnipeg was part of a business that eventually operated from one end of Canada to another, and although the history of that company was, for several decades, a classic example of commercial success, the Winnipeg store established a unique bond with the community it served. And, although the company would eventually open three additional stores in Winnipeg, the name "Eaton's," for most Winnipeggers, immediately brought to mind the huge red brick store at Portage and Hargrave.

Success from the beginning

FROM THE VERY FIRST DAY THE BIG STORE (as it was affectionately called) opened its doors to the public, people flocked there to meet their friends, to spend the day, to eat, to browse, and, above all, to buy. Sales in the first year were estimated at $2.5 million. By 1915, they exceeded $14.4 million.

The decision to build the landmark red brick building on Portage Avenue is an illustration of the boldness of the Eaton family. In addition to operating a successful department store in Toronto, the family-owned company was doing a significant amount of business in western Canada through its thriving mail order service. The question facing founder Timothy Eaton and his

For the comfort of Manitobans and visiting Americans driving across the international boundary, Eaton's provided "Tourist Rest Rooms" near the Town of Emerson. Travellers were welcomed to pull off the highway and take advantage of the easy chairs and washroom facilities. The cottage-like structure featured awnings to withstand summer heat and a fireplace for cold winter days.

Prologue

Labels on image: MAIN STORE BUILDING · MAIL ORDER BUILDING Nº2 · FARM IMPLEMENT HARNESS AND AUTO ACCESSORY SECTION · MAIL ORDER BUILDING Nº1 · STABL[ES] · POWER HOUSE · GARAGE · CARPENTER SHOP

This sketch shows the buildings in 1926. It was estimated in 1937 that the total area of all of the Eaton's buildings in Winnipeg was 44.87 acres. This meant that the entire population of Manitoba at that time (711,056) could be accommodated in these buildings (allowing two square feet for each person). On that basis, there would have been enough space left over to accommodate an additional 250,000 people.

son John in 1904 was whether they should establish a mail order distribution centre or open a department store in Winnipeg. Their decision was to do both.

The very location of the store was an illustration of their willingness to take risks and of their confidence in Winnipeg and western Canada. Rather than settling on Main Street, where almost all of the major businesses of the day were located, they chose to purchase property on the south side of Portage Avenue between Donald and Hargrave Streets, a relatively isolated area. Rather than beginning with a small store to test the market, they constructed the largest building in Winnipeg. Their decision turned out to be a wise one.

Unrivalled domination

ACTUAL FIGURES ON THE EXTENT to which Eaton's dominated the retail scene are elusive and somewhat speculative. As a family-owned enterprise, the sales figures of the T. Eaton Company were well-kept secrets for most of the life of the company. The passage of time and the inaccessibility of the receipts of competitors are other factors that make accurate assessments difficult.

John Craig Eaton, a great grandson of the founder, recalls being told that when the store opened, or shortly thereafter, it had about eighty percent of the retail trade in Winnipeg. "That slowly eroded over time as the city grew, but that was an enormous amount of the department-store type of merchandise. It didn't leave much for the others. It was just a success from the word 'go'."

The success of Eaton's in Winnipeg was impressive not only from a local perspective but also on a wider basis. John M. Bassett, in his 1975 publication *Timothy Eaton,* claims that "From the first it was an amazing success, and for years it had a greater percentage of the city's business than any other store in the other Canadian cities."

Even in the 1960s, it was estimated that on a busy day at Eaton's, one out of every ten Winnipeggers visited the Big Store.

There are suggestions that, at its peak, Eaton's in Winnipeg was the most successful department store in North America. Ken Gibson, who worked in management in both Winnipeg and Toronto, declares "there is no doubt that it was the most dominant in North America in share of market."

Tom Gladney, who worked as a manager and buyer in Winnipeg home furnishings in the early 1970s before being transferred to Toronto, sums it up: "Nobody ever gets its market share as large as that in anything unless you've got the monopoly on something. Even though the Hudson's Bay Company had their rather impressive store down the street, they just never ever held a candle to Eaton's for many years."

A city within a city

EATON'S WAS HUGE, covering an entire city block. It had its own hospital clinic, fire department, water supply, library, and, of course, restaurants. It even had its own neighbourhoods – beyond the main store was the towering Catalogue building, as well as smaller structures like the power house, the parkade, and the bus depot.

For several generations of many Winnipeg (and Manitoba) families, Eaton's might as well

There are suggestions that, at its peak, Eaton's in Winnipeg was the most successful department store in North America.

RURAL CUSTOMERS FOUND it convenient to walk across Graham Avenue from the Winnipeg Bus Depot to Eaton's. The fact that the bus depot was located so close to the Big Store was not just coincidence – Eaton's owned the depot. Bus lines that used the facilities benefited from reasonable user fees, and rural shoppers were sometimes given discounts on bus fares to make the store their destination. As one Eaton's executive chuckles, "We didn't want them to know where the Bay was."

PARCEL POST
MAIL COLLECTIONS

OFFICE

The post office, although it operated at a deficit for the company, attracted many customers — and the location enticed them to look at what else the store had to offer as they made their way to and from the sixth floor.

Some visited the store in person, others telephoned in their orders for delivery, and many used the catalogue service to do their shopping.

have been the only store in town. These families purchased their furniture, their appliances, their clothing, their tools, their groceries, and almost all of their other everyday needs from Eaton's. Some visited the store in person, others telephoned in their orders for delivery, and many used the catalogue service to do their shopping.

When Eaton's first opened its Winnipeg store, there was little competition in terms of full-service department stores. The Hudson's Bay Company, which was to become Eaton's major competitor in later years, had a small store on Main Street at the time, but it would not be opening its Portage Avenue and Memorial Boulevard store until 1926. Some locally owned retail businesses were already in operation on Main Street, but they carried limited lines of merchandise and were in no

UNDER THE CLOCK

ALTHOUGH MANY VISITORS to the store made the area in front of the statue of Timothy Eaton their meeting place of choice, some preferred to meet "under the clock." A large four-faced clock hung from the ceiling in a wide centre aisle of the main floor, and the floor area beneath it was often crowded with people who expectantly scanned the faces of passing customers. Because this clock was located in the area of the jewellery department (and for some years the candy counter), there were pleasant distractions for browsing while waiting to meet a friend.

Gary Filmon came from an "Eaton's Family." His mother began working at Eaton's when Gary was in junior high school, and he later became a Junior Executive. "We were completely captured by Eaton's in terms of our spending dollars. Everything including the furniture and appliances in our home was bought from Eaton's." His wife, Janice, on the other hand, came from a "Bay family." Her father was a Bay executive for more than twenty years, and she had never set foot in Eaton's until she met Gary.

JUNIOR COUNCILLORS AND JUNIOR
EXECUTIVES

"Winnipeg's elite shopped at Eaton's to be the very first to have the very latest, and they were willing to pay a premium for that distinction."

BEGINNING IN THE EARLY 1940s, high schools throughout Winnipeg were invited by Eaton's to nominate suitable grade eleven and grade twelve students to serve in prestigious positions with the company for a one-year period. Male students who were appointed were known as Junior Executives, while their female counterparts were called Junior Councillors.

In addition to providing part-time employment, this program was an opportunity for students to learn more about retailing and business administration. In return, Junior Councillors and Junior Executives served as valuable sources of information for the company on the buying needs and preferences of younger shoppers. Smartly dressed in blue blazers and grey trousers or skirts, these attractive young people brought a fresh and energetic presence to the store. Academic excellence was not required to be accepted for the positions (although many were outstanding students); outgoing personalities and enthusiasm were considered more important. One prominent Winnipeg lawyer still chuckles about the fact that his high school turned down his request to nominate him to become a Junior Executive. They felt he was too short.

Junior Executives and Junior Councillors became involved in community activities on behalf of the company, including Christmas carolling and toy distribution at the Children's Hospital, canvassing for the Salvation Army, marching in the Santa Claus Parade, and delivering Yuletide poinsettias to seniors in retirement homes and hospitals.

Many of the participants in the program went on to distinguished careers in later years. Some, like Gary Filmon, went into political life. Lloyd Axworthy, who was a Member of Parliament and federal cabinet minister before becoming the President of the University of Winnipeg, preceded Gary Filmon by two years in representing Sisler High School. Bill Norrie became the Mayor of Winnipeg. Reverend Carl Ridd was an Olympics basketball player, established the Religious Studies Department at University of Winnipeg, and was highly regarded as a social activist. Other Junior Executives included actor Len Cariou, and Frank Rossi, who would eventually become the manager of the store.

position to compete with all that Eaton's had to offer.

As time went on, the two major choices for Winnipeg shoppers were Eaton's and the Bay. Many individuals (and even families) developed strong loyalties to one store or the other, and to some extent, the population was divided into two camps: "Eaton's shoppers" and "Bay shoppers." Although some people would visit both stores to compare the prices, attractiveness, and quality of their merchandise, many automatically took their business to the store that had won their allegiance. Even with Eaton's gone, people like thirty-eight-year Eatonian Mel Jenkins continue to remember the rivalry. "We never went to the Bay. My wife still can't shop at the Bay."

The huge assortment of merchandise was well-displayed and easy to find. Prices and quality ran the gamut from basic and bargain to extravagant and expensive. New immigrants and working people were able to find durable and reliable items within reach of their limited budgets. Winnipeg's elite shopped at Eaton's to be the very first to have the very latest, and they were willing to pay a premium for that

One of the youngest performers at a Good Deed Club event at the Metropolitan Theatre in 1950 was four-year-old Garry Peterson. His drum solo of C Jam Blues led to his being dubbed a "youthful Gene Krupa." The ovation he received for his first number led to a special encore later that morning and previewed the acclaim he would receive in later years as the drummer in The Guess Who.

THE CAT LADY
TRIUMPHS

ONE OF WINNIPEG'S MOST COLOURFUL CHARACTERS in the 1960s was the "Cat Lady," Bertha Rand. This cantankerous woman lived in a small house on Queen Street with fifty or more cats that she rescued from abandonment. Bertha regularly visited the pet department of the store, where there was a standing arrangement that she could be sold any broken bags of kitty litter or dry cat foods for a minimal charge. Whenever a bag broke, staff members set it aside for her. One day she arrived in the department and was told that there were no broken bags available. Bertha's reaction to this news was both emotional and loud. One of the Eaton brothers was in the area and, after watching the manager being harangued for several minutes, delivered a sharp kick to a bag of cat food. He pointed the now-punctured bag out to Bertha and said, "There's one for you."

THE GOOD
DEED CLUB

IN 1939, EATON'S INTRODUCED the Good Deed Club to Winnipeg, and it enjoyed extraordinary success. In its first five years, the club attracted more than thirty thousand children to its membership. On Saturday mornings, thousands of Manitoba children sat glued to their radios as the cheery theme song was beamed out on radio station CKY (later CBW).

Theatre parties held initially at the Capitol Theatre and later at the Metropolitan (both within a stone's throw of the store) attracted capacity crowds of youngsters. Packed club meetings were also held in other Manitoba communities where there were Eaton's stores. Dauphin, Brandon, and Portage la Prairie were the locations of theatre parties and broadcasts during the 1930s and 1940s.

On May 13, 1955, the Good Deed Club made broadcasting history in Winnipeg by participating in the first radio-television simulcast in the city. Scholarship winners and the Good Deed Club Choir's Senior Ensemble performed on both radio station CBW and television station CBWT.

In keeping with its basic purpose of encouraging children to be helpful to others, the club regularly presented awards to youngsters who performed acts of special kindness or bravery. These were generally wristwatches, but during the war years, War Savings Certificates were given.

Do a Good Deed every day,
Obey the Golden Rule;
Never say an angry word,
Or be unkind or cruel.
Scatter seeds of happiness,
At home, at play, at school, and
You'll find there's sunshine everywhere,
Obey the Golden Rule.

distinction. Many shoppers came to rely on items that carried the familiar and trusted names of Eaton's branded lines, regarding them as reliable and well-priced. Others appreciated that Eaton's, through its buying offices in the United States, Europe, and Asia, brought distinctive items to Winnipeg that couldn't be found in any other store in the city. Eaton's own factories produced lines of merchandise that were exclusive to Eaton's and enabled the company to offer attractive prices by bypassing the markups of outside manufacturers and wholesalers.

One of the reasons that the downtown store became a one-stop destination for so many shoppers was that it offered such a complete range of services. The drug department was, at one point, one of the largest in the Prairie Provinces, and reasonable prices (as well as the feeling of confidence inspired by anything associated with Eaton's) attracted many shoppers to fill their prescriptions there. The independently-owned Attractions Ticket Office was a supplier of tickets for sports and entertainment events. Eaton's car rental service offered General Motors vehicles and the convenience of using an Eaton's credit card. The travel service was used by customers as well as Eaton's buyers embarking on trips. The busy beauty salon was

ONE OF THE THOUGHTFUL TOUCHES provided by the Big Store was the uniformed doormen who were stationed at the main entrances. Their role was to open doors, greet customers, and be of general assistance to people as they arrived and departed. Among the most memorable of these was the legendary Ed Logan, who became as much of a fixture at the South Hargrave Street entrance as the heavy glass doors he opened for customers.

This charming and outgoing doorman with a ruddy complexion seemed to know all of the regular customers by name (especially the ladies) and often regaled them with humorous (even slightly risqué) stories told in his heavy Irish brogue. Ed Logan had the reputation of looking after customers and they, in turn, always remembered him at Christmas time.

The exterior of the Big Store was decorated
to mark significant events.

During the 1940s, Eaton's aired their "Home Service League" on radio station CKRC. These programs provided practical tips to homemakers during wartime and kept them informed about what was new at Eaton's. The topics of the sometimes dramatized broadcasts included information on beauty tips, fashions, home sewing, and handling salvage. By 1947, Eaton's had a staff of four full-time employees to produce and perform in these broadcasts.

EATON'S

CKRC

HOME
SERVICE
LEAGUE

RADIO PROGRAM
OVER
CKRC
9:00 to 9:30 A.M.

MONDAY *through* SATURDAY

February 14th, 1944

Today . . .
"THE TYPE TALKS"
Through the Modern Miracle of Radio

another service that attracted many clients to visit the store.

Service was one of main attractions of Eaton's. Knowledgeable and dedicated salespeople went out of their way to ensure customer satisfaction, and many shoppers had favourite salespeople with whom they dealt regularly. Until changing economic conditions necessitated staff reductions, salespeople were able to spend almost unlimited time with customers (and even to accompany them to other departments to provide advice on related purchases).

For those who chose not to carry their purchases home, or preferred to shop by telephone, Eaton's provided reliable home delivery by friendly drivers who, like the sales clerks, were willing to make extra efforts to keep their customers pleased. As telephone shopping became more popular with city and rural customers during the 1960s, Eaton's Buy Lines remained open from 8 a.m. to midnight.

And, if there was any chance that a purchase might not be exactly what a customer wanted (and would continue to want), there was the famed Eaton's guarantee of "goods satisfactory or money refunded." Many customers knew that the company would go to almost any lengths to honour their commitment to customer satisfaction.

Sales events were especially popular among Winnipeggers, who have traditionally taken pride in their self-ascribed reputation as bargain hunters. They came to know that Eaton's highly ethical regulations on sale prices guaranteed that

there was no deception. In "wholesale city" Winnipeg, the store was routinely mobbed during these events. As one manager comments about customers waiting for the store to open during a Trans-Canada sale, "You could walk on people's heads to cross Portage Avenue." Shouting matches and even minor scuffles among customers competing for the same articles were not uncommon.

The store was much more than just a place to shop. The statue of Timothy Eaton and the centrally-located clock on the main floor provided places to meet. The restaurants (ranging from economical to elegant) provided havens to relax and enjoy well-prepared food. The displays in the show windows and inside the store were the subject of many hours of browsing, and demonstrations of products within the store provided free entertainment.

Eaton's knew its clientele and offered small but appreciated services that made visits to the store even more pleasant. When more women shoppers began to drive to the store instead of taking the bus or streetcar, they appreciated the Women's Parking Lot on Hargrave that featured uniformed valet parking (and allowed no tipping). Gerry Murray, who was one of the young car jockeys, explains that, in addition to this being a service to women drivers, it was also a way

Eaton's knew its clientele and offered small but appreciated services that made visits to the store even more pleasant.

Attracting rural customers

AS MORE RURAL RESIDENTS became car owners, and as Manitoba roads improved, visiting Winnipeg to shop became more common. Customers who previously ordered from the catalogue were now also able to visit the Big Store in person. For many families, visiting Winnipeg for a day meant spending the day in Eaton's.

Farmers who brought their eggs to the egg-grading department in Mail Order Building Number Three were paid with vouchers that could be spent on merchandise in the store.

From the early days of the store, a farmers' waiting room was provided as a free service to rural visitors. Here, at the rear of the annex, visitors from outside Winnipeg could relax on benches and chairs and freshen up in washrooms before or after a busy day of shopping. A small coffee bar was also provided. Many of these visitors spoke English as they enjoyed the facilities, but others chatted about their shopping adventures and the year's crops in Ukrainian, German, Polish, French, or Icelandic.

Supporting the community

ONE OF THE WAYS THE T. EATON COMPANY gained a high level of respect in Manitoba was through its generous support of community activities.

For many years, the company sponsored luncheons, dinners, and social events for a number of community organizations and activities, including the Tuxis and Older Boys'

KEEPING A SECRET

IT WAS WIDELY ASSUMED that there was an intense rivalry in the city between the T. Eaton Company and the Hudson's Bay Company, and that both businesses were determined not to have their competitor find out their trade secrets. From this belief emerged an expression that was used by Winnipeggers who didn't want to disclose confidential information. They simply asked, "Does Eaton's tell the Bay?"

---

of maximizing the capacity of the lot. It was designed to hold 140 cars, but the jockeys could squeeze in 200 by parking the cars so close together that they barely had room to open the doors. In 1956, the site of the lot was taken over by a newly-constructed parkade with a capacity of 600 cars.

Another factor that contributed to the popularity of Eaton's in Winnipeg was that it was one of the largest private employers in the province, so almost everyone in Winnipeg had a personal connection with the store. Greg Purchase estimated that, in the 1950s, about 15,000 full-time and part-time employees worked in the store, with another 12,000 in the Catalogue. Sales events and the Christmas season provided temporary jobs for untold thousands over the years. It used to be said that nearly every person in Winnipeg worked for Eaton's at some point in his or her life. And the small number of people who didn't fall into this category generally had a relative or friend who did. The fact that so many had these ties to Eaton's resulted in a high degree of loyalty. Employees, of course, had the benefit of discounts, but, as secretary Hazel Workman emphatically states, "I didn't look anywhere else. It wasn't the discount, it was the loyalty."

Parliament, the provincial high school curling bonspiel, the Manitoba Dairy Association, and the Manitoba postmasters.

In rural areas, the company was a strong supporter of 4-H Clubs and made a point of purchasing livestock owned by club members, sometimes at premium prices. The meat that was processed from the animals was sold (often at a loss) in the store's meat department.

The Community Chest (and later the United Way) received generous contributions from both the employees and the company. One example of this was that in 1949, the largest single donation received to that point by the Community Chest during its campaigns in Greater Winnipeg was made by the T. Eaton Company Limited and its staff and management, with a total contribution of $45,000.

The seventh-floor Assembly Hall was the location of thousands of teas and other social events. This spacious facility was provided free of charge to churches and other community organizations, as were coffee, tea, dishes, and coffee urns. *Contacts*, the company's Winnipeg employee newsletter reported in 1935 that this hall was used in the fall of 1934 for silver teas by 69 churches and societies, with another 120 booked for the spring season. During that same fall season, more than 80,000 cups of Eaton's Grill Room Blend Tea were served. ("And," *Contacts* boasted, "not one complaint!"). This facility continued to be used for community events for several decades, and it was estimated in the 1960s that 250,000 people annually attended functions held there. Truly, Eaton's was a fundamental part of the community of Winnipeg. ■

ELEVATORS AND
ESCALATORS

T HE FOUR ELEVATORS INSTALLED in the store when it was first constructed were considered marvels of modern technology. The cage-like black iron doors provided an open view of their surroundings, and they clanged reassuringly as they were opened and shut by uniformed operators. These slow-moving conveyances enticed people of all ages to ride up and down, especially out-of-town visitors seeing them for the first time.

The open design of the elevators had a special attraction for young boys who discovered that, if they dropped coins on the floor near the elevator entrances at just the right moment, a glance upward into a loaded car could provide revealing glimpses of the limbs of long-skirted ladies.

In the 1950s, there were two banks of elevators (one on the Portage Avenue side and on near Donald Street) with a total of seventeen cars. Hydraulically-driven cage elevators were eventually replaced by air-conditioned electronic versions. By the early 1980s, only one bank of five elevators remained – clean and shiny cars surrounded by beige marble and shiny brass. Despite changes in technology, Eaton's continued to provide well-groomed and outgoing operators, who always looked their polyester best in grey in the summer and maroon in the winter as they greeted customers and called out the departments upon arrival at each floor.

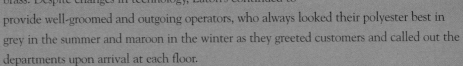

The first two escalators the Big Store were installed in 1916 and were believed to be the first in western Canada. They had black deeply grooved tire-tread-like steps that encouraged women wearing high heels to take elevators, and were so narrow that passengers usually couldn't stand side-by-side. Precariously steep, and with a bumpy, hesitant ride, they bordered on the frightening for young children and the elderly. By the 1950s, two streamlined banks of stainless steel and aluminum escalators with shiny enameled sidewalls were capable of gliding 8,000 passengers an hour from the basement to the eighth floor.

By April 11, 1905, the steel frame of the
five-storey building was virtually complete.

BIG STORE

Jack and Flora arrive in Winnipeg

THE RAILWAY JOURNEY FROM TORONTO TO WINNIPEG in the spring of 1904 was an adventure for the young married couple. From the observation car and the rear platform of the train, Jack and Flora admired the shining waters of Lake Superior, the seemingly endless forests of northern Ontario, and finally the flat and predictable prairies of Manitoba. A fellow passenger turned out to be Sir Daniel Hunter McMillan, the Lieutenant-Governor of Manitoba, and the pair was welcomed to what would later be called "Friendly Manitoba" with an invitation to Government House.

But this was not a holiday, and this was no ordinary couple. John Craig Eaton was the son of Timothy Eaton, the legendary founder of the Eaton's retail chain. He had watched his father's business grow, and now he was going to Winnipeg to find a location for a new outlet for the T. Eaton Company Limited.

One of Flora's first memories of their arrival in Winnipeg was the mud. Half a century later, in her autobiography, she described it as "of a gluey consistency, dirty yellow in colour" and recalled how difficult it was to remove mud stains from clothing. She visualized the "board sidewalks, little houses of new lumber, and the generally sprawled, busy, disorganized look of a city in its birth throes."

Jack was different from his father in many ways. In contrast to Timothy's simple upbringing and his apprenticeship at age thirteen, Jack grew up in luxury and become accustomed to the convenience of servants. Timothy was a strict teetotaler and strongly opposed to smoking; Jack enjoyed whisky and monogrammed cigars. Timothy was regarded as a stern and humourless autocrat; his son was outgoing and approachable. Jack was handsome, always fashionably dressed, and overwhelmingly charming.

Jack did share one very important characteristic with his father – an aptitude for business. At the age of six, "Master Jack" was happily demonstrating tops during the Christmas season in the toy department of his father's store.

John Craig Eaton and his wife Flora, on board the *Lusitania* on its maiden voyage from New York in 1907.

Chapter 1

An advertisement in the *Winnipeg Tribune* on July 27, 1904, put out a call for 50 teams of horses and 100 men. Before the excavation was complete, 29,000 loads of earth were removed at the rate of as many as 800 loads per day by men and teams of horses from as far away as Brandon.

When he was nineteen, he was sent on a buying trip to Asia and England. By the time he and Flora were married in 1901, Jack was vice-president of the company, and clearly destined to succeed his father.

Finding the location

WINNIPEG IN 1904 WAS DESCRIBED AS "The Chicago of the North." From a population of just 241 in 1871, the city had grown to more than 67,000 in 1904, and would exceed 136,000 by 1911. The growth of Winnipeg was so rapid that it acquired city status almost immediately. As the major urban centre west of Toronto, it was to become the western headquarters of the Canadian Pacific, the Grand Trunk Pacific, and Canadian Northern Railways.

Although there was some manufacturing industry in Winnipeg, the economy of Manitoba and the other western provinces was primarily agricultural. The availability of cheap (or even free) farm land attracted many Canadians from Ontario, joining the steady stream of arrivals from the United Kingdom. More significantly, a wave of immigrants from southern and eastern Europe was well underway by 1904. In pursuing new and better lives for themselves and their children, these new Canadians were weaving a fundamental change in the social fabric of Canada. In 1901, Manitoba welcomed approximately 11,000 immigrants; in 1903 nearly 40,000 arrived.

Winnipeg had the advantage of location. The stream of people and goods that was moving west passed by necessity through Winnipeg, and

The site chosen in 1904 for the new store (shown here on August 2, 1904) was made up of several small lots. Eaton's was concerned that the owners would ask inflated prices if they knew that the T. Eaton Company was interested in their property, so they quietly arranged for agents to make offers on the lots without disclosing the identity of the purchaser. The strategy was successful, and most of the properties were acquired with minimal bargaining.

the growing city served as the distribution centre for all of western Canada. As a Chicago newspaper columnist was to observe a few years later, "All roads lead to Winnipeg. It is the focal point of the three transcontinental lines of Canada, and nobody, neither manufacturer, capitalist, farmer, mechanic, lawyer, doctor, merchant, priest nor labourer, can pass from one part of Canada to another without going through Winnipeg. It is a gateway through which all the commerce of the east and the west, and the north and the south must flow."

As Jack and Flora assessed potential sites, they recognized that the key business district of

ONLY A TEMPORARY BUILDING

ALTHOUGH THE BIG STORE eventually occupied its site for ninety-five years, there are indications that it was intended to be demolished and replaced not long after it was built. In 1916, at the same time that the construction of Mail Order Building Number One was announced, the company disclosed its intention to replace the store with a new building over a period of fifteen years. Dismissing the red brick store as a "test structure," a newspaper advertisement included a sketch of "Winnipeg's Shopping Home of the Future," which showed an entirely new building on Portage between Hargrave and Donald, connected by an overpass crossing Graham Avenue to the new Mail Order Buildings. This plan never became a reality, perhaps due to the death in 1922 of president John Craig Eaton and his succession by his conservatively-inclined cousin Robert Young Eaton.

Bricklayers, having proudly reached the "last lap" in their work, stopped for a group photograph. This phase of construction was accomplished in just two months.

Construction workers posed with their bicycles
at the Thomson Brothers Contractors site office
at 269 Hargrave Street.

Winnipeg was Main Street. The Hudson's Bay Company retail store was located at "Main, York and Fort Streets." Entrepreneur Jerry Robinson moved from Emerson to Winnipeg, and opened his Robinson and Company department store at Main and Albert. Another major retailer, the George Craig Company Limited, had its store at 532 to 536 Main Street. The hardware emporium of James H. Ashdown, a well-known businessman who was to become the mayor of

Winnipeg in 1907, was located at 476 Main Street at Bannatyne. Because of the popularity of Main Street as a location for commercial and banking establishments, property prices were high.

Jack's recommendation to purchase property on the south side of Portage Avenue between Hargrave and Donald was a clear departure from the established pattern. Although there were other buildings in the vicinity (including Wesley College, Holy Trinity Church, and the YMCA

building at Portage and Smith), this was clearly not the recognized centre of business in the city at the time. Part of the site chosen for the new store was previously a brick yard owned by Thomas Kelly, the controversial contactor who built Manitoba's Legislative Building at Broadway and Osborne. Other portions of the property were occupied by homes and small commercial buildings, and some of the lots were vacant.

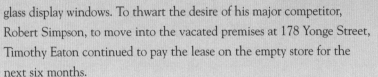

THE ORIGINS OF THE
T. EATON COMPANY

TIMOTHY EATON WAS A MAN of humble origins with a strong desire to succeed in business. After serving his apprenticeship in a general store, he escaped the poverty of Ireland in 1854 at the age of twenty and joined his brothers and sisters to pursue his dreams in Canada. His first business venture in his new country was a small general store that he operated with his brother James in Kirkton, Ontario. In 1860, the two brothers moved their business to the nearby town of St. Marys. In 1868, disagreements with James resulted in the end of the partnership and Timothy's decision to move to Toronto. Here, in a community of 50,000 with a large percentage of Irish immigrants, Timothy opened the first store to bear his name in rented premises at 178 Yonge Street in 1869. The staff of T. Eaton and Company initially consisted of two men, a woman, and a boy.

Timothy utilized a number of innovative business practices, including having fixed prices for goods (in contrast to bargaining) and buying and selling for cash only (in contrast to credit). Although these practices were not originated by Timothy Eaton, he was instrumental in popularizing them. Dissatisfied by his dealings with wholesalers in Toronto, he travelled to Britain to purchase goods directly from manufacturers. Extensive advertising and eye-catching displays were successful in attracting the business of Torontonians of all economic levels. The famous "Goods Satisfactory or Money Refunded" policy was introduced in 1870.

In 1883, the success of the store necessitated a move to much larger premises at 190-196 Yonge Street, a three-storey row of stores with more than fifty feet of frontage, twenty-five thousand square feet of retail space, and impressive plate glass display windows. To thwart the desire of his major competitor, Robert Simpson, to move into the vacated premises at 178 Yonge Street, Timothy Eaton continued to pay the lease on the empty store for the next six months.

By the time Jack and Flora made their way to Winnipeg, additions to the Yonge Street store in Toronto had more than doubled its square footage, business was thriving, and the Company had 5,500 employees (who proudly called themselves Eatonians). Timothy had established buying offices in Paris, France and London, England, and Eaton-owned manufacturing facilities supplied the store with a variety of goods, including window shades, shirts, comforters, and horse harnesses. The first mail order catalogue, published in 1884, introduced residents of western Canada (thanks to the completion of the trans-continental railway) to the wide range of merchandise offered by Eaton's. The result was a base of loyal western Canadian customers who had never shopped on Yonge Street but recognized that the T. Eaton Company provided quality merchandise, reasonable prices, and outstanding service.

The *Winnipeg Telegram* reported on July 4, 1904, that "The T. Eaton Company of Toronto, the largest and wealthiest department store in Canada, will commence at once to build a large block of stores on Portage Avenue to control its western trade."

As might be expected, when it became known that Eaton's was going to build on Portage Avenue, other developers announced plans to erect buildings close to the proposed new store, and vacant lots on Portage took on a new appeal for potential purchasers.

Not long after Jack returned to Toronto and persuaded his father to purchase the Portage Avenue property, an advertisement in the *Manitoba Free Press* asked in its headline "Who Is Eaton?" It then provided the answer: "The man who built up Yonge Street, Toronto, and who is now about to do the same for Portage Avenue." The advertisement went on to encourage prospective buyers to purchase seven acres on Portage Avenue with over two hundred feet of frontage for just $8,500, with the added caution: "Don't wait until he puts up that million dollar building, but buy now."

An advertisement for the Hugo Ross Realty Company in the *Winnipeg Telegram* of July 16, 1904, offered various Portage Avenue properties for sale. These included 88 feet of frontage on the south side of Portage between Carlton and Edmonton for $450 per foot, and a 44 by 130 lot on the north side between Hargrave and Carlton for $500 per foot.

The *Manitoba Free Press* carried a page one story on August 6, 1904, with the headline "Simpson Co. Want Location." It referred to "a persistent and apparently well-founded rumour for some time that the Robert Simpson company, of Toronto, did not intend to allow their Eaton rivals to secure much of a lead over them in establishing in the west." The article claimed that the Simpson company was considering the purchase of property on the north side of Portage Avenue between Hargrave and Carlton, with a

AT THE TIME THE SITE of the new store was purchased, the company also bought a large home on Donald Street known as Strevel House (the future site of the Donald Street Annex of the Eaton store). This impressive brick home with its wooden gingerbread trim served not only as a residence for employees, but also as temporary accommodation for the members of the Eaton family when they came to Winnipeg for the official opening of the store. By 1906, Strevel House became a residence for unmarried male Eatonians who moved from Toronto.

A STORE LIKE NO OTHER · EATON'S OF WINNIPEG

On May 18th, 1905, John Craig Eaton (left) and Harry McGee (right) ceremoniously laid the last brick on the roof parapet.

Managers knew that they had achieved success when they were given the privilege of parking in the company garage. The upper floors housed the paint and carpentry shops.

depth of 150 feet. Had this rumour become a reality, a Simpson store would have been located across from the Eaton Store and only one city block over. However, it would prove to be many years before Simpson's would provide significant competition for the T. Eaton Co. in Winnipeg.

A major decision that had to be made by the Eaton directors was the type of business to be established. Would this be only a mail order building to expedite the shipment of goods to customers in the western provinces, or should it be a combination of a department store and a mail order operation? There were concerns that

Montgomery Ward might expand its operation from the United States into Canada to follow the large number of American immigrants who had relocated to western Canada. If this were to happen, the Eaton company could miss out on a major opportunity.

When John Craig Eaton returned to Toronto, he demonstrated that he had inherited his father's willingness to think big, and to take calculated risks. He recommended that the Eaton presence in Winnipeg should be a massive department store as well as an extensive mail order operation.

Planning the store

THE PROPERTY PURCHASED BY THE T. EATON CO. Ltd. was bordered by Portage Avenue, Donald Street, Graham Avenue, and Hargrave Street, and measured 266 by 490 feet. The original recommendation of "Mr. J.C." (as John Craig Eaton was called within the company) was a six-storey store. However, cautious advisors convinced Timothy to scale back the project to a store of only five floors.

Supervision and co-ordination of the building project was entrusted to Harry McGee. McGee's origins, like Timothy Eaton's, were humble and Irish. He began his long career with the Eaton company in 1883 as a floor sweeper and furniture mover. Within only a few days, he became a salesman for $6 a week, and within a couple of weeks his salary was increased to $7.

His rapid rise continued with his promotion to carpet department manager at $8 per week, plus commission, within seven months. At the time of the planning of the Winnipeg store, McGee was a company director; he was later to be appointed a vice-president, with responsibility for construction, engineering, and carpentry. A clear indication of the high regard in which McGee was held by the company was the presentation to him in 1928, on his 45th anniversary, of a Rolls-Royce automobile by then-president R. Y. Eaton.

Similarly, responsibility for specific aspects of the Winnipeg construction project was given to people known and trusted by the Eatons. Excavation, masonry work, and brick-laying

THE SOD-TURNING

A SOD-TURNING CEREMONY TOOK PLACE AT 8:00 a.m. on Wednesday, July 27, 1904. Watched by a large number of spectators, some Eaton officials, and the workers who were standing by to begin the excavation of the basement, John Craig Eaton enthusiastically wielded a shovel and began the digging in earnest. The shovel he chose was not plated in gold or silver, as was often seen at such events; it was described by the *Manitoba Free Press* as "an honest every-day shovel." Along with some Manitoba sod, the shovel was subsequently sent to Toronto to be placed on display.

According to the *Winnipeg Daily Tribune*, Eaton was spurred into action by a friend who said (as the city bell rang out 8:00 a.m.): "Now, Jack, there's the eight o'clock bell, step up and turn the sod promptly. You know your father would be right on the second if he were here and he would fire anyone who was three seconds late."

Before pushing the shovel into the earth, Jack removed his hat and said: "Gentlemen, we are about to erect a great building in Winnipeg for the T. Eaton Company. The dimensions are large, and the structure will be ample for the requirements of this great country."

The keynote speech at the event was made by Chancellor Burwash of Victoria University in Toronto, a longtime friend of Timothy Eaton. He spoke of the growth of the company and praised its exemplary approach to business. Burwash pointed out how the decision of the Eaton company to begin such an ambitious project in Winnipeg was evidence of both the progressive attitude of the business and of the ongoing development of western Canada. His address was followed by enthusiastic cheers for the the King, for Manitoba and the west, and for the T. Eaton Company.

Also in attendance for the event were the mayor of Winnipeg, Thomas Sharpe, and several representatives of the Eaton company including G. W. Thompson, G.S. Hannah, and, of course, Harry McGee.

It should be noted that some reports of the sod-turning indicate that it took place on July 24, but newspaper coverage of the event in the *Manitoba Free Press* and the *Winnipeg Daily Tribune* verify that the date was Wednesday, July 27th, 1904. Another factor is that July 24, 1904, was a Sunday. Considering the attitude of Timothy Eaton (and therefore The T. Eaton Co.) on the sanctity of the Sabbath, it is unlikely that the ceremony and the beginning of the actual excavation would have taken place on a Sunday.

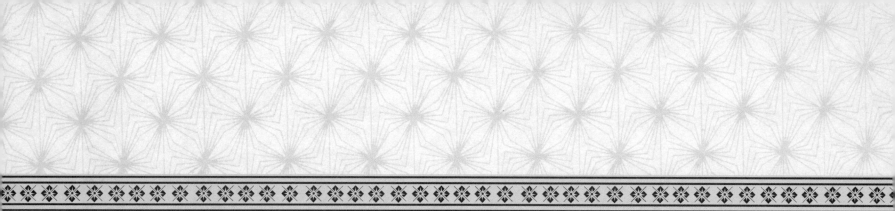

In order to focus attention on the displays of merchandise, there was extensive open space.

were carried out by Thomson Brothers Contactors of Toronto, who had seventeen years of experience in building for the Eaton company. George. W. Thompson, Chief Engineer of The T. Eaton Co., was placed in charge of steel and iron work, and G. S. Hannah, the company's carpenter foreman, was made superintendent of the wood framing.

The architect was Winnipegger John Woodman and his design was practical, flexible, and progressive. Built on a structural bay system, the store would allow for additions and interior changes to be carried out relatively easily and with no compromise of the building's structural integrity.

Inspired by the Chicago style of architecture, the perimeter of the store utilized light walls known as "curtain walls." This allowed for the installation of large window openings, which permitted a great deal of natural light to enter the store.

The floors were made of wood, and designed to bear very heavy loads. The strength of the floors permitted the display of many heavy items over the ninety-four years that the store was open, including large appliances, cast-iron bathtubs, and even automobiles. This was in addition, of course, to the combined weight of thousands of shoppers.

The exterior of the store emphasized simplicity. Woodman chose to minimize elaborate decorations and, instead, incorporated horizontal and vertical lines in a clean and distinctive design. He also chose simplicity in the actual building materials, using only red brick and Bedford stone. One of the most memorable features of the building was the 42 massive show windows at the street level; each of these was the width of one of the structural bays.

The interior of the store was similarly simple and functional. In order to focus attention on the displays of merchandise, there was extensive open space. Because of the structural system, display cases and temporary partitions could be used flexibly to define different areas of the store. Steel beams, iron columns, and the sprinkler system were left exposed. The pressed metal ceiling tiles with their distinctive "Diamond 'E'" were one of the few exceptions to the basic simplicity of the interior.

Another very functional feature was the store's sprinkler system. Approximately 8,000 sprinkler heads provided fire protection (with one nozzle for every one hundred square feet). Designed to activate at 155 degrees Fahrenheit, they were provided with water by two artesian wells located more than 300 feet beneath the building. These wells also had the capacity to provide approximately 100,000 gallons of clear cold drinking water each day. Two storage tanks could hold a total of 25,000 gallons of water, and two pumps could provide 3,000,000 gallons of water in twenty-four hours.

The original power house building, located on the east side of Hargrave Street on the same lot as the store, used four boilers capable of providing a total of 1,000 horsepower. Four electric generators provided electricity for 230 arc lights and 2,000 incandescent lights. By 1910 seven boilers were delivering almost 2,500

horsepower, and the number of lights had leaped to 25,000.

Timothy Eaton took great pride in his utilization of modern technology. In Toronto, he had pioneered the use of electric lights, passenger elevators, and telephones in his store. The newly-opened Winnipeg store included four water-powered passenger elevators (each with a capacity of twenty people) and four freight elevators, telephone and telegraph facilities on the first floor, and a totally modern fire protection system – an essential component of a building that many years later would be described by its critics as a fire-trap.

The design featured an innovation to enhance the comfort of arriving and departing customers. Hot air blowers in the floors of the "porches" at the entrance doors were included to keep Winnipeggers warm on frigid winter days.

This, of course, was at a time when such conveniences as electricity, indoor bathroom facilities, and telephones were uncommon for city dwellers and a rarity for rural residents. For many, a visit to the Eaton store was like entering a palace of luxury and modern convenience.

Building the store

EXCAVATION OF THE BASEMENT by teams of men and horses started immediately after the sod-turning on July 27, 1904, followed by construction of the frame of the building. Brick-laying commenced March 17,

1905. Appropriately, the first brick was laid by Harry McGee and the event took place on St. Patrick's Day.

By the time construction was completed, six million pounds of iron (from Toronto) and steel (from Pittsburgh) had been used. Seven thousand barrels of Portland cement, more than two million of the distinctive red bricks, and somewhere between two and three million feet of lumber were incorporated in the project. There were 1,021 steel beams and 876 cast iron pillars and bases.

The total floor space of the store was estimated to be more than $5^{1}/_{2}$ acres. This made it the largest building in Winnipeg and resulted in its being nicknamed "the Big Store." When combined with the power house and the stables, Eaton's total floor area exceeded $6^{1}/_{2}$ acres. The cost of the building was reported at the time to be $350,000.

Although the completed building at 320 Portage Avenue was only five storeys (with a partial sixth storey), the structure was designed for the eventual addition of three more floors. Its Portage Avenue frontage of 266 feet covered the entire block from Hargrave to Donald, and its depth was 158 feet. The lot itself was 490 feet from Portage Avenue to Graham Avenue.

Staffing the store

ONE OF FIRST STEPS IN providing capable staff for the new store was the appointment of the general manager. Alfred Alleston Gilroy had been a school teacher in his

The Big Store was largely self-sufficient when it opened. Generators in the power house supplied electricity, and artesian wells provided water.

At the luncheon hosted by Timothy and Margaret (right foreground), Mayor Thomas Sharpe welcomed the company to Winnipeg and wished it success. Premier Rodmond Roblin described Timothy Eaton as a king in the commercial world. Harry McGee, after a rousing ovation, declined to make a lengthy speech and simply announced that the opening ceremony would be taking place shortly. With similar brevity, John Craig Eaton ignored requests that he make a speech. He reminded the luncheon guests that the citizens of Winnipeg were waiting for the promised opening at 2:30 p.m. and shouldn't be disappointed by any delay.

home town of Port Credit, Ontario, but he soon discovered his preference for the world of business and he joined the Eaton company. Having established a reputation as "a thorough business man" (Timothy Eaton's words) in Toronto, Gilroy was chosen by John Craig Eaton to manage the new Winnipeg store.

A small classified advertisement appeared in the *Winnipeg Daily Tribune* on June 8th, 1905, with the heading "Wanted for our Winnipeg store." It requested that "Salesmen, saleswomen, lunch-room help, drivers and parcel hands" apply to the T. Eaton Co Ltd. at 269 Hargrave Street.

As a result of this type of advertisement, approximately 450 new employees were hired locally and were trained in the T. Eaton way of doing business. This training was conducted by experienced Eatonians, twelve men and five women, who were sent from Toronto.

The backbone of the staff, however, was the more than 250 employees of the T. Eaton Co. who came from Toronto in time for the first day of business of the Winnipeg store. Often referred to as "the Originals" (and sometimes as "the Pioneers"), these men and women were recruited on the understanding that they could return to Toronto and their former positions after one year if they wished. Fewer than 20 of the Originals eventually opted to move back to Toronto.

One of the Originals was interviewed in 1955 by Lillian Gibbons for a series of nine articles that appeared in the *Winnipeg Tribune* to mark the Golden Jubilee of the Big Store. Miss Vivian Foote had been the assistant cashier in the Toronto store, but became the chief cashier

in the new store in Winnipeg. "I came on the boat and the train, with a chaperone, everything was very nice. There were 20 in our party," she recalled. "We left July 4 and arrived here July 7. Eaton's had places arranged for us to stay. Everything was thought of."

For management personnel (and their families) from Toronto, the company arranged comfortable and convenient accommodations. Luxurious homes, mainly on Donald Street between Portage and Broadway, were found and were considered quite satisfactory by these newcomers.

The boarding arrangements made by the company for employees who were not in management positions, however, were not to everyone's liking. Not satisfied with the quality of the existing boarding houses, some of the more adventurous women approached the owners of private homes in desirable parts of the city and asked if rooms might be made available to rent. Winnipeggers were pleased to open their homes to "some of the people come up to work at Eaton's," at least until alternative accommodation became available. These acts of kindness illustrated the hospitality of Winnipeggers, as well as their high regard for the morality and integrity of Eaton's employees.

The store opens

A WINNIPEG CONTRACTOR WAS TOLD that the company planned to have the store open for business one year after construction began and responded by saying,

The boarding arrangements made by the company for employees who were not in management positions, however, were not to everyone's liking.

BELLS, GONGS, AND
BUZZERS

BECAUSE, FOR MANY YEARS, THE BIG STORE was not equipped with a public address system, staff members relied on a system of bells, gongs, and buzzers for basic messages. Some of these signals might have puzzled customers, but employees were expected to be familiar with their uses and meanings.

The signal that was probably the most familiar to early-bird customers was the one that announced that the store was open for business. Each morning, customers waited patiently near the entrances for a floorwalker to sound the gong that told them they were welcome to come in. At the same time, bells were rung twice on each floor and in the annex to alert staff that the business day was beginning.

Each floor had a bell in the centre aisle which could be used by staff members to signal for assistance. One ring chime would summon a floorwalker, two would alert the investigation department, and three rings would bring a sweeper.

Promptly at closing time, buzzers signaled floorwalkers to lock the entrance doors, allowing customers to leave but not enter the store. The south Hargrave doors were kept open after that time to admit customers who had a good reason to go in (such as picking up checked parcels). Dismissal bells were used to inform clerks that they were expected to complete their closing routines (one ring to turn off showcase lights, two to cover the counters, and three to sweep behind the counters).
All of these were conditional on there being no more customers to be served.

The gong that was used by Timothy Eaton and his grandson to signal the opening of the store in 1905 remained in active service until 1953. When this gong was retired to be replaced by a bell with a less jarring tone, it was estimated that it had been struck approximately 400,000 times.

"You could not build a bandbox in Winnipeg in that length of time." Exactly 353 days after men and horses began the laborious excavation of the basement, the Big Store was ready to open its door to the public. The date chosen was Saturday July 15, 1905. Timothy Eaton and several family members arrived on July 10th to spend a few days in Winnipeg prior to the opening.

In her memoirs, Flora McCrea Eaton recalls how they travelled in a private railway car (named "Iolanthe") and a chartered sleeper car. "Our party consisted of Mr. and Mrs. [Timothy] Eaton, Mr. E.Y. Eaton, Mr. and Mrs. C. E. Burden, my husband and myself, and our little Timothy. Mr. Eaton's physician, Dr. Edmund E. King, and a masseur accompanied him."

As the Eaton family and their entourage stepped from the train on the morning of Monday, July 10, 1905, A. A. Gilroy led bystanders in three cheers and a tiger. The new arrivals rode in open horse-drawn carriages down Main Street and Portage Avenue to Strevel House.

The arrival of Timothy Eaton in Winnipeg made the front page of the *Winnipeg Daily Tribune* that same day. A headline read: "The Canadian Napoleon of Retail Commerce Reaches the Capital – Views His Great Store for First Time – Well Pleased." The first sentence of the news article simply read: "The great man arrived today."

Saturday, July 15, 1905, turned out to be a beautiful summer day in Winnipeg, with a temperature of 76 degrees Fahrenheit. The previous day's newspaper advertisements had

invited the people of Winnipeg to "Our Public Reception" on Saturday at 2:30 p.m. "On that occasion we will supply guides competent to explain the workings of the many labour-saving appliances to be found in our store to all who may be interested. On the reception day we will sell no goods, and we will close at 6 o'clock, as we purpose to do on all Saturdays in the future."

The choice of July 15th for the store opening was not based solely on the completion of the building to the point where it was able to be open to the public. That weekend also saw a large number of people from outside of Winnipeg attending the Western Industrial Fair, and it was correctly assumed that many of them would visit the new store.

Before the store was opened to the public, Timothy and Margaret Eaton hosted a luncheon on the fifth floor for dignitaries and company officials.

The Governor paid tribute to his son John, to Harry McGee, and to manager A. A. Gilroy. The usually finicky Timothy spoke of his inspection of the new building the day before and observed that he could not find a single fault or think of any suggestions he might make. He concluded his comments by saying, "I am very much pleased."

Just before 2:30 p. m., Timothy Eaton was wheeled to a waiting elevator to carry out the official opening. The Governor (as he liked to be known – and therefore was known – throughout the company) had suffered a broken hip several years earlier and largely depended on a wheelchair for mobility. On his lap was his grandson and namesake, Timothy Craig Eaton, the first child of John Craig and Flora.

Attendants stood at each of the store's four entrance doors (two on Portage and one each on Hargrave and Donald) and at the show windows, anxious to hear the signal that it was time to admit the crowds of eager Winnipeggers waiting outside.

Holding his watch in his hand, The Governor waited until exactly 2:30 and then guided the finger of his grandson to push a pearl button. A gong sounded three times, 42 show windows were unveiled, the doors swung open, and three cheers rang out.

A young boy was the first person to cross the threshold and reach Timothy Eaton. He received a five dollar bill for his achievement and followed Mr. Eaton around the store for the rest of the afternoon. Newspaper reports estimated that between 20,000 and 25,000 people passed through the store in three and a half hours that Saturday afternoon. The aisles, stairs, and elevators were so congested with curious visitors that there was barely room to move. The store was open until 6:00 p.m. and the display windows remained lit until 11:00 p.m.

The first day of business

SATURDAY EDITIONS OF WINNIPEG newspapers included *Eaton's Daily Store News* advertisements proclaiming that the store would be open for business on Monday, July 17 at 8:00 a.m.. A large number of bargains were listed,

A gong sounded three times, 42 show windows were unveiled, the doors swung open, and three cheers rang out.

GOLDEN JUBILEE
1869·1919

including "New York's Latest Creations" for fashion-conscious ladies.

Obviously sensitive to the competition, the *Hudson's Bay Store News* in the same newspapers promised "great price reductions never before equalled" to shoppers who arrived at their store at 8:00 a.m. Monday.

When the Big Store opened on Monday morning at 8:00 a.m., several prominent people could be found serving as temporary employees (and wearing the mandatory black and white attire). Timothy's wife, Margaret Eaton, took on the role of a floor walker and her daughter, Mrs. Charles Burden (formerly Margaret Elizabeth Eaton), was a cashier. Two of Timothy and Margaret's daughters-in-law were involved, with Mrs. E. Y. Eaton looking after a cash register, and Flora in the ribbon circle. These honourary employees were given one day's pay for the jobs they performed during the opening. Flora received a cheque for fifty cents and, fifty years later, she still treasured it as a memento.

Winnipeg newspaper reports indicated that an estimated 50,000 shoppers passed through the doors that day to participate in the Big Store's first day of business and were reluctant to leave at closing time. This figure is noteworthy in view of the fact that the population of Winnipeg at the time was approximately 78,000. For the next several days, *Eaton's Daily Store News* advertisements apologized for the inexperience of the staff and the presence of workers who were still putting the finishing touches on the interior.

The store's layout and services

WHEN THE BIG STORE WAS COMPLETED in 1905, it was clearly the largest building in Winnipeg. It was fully stocked with merchandise that had been shipped from Toronto, along with all the necessary counters and display cases. These had been stored in railway cars and sheds while the store was under construction.

None of the merchandise was available on a "self-serve" basis when the store first opened, and this explains the need for a large number of clerks to assist customers with their purchases.

The basement was not open to the public. In part, it was utilized as a place where employees, after entering by the Donald Street doors, could leave their outer clothing in the cloak room. A card system was used to keep record employees' arrival and departure times so their pay could be calculated. A "toboggan slide" was used to send merchandise received by the store down to the basement, where it was unpacked and placed in store rooms assigned to each department in the store. The mail order shipping and home delivery services were located in the basement as well.

The main floor, the busiest place in the store, featured an island of palm trees in the centre. Among the departments on the first floor were men's clothing, stationery, books, drugs, jewellery, and staples. The second floor offerings primarily focused on women's needs and included women's and children's clothing, coats, corsets, boots and shoes, millinery, and whitewear.

"From the very first day the Big Store (as it was affectionately called) opened its doors to the public, people flocked there to meet their friends, to spend the day, to eat, to browse, and, above all, to buy."

The third floor housed the general offices and the mail order office, which provided service to all of western Canada. Trunks, saddlery, glassware, and kitchen utensils as well as a well-stocked grocery department (including both fresh and dried meats) were also located on the third floor. Grocery customers were provided with tables and chairs where they could sit as their orders were written out by a clerk. On the fourth floor, customers could find carpets, rugs, paints, and other home decorating and furnishing items.

The fifth floor proved to be particularly appealing to customers because it housed a restaurant with seating for several hundred patrons. The huge kitchen was proudly opened for public inspection each morning. The fifth floor also featured the toy department and furniture show rooms.

The new store offered a wide range of services and conveniences for its customers. A comfortably-furnished "resting room" on the second floor was provided for the use of the public and Eaton advertisements encouraged prospective customers (and others who wanted to visit the store even if they had no plans to make purchases) to meet their friends there. This room included tables and chairs, was well as writing paper, pens, and ink.

Valises and parcels could be checked at no charge, and, on rainy days, customers' umbrellas could be left at the main entrances. Telephone and telegraph services were available for customer convenience, as well as train schedule information. A hospital ward, complete with cots, a stretcher, and two attendants, was available to meet any urgent needs of staff members and customers.

For those who preferred the convenience of home delivery, fifteen horse-drawn wagons provided this service to Winnipeg homes three times a day, at 7:30 a. m., 12:00 noon, and 3:30 p.m.. Out-of-town visitors could have their purchases delivered to their Winnipeg hotel or railway station if they wished.

An overwhelming response

THE RECEPTION THAT THE T. Eaton Company received in Winnipeg dramatically exceeded the expectations of the company directors. On the first day of business, the store's receipts were $13,500, a figure estimated as five times the amount normally taken in by any other business in Winnipeg. The initial staff of 750 was increased to more than 1,200 within a few weeks of the opening of the Big Store.

Similarly, the decision to build only five storeys and a basement (with a partial sixth storey) was quickly proven to have underestimated the demands that would be placed on the facility. Only a couple of weeks after the store opened, planning was underway to add to the building.

Over the next few years, a number of additions to the store took place. The original building (as completed in 1905) spanned the entire frontage on Portage Avenue between Hargrave and Donald Streets, but extended

Out-of-town visitors could have their purchases delivered to their Winnipeg hotel or railway station if they wished.

south only about a third of the way to the point it would eventually reach. The remainder of the sixth storey was completed in 1906. In 1907, a six-storey section was added at the rear of the existing store extending south along Donald Street and west approximately half way to Hargrave Street. This addition brought the east rear half of the store to its final limit. In the same year, the basement was extended at the rear of the store in the vacant section at the centre of the property. In 1909, a seventh floor was added to the original section of the store and a two-storey building was erected over the extended basement section in the centre.

As well, in 1909, a four storey building was constructed next to the new two-storey building. In 1910, yet another section, this one having eight storeys and a basement, was added and all of the other sections of the store were brought up to the same height of eight floors. There was also a ninth storey over part of the building. This brought the total floor area of the store to 702,938 square feet (more than 16 acres). The cornice of the massive store was 124 feet above the sidewalk of Portage Avenue, and the flag poles extended an additional 66 feet towards the sky.

Although some discrepancies exist in reports of the sequence and dates of expansions to the store, there is no doubt that a rapid and ambitious series of additions took place during the period from 1906 to 1910. Because the design of the store anticipated expansion, the additions to the building blended in so well with the earlier sections that the exterior provided a completely

A FUTURE
PRESIDENT

BY 1910, JOHN AND FLORA'S OLDEST SON Timothy Craig was seven. John David, only a few months old in this family portrait, would serve as company president from 1942 to 1969.

uniform appearance. On the inside, some of the exterior brick walls that became interior walls created special challenges in later years for electricians trying to string cable from one section to another. As well, different sizes of pillars meant that display personnel had to modify brackets that hung from the pillars.

The expansion of the Big Store necessitated the relocation of the power house. The original power house was in the eventual location of the south Hargrave Street doors. In 1910, a new power house of two storeys and a basement (38,688 square feet) was constructed near the northwest corner of Hargrave and Graham. Its distinctive chimney rose 185 feet in the air and it boasted a flue of seven feet six inches. Also completed in 1910 was a 27,000 square foot single-storey shed that was used for receiving and delivery purposes. The Hargrave Street and Donald Street Annexes at the rear of the store were completed by 1919. Clearly, this was a store growing with the city it served. ■

FALL
AND
WINTER
1905 & 6

WINNIPEG
CATALOGUE
No. 1

THE T. EATON C?. LIMITED.

WINNIPEG, CANADA.

Muff
No. 66-M,
Page 31....25.00

Skirt
No. 4368,
Page 40......6.00

Hat
No. 10-1,
Page 67.....6.50

Coat

BOOK

A woman and a boy

THE FIRST CATALOGUE ISSUED by the T. Eaton Company was a simple six by nine inch booklet. Distributed free of charge to visitors at the Industrial Exhibition – forerunner of the Canadian National Exhibition – in Toronto in 1884, it consisted of only thirty-two pink newsprint pages and was titled *The Wishing Book*. This modest first effort included no illustrations (except for a drawing of the Yonge Street store on the cover), but it did provide detailed descriptions of the merchandise it advertised.

This was not actually the beginning of the mail order business for Eaton's. In previous years, some customers had chosen to order items by mail from the company's store in Toronto, and a staff of two people was charged with filling these requests. A woman was responsible for locating suitable merchandise within the store, and a boy wrapped items and delivered them to the post office to be sent on their way.

Once it became more formalized and publicized, the mail order business expanded rapidly, and so did the number of employees needed to fill the orders. The completion of the Canadian Pacific Railway in 1885 meant that merchandise could be shipped from Toronto to all parts of Canada. The settlement of the prairies saw thousands of families move to farms and small towns, and the T. Eaton Company mail order service became the main shopping source for many.

By 1890, more than a hundred clerks were needed to fill the orders. Although merchandise was described in the catalogue, customers could order anything that the store stocked, and the clerks who were responsible for filling orders frequently had to use their judgement in selecting colours, styles and sizes. To increase the number of people receiving catalogues, Eaton's offered free gifts to customers who sent in the names of friends and neighbours to be added to the mailing list.

Beginning in 1893, there were two editions of the catalogue each year – one for the spring and summer, and another for fall and winter. Approximately 75,000 copies of the 1895 spring

By 1890, more than a hundred clerks were needed to fill the orders.

Chapter 2

Because of volume of mail order business, a separate
building was needed. In 1916, men and horses were
busy excavating for Mail Order Building Number One.

May 5th

48   A STORE LIKE NO OTHER · EATON'S OF WINNIPEG

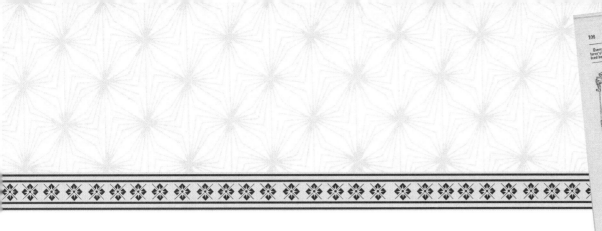

and summer catalogue were printed – double the number of the year before. In 1896, the publication contained 400 pages. By the turn of the century, several smaller issues of the catalogue supplemented the two major editions, offering groceries, hardware, and, of course, items for the Christmas season. Better quality paper was used and illustrations portrayed the vastly-increased offerings.

The Winnipeg Mail Order opens

ALTHOUGH EATON'S HAD thousands of mail order customers in western Canada prior to 1905, the opening of the Winnipeg store was seen as an opportunity to increase sales in the West. By having goods shipped to western mail order customers from Winnipeg rather than Toronto, it was expected that shipping time would be cut in half and that the volume of orders would increase considerably.

When the Big Store opened in 1905, the mail order service was an integral part of the store. Utilizing a portion of the third floor, the department received orders and filled them with merchandise gathered from departments within the store. By 1907, the mail order acquired its own stock of merchandise. The volume of mail order business increased so much that large sections of the newly added sixth, seventh, and eighth floors were soon needed.

By 1917, the nine-storey structure known as Mail Order Building Number One (located behind the store at Graham and Hargrave) was open for business. By 1921, a second and almost identical structure, (Mail Order Building Number Two) was constructed on the south side of Graham at Donald, immediately east of the first structure. The two buildings, which occupied the entire block on the south side of Graham Avenue between Donald and Hargrave became known as "the Mail Order" or, in later years, "the Catalogue." A light-well originally separated the upper stories and there were two connecting walkways on each floor, but this was eventually filled in and the buildings functioned as one. Mail Order Building Number Three, which was actually a four-storey annex to the other structure and housed the horse stables, was constructed in the 1920s.

To expedite the delivery of some items to customers in Saskatchewan and westward, a distribution warehouse was opened in 1916 in

When the Big Store opened in 1905, the mail order service was an integral part of the store.

EATON PLACE

AFTER THE CLOSING of the catalogue operation, an ambitious plan was announced by Eaton's in June 1976 to convert Mail Order Buildings One and Two (which, in effect, had been joined to become one building) to a combination of a retail shopping centre and office tower, complete with its own spacious parking facility. Eaton Place was officially opened in 1979. It was linked to the main store by a pedestrian bridge over Graham Avenue, and long-range plans even provided for the construction of a nearby hotel. Not only did the hotel not materialize, but Eaton Place was one of the properties that were eventually sold in an effort to raise funds to shore up the failing business.

LEGENDS
OF THE BOOK

AS THE T. EATON CATALOGUE became a valued tool in thousands of Canadian households, stories of almost legendary quality were told, re-told, and believed.

The book itself acquired a number of nicknames. "The Wishing Book," "The Wish Book," and "The Book of Dreams" were among the most common. These reflected the ability of the catalogue to provide many hours of wistful browsing for people of limited means, particularly those who lived far from stores. Many older people reminisced about spending long winter evenings in farm homes, leafing through the catalogue by the flickering light of coal oil lanterns. For men, it promised tools and utensils that they dreamed of owning. For women, it was a glimpse of high fashion (and indoor plumbing) about which they could only fantasize. For children, it was page after page of all the Christmas gifts they could ever want Santa Claus to bestow on them. Even if purchasing the items portrayed in the catalogue was not a possibility, leafing through the book liberated people of all ages to dream of a different and better life in the kind of world populated by the shiny, happy, and always appropriately-attired models.

"The Farmer's Bible," "The Prairie Bible," and "The Homesteader's Bible" were nicknames that stressed the importance of the book to rural families. It was sometimes said that the libraries of many rural families consisted of a Holy Bible, a Farmer's Almanac, and the latest Eaton's catalogue. It was a source of virtually all of the clothing, implements, and furnishings they would ever need. Eaton's provided farmers with awareness of the latest household and farming conveniences, as well as an estimate of their fair market value. For those who were considering making purchases at their local store, the Eaton's catalogue was an easily-consulted reference for price comparison (and a way of discouraging local merchants from charging inflated prices to customers in their communities). This led to another nickname – "The Price Guide of the West."

Some stories about the almost-naïve trust that customers placed in Eaton's have been told for decades, and it is difficult to know if they are based on fact of if they qualify as urban (or, at least, rural) legends.

Some early customers apparently believed that they were dealing directly with Timothy and Margaret Eaton. One farm woman in Ontario sent a basket of fresh plums from her orchard (addressed to Mrs. Eaton) in appreciation for the shopping opportunities she had enjoyed though the use of Mr. Eaton's catalogue. Another customer is reported to have requested that "Mrs. Eaton or one of her family" try out a particular piece of sheet music on her own melodeon to determine if the customer would enjoy it. Some customers asked for Mr. Eaton's advice on their clothing selections. Others wrote letters that requested merchandise, but also included chatty accounts of their own families as well as friendly inquiries about the members of the Eaton family.

Three fairly similar stories can be found of men whose loneliness led them to misunderstand what even Eaton's was capable of providing. One is that an Inuit man living on Herschel Island in the Yukon spotted an afternoon frock that was modeled by an attractive young woman and placed his order. When the dress arrived, he wrote a letter to Eaton's asking "Where is the woman?" A similar but more poignant story tells of an Ontario farmer who, after being informed that Eaton's could supply anything that was requested of them, wrote to tell them of the recent loss of his wife. Pointing out that he was very lonely living alone, he requested that he be sent a woman ("not too old"). To provide some incentive for his anticipated companion, he pointed out that he owned his own house and had a monthly income of sixty-seven dollars. The third tale reports that a lonely northern prospector asked the catalogue order-fillers to send him a "real live model, just like the one illustrated on page nine."

Some children showed such confidence in the ability of the T. Eaton Company to supply virtually anything that they wrote letters requesting the delivery of baby brothers and sisters. (Perhaps they also had in mind the company's liberal "goods satisfactory or money refunded" policy.)

Some stories are of customers with complaints that were eventually rectified. One Saskatchewan farmer is reported to have written that the bath tub he ordered and received must have been damaged in transit because it had a hole in the bottom. When a second tub was immediately shipped to him, his frustration increased because, according to his second letter, it had exactly the same defect. It was then that an astute mail order staffer realized what the problem was and wrote to the disgruntled customer that the hole was a feature found in all bathtubs. It was the drain.

Another customer wrote an angry letter (in French) to complain that the stove he had ordered arrived in excellent condition but was missing its legs. His letter went on for several pages, venting his wrath on a company that could be so incredibly incompetent that it would fail to ship legs with a stove. By the time he reached the end of the letter, he had managed to solve the problem on his own, and the postscript after his signature reported that he had found the missing legs in the oven.

EATON'S *Summer Catalogue*

(A) **Classic Slack Suit** of Spun Rayon—Joy of your wardrobe for work, play or carefree lounging! Jaunty Jacket has a smart set-in belt that cinches your waist for the new look; broad rounded shoulders, two patch pockets. Slimming Slacks with roomy pleat in front, set-in pocket and button side closing. **Colors:** Blue or Rose. **Sizes:** 12, 14, 16, 18, 20.

46-K11—Suit, deliv...**6.98**

(B) **Girls' Busy Little Two-Piecer** for active days 'n' Summer beach play! Honey of a Slack Suit of Cotton-and-Rayon Hopsacking—wear the Top out or tucked in—comfy and smart either way. Pointed collar with gay motif, button front and breast pocket. Trim-fitting slacks with set-in pocket; button side opening. **Color:** Medium Blue. **Sizes:** 10, 12, 14, 14X.

11-K013—Suit, del...**2.98**

(C) **Peppy Little Pullover** that's an in or outer for up-and-coming little tykes. Cotton knit in novelty stitch with p collar and two buttons at Ribbed bottom, and cuff long sleeves. **Colors:** or Powder Blue. Size

10-K070—Deliv..

(D) **Snappy Slacks,** fo lass, in new style! Sturdy Cot that'll stand a lot of rum wide band in front, e bac patch pocket t with Red stitching. Blue Sizes: 3, 4, 5, 6, 6X.

10-K066—Delivered..**79c**

(E) **Boys' Short Pants Suits** of Cotton Linene to suit a little he-man age 2 to 7 years! White top with Navy trim on the collar, breast pocket and short sleeves, three-button front. Navy short pants button on to the top. **Sizes:** 2, 3, 4, 5, 6, 7.

10-K071—Suit, del....**79c**

COLLECTING
CATALOGUES

L IKE MANY OTHER ITEMS of Eaton's memorabilia, catalogues have become collectible. The issue commonly found in many closets across Canada is the Spring and Summer, 1976 edition, carefully set aside by thousands who realized that it was the last one to be published. While some may have decided to save it for reasons of nostalgia, other probably assumed that it could be sold for a handsome price a few years later. Like Canadian one-dollar and two-dollar bills, so many people have saved these catalogues that no one will soon become wealthy selling them. Older catalogues in good condition do sell for higher prices in antique stores and on Internet sites.

Reproductions of at least two early catalogues were published many years later. The 1901 and 1927 catalogues were reprinted in the early 1970s by the Musson Book Company of Toronto.

Many libraries and archives across Canada (including the Archives of Ontario which houses the extensive Eaton Collection) have actual catalogues or have preserved them on microfilm.

From the point of view of historians, Eaton's catalogues contain a wealth of information because they reflect so many aspects of Canadian society during the periods in which they were issued. The covers are also valued for their historical depictions and artistic merit.

*The first catalogue
specifically designated
for western Canada
was issued in 1905.*

Saskatoon, and a similar facility in Regina in 1918. These were used for the storage of "heavy goods" (including appliances and furniture as well as buggies and farm implements), but all mail orders continued to be processed in Winnipeg, and most merchandise was shipped from Winnipeg.

The first catalogue specifically designated for western Canada was issued in 1905. Although it was printed in Toronto, the 178-page book was intended to appeal to customers in Winnipeg and all points west. Unlike the 290-page eastern catalogue printed at the same time, the western version paid less attention to high fashion and placed more emphasis on practicality. In recognition of the harsh realities of the prairie climate, the book featured a wide selection of warm coats, muffs, mitts, long underwear, and flannel nighties. The western catalogue also devoted considerable space to farming implements and equipment.

The catalogue of the following year provided even more incentives for western Canadians to do their shopping through Eaton's mail order. For those who were concerned that they might not like what they received, the company offered to prepay the shipping charges on exchanges.

In 1919, the company's Golden Jubilee year, the western catalogue contained 586 pages. Free delivery was offered on all orders of five dollars or more, and this was later lowered to two dollars.

A book of many uses

THE EATON'S CATALOGUE had a variety of uses that went far beyond its primary function as a comprehensive listing of merchandise that could be ordered from the company.

There are many stories of its educational value. New settlers, particularly those from Eastern Europe, discovered that it was an excellent English-as-a second-language textbook. The numerous illustrations with adjacent sections of descriptive text enabled new Canadians to expand their vocabulary of words and phrases referring to everyday household items. In fact, some immigrants were disparagingly accused of speaking "Eaton's Catalogue English" because of their reliance on expressions utilized by the company's copywriters.

Teachers in one-room schools kept Eaton's catalogues as a tool for teaching immigrant children their new language, as well as mathematics (placing hypothetical orders for catalogue items and calculating the totals) and social studies (learning more about Canadian lifestyles). A priest who taught in northern Manitoba once wrote a letter to president John David Eaton asking if he could spare a dozen copies of the catalogue "for the instruction of the children of the parish." It has even been claimed that Queen Mary utilized an Eaton's catalogue to teach her granddaughter Elizabeth (the future Queen Elizabeth II) more about the Canadian way of life.

FOUR CATALOGUES
AT A TIME

IN THE EARLY DAYS of air mail service to remote northern communities, one of the most eagerly-arrived pieces of mail was the Eaton's catalogue. Because the weight of cargo the tiny aircraft could carry was quite limited, pilots would allow a maximum of only four of the weighty catalogues on each flight. These coveted volumes were passed from family to family in the communities.

In the late 1940s, "Displaced Persons" sought refuge and employment in Canada after the war. Eaton's encouraged people who were responsible for the orientation of these new arrivals to give each one a copy of the latest catalogue. This was advocated partly for the purpose of obtaining new customers, but primarily because of the usefulness of the books for learning English.

Illustrations in the catalogue were helpful examples of various clothing styles, and some women who sewed clothing for themselves and other family members copied from illustrations in the catalogue instead of spending money on patterns.

Some recall the catalogues' usefulness as door stops or book ends. Others found that catalogues soaked in salted water, then rolled up and tied, worked very well in their fireplaces as Yule logs. When carefully heated on a wood stove, an Eaton's catalogue became an effective bed-warmer on a cold winter night. There is also the inspiring winter tale of a young woman whose husband was seriously injured and needed to be taken to the nearest doctor. Although she had never before hitched their horse to their sleigh, she used the drawings in an Eaton's catalogue to guide her, and her husband's life was saved.

Women's Wrappers and House Dresses

0560 $1.75

0550 $1.50

0559 $1.00

0562 $1.85

0563 $1.25

8922 $3.00

0558 $1.00

0553 $1.85

1905

Men's and Women's Boots and Slippers.

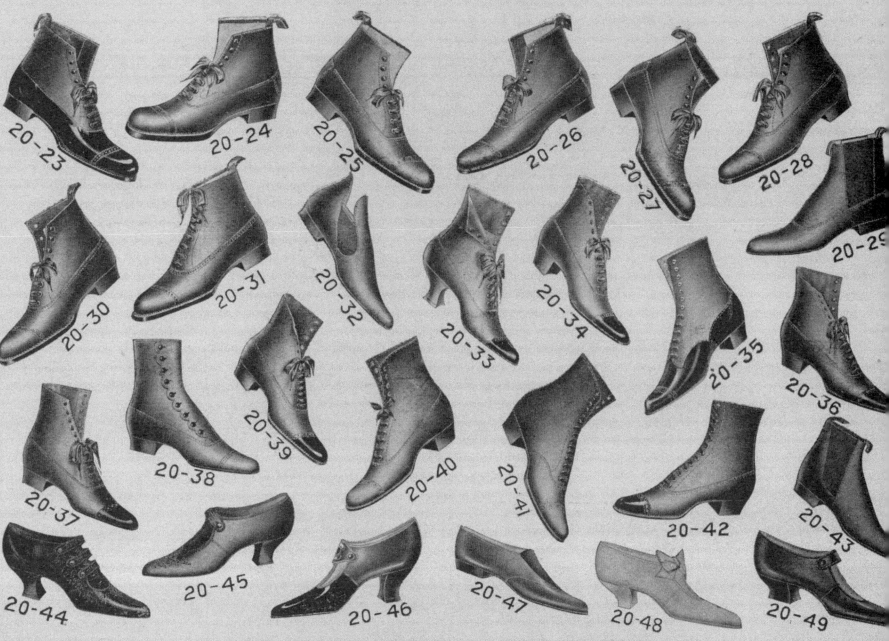

MEN'S BOOTS.

23. Men's extra fine selected Patent oltskin, Goodyear Welted Soles, very essy, size 5½ to 10............ **4.50**

4. Men's "Police Boots" made om genuine Box Calf Skin, extra avy, Goodyear Welted Soles, Calf ing, size 6 to 11, width EE **4.00**

5. Men's selected genuine Box ltskin, leather lined, solid Good-ar Welted Soles, size 6 to 11 **3.50**

6. Men's choice Vici Kid, Good- sewn soles, very soft and easy

20-30. Our special Men's best quality black oil-tanned buff, heavy solid leather soles and heels, sizes 6 to 11..
.... **2.00**

20-31. Men's selected black buff leather extension standard screw soles, sizes 6 to 11.. **1.50**

20-32. Men's choice black Dongola Kid Slipper, elastic sides, turn flexi-ble soles, sizes 6 to 10 .... **1.75**

LADIES' BOOTS.

20-36. Selected jet-black Vici-Kid patent tip, genuine Goodyear welted walking soles, sizes 2½ to 7.... **3.00**

20-37. Choice Dongola Kid, medium light weight soles, patent leather toe cap, sizes 2½ to 7.................... **2.50**

20-38. Soft jet-black glossy Kid, med-ium weight soles, extra wide fitting, very soft, for tender feet, sizes 2½ to 7.. **2.25**

20-39. Extra fine Dongola Kid, patent tip extension McKay sewn soles

20-43. Ladies' prunella cloth sides, for house-wear, sizes 3

20-44. Ladies' extra selected Patent Coltskin, American fancy black beaded, high Lo heels, hand-turned flexible size 2½ to 7.

20-45. Ladies' extra fine Vi one strap, fancy beaded, hand soles, sizes 2½ to 7.

20-46. Ladies choice Patent one strap, two buttons, medi

TOP OF **THE PILE**

IN THE MID-1960s EATON'S DECIDED to reduce the size of its catalogues from the conventional size of 9" by 12" to a smaller 8" by 11". Although this undoubtedly reduced the amount of paper, ink, and glue used in the printing process, the main rationale was not to save money or conserve resources. Instead, it was reasoned that customers (primarily women) received numerous catalogues from different stores and would probably keep all of them in the same place. Assuming that they would be placed in a pile and that the neatness of the pile would be a consideration, then the smallest book (the Eaton's catalogue) would be at the top of the pile – and that would be the one most likely to be used.

Although Eaton's made many efforts to ensure that illustrations in the catalogue were in the very best of taste and would not offend even the most conservative customers, adolescent boys found the undergarment and lingerie sections especially enticing.

For children, the arrival of a new Eaton's catalogue liberated the previous tattered and dog-eared issue for all kinds of fun. Rolled-up catalogues served as shin pads for young hockey players. An empty cardboard box, with the addition of pictures of furniture, appliances, rugs, accessories, and people carefully cut from the catalogue, turned into a fabulous dollhouse. A pair of scissors and a catalogue produced paper dolls. For children with a mischievous bent, crayons were used to add moustaches, beards, and any other embellishments their imaginations could inflict on the catalogue's helpless inhabitants. A game called "Eatonia" saw children flip the book open and slap pages at random, the winner being the one whose hand most often landed on an Eaton trademark. And, when spring arrived, an old catalogue simmered in boiling water yielded dye to colour Easter eggs.

Although Eaton's made many efforts to ensure that illustrations in the catalogue were in the very best of taste and would not offend even the most conservative customers, adolescent boys found the undergarment and lingerie sections especially enticing. There is no doubt that many pleasurable hours were spent furtively studying these tame precursors to *Playboy*.

And, of course, there are numerous stories of how Eaton's catalogues could be found in outhouses throughout western Canada. Although they undoubtedly served as toilet tissue for families of limited means, the smooth and heavy paper on which they were printed must not have provided much comfort for the users. At the very least, Eaton's catalogues served as interesting browsing material in countless biffies.

Catalogue shopping in person

AFTER THE MAIL ORDER acquired its own premises and stock, customers who wanted to purchase merchandise offered in the catalogue were given the opportunity to shop in person.

A spacious and comfortable Mail Order Salesroom set up on the main floor of the Winnipeg Mail Order Building enabled customers to browse through catalogues and place orders. Young clerks, sometimes on roller skates, would bring merchandise for a customer to examine.

Eaton's Clothing and Mail Order

By 1970 there were sixteen Catalogue Sales Offices in rural communities across Manitoba. Here too, catalogues were available and orders could be placed for later delivery. In some of the larger locations, a limited stock of merchandise was displayed. These stores offered the advantage of having knowledgeable local personnel on hand to discuss the merchandise with customers.

The implementation of telephone ordering (using a convenient toll-free phone number) proved to be very popular with mail order customers, and eventually telephone orders exceeded those received by mail. In fact, it was the increase in personal and telephone sales, and the decrease in mail orders that led to the entire operation becoming known as "the Catalogue" rather than "the Mail Order."

A temporary Catalogue Bargain Centre was opened in 1968 at the corner of St. Anne's and St. Mary's Road in a former Safeway supermarket. This brief arrangement was needed while an addition was being constructed to the Donald and St. Mary location. After the Catalogue closed in 1976, a small storefront location in a strip mall at McPhillips and Logan was used to clear out merchandise.

Printing the catalogue

WHEN EATON'S FIRST BEGAN publishing its catalogues in Toronto, the printing was done by an outside firm. In 1901, a printers' strike, coupled with Timothy Eaton's negative feelings about unions, led to a swift decision to set up a company-owned printing plant. It was staffed by Eaton's employees, including a dozen men's wear salesmen who were quickly trained in typesetting. The 1901 catalogue was completed on time, and the company acted as its own printer for more than fifty years.

Although the first few editions of the western catalogue were printed in Toronto, Eaton's soon established its own printing plant

Eaton's
HOUSES

ONE OF THE PRODUCTS OFFERED from 1911 to 1932 to customers in Manitoba, Saskatchewan, and Alberta was complete ready-to-build houses. Featuring pre-cut British Columbia lumber, the materials (shipped by boxcar from Vancouver) included shingles, white oak hardwood floors, windows, doors, and even nails. Some included verandahs and back porches. Prices started as low as $505, with building plans available for a small extra charge. "Eaton's houses" were recognized as quality homes offered at reasonable prices, and examples of these early homesteads can still be found on farms and in small towns throughout western Canada. Barns, other farm buildings, and even school-houses were also available at very reasonable prices.

ESTABLISHING
FAIR PRICES

DURING WORLD WAR II, the Wartime Prices and Trade Board used the Eaton's catalogue as a guide to set ceilings on prices and to check inflation. The Board regarded the catalogue as a useful way to determine fair prices for consumer items. In a later local variation on this, the relief fund established after Winnipeg's devastating 1950 flood used the current Eaton's catalogue to determine replacement values as they compensated householders for furniture, appliances, and other possessions that were destroyed during the flood.

For children, a Fall catalogue was like Toyland on paper.

in Winnipeg. Originally located in Mail Order Building Number One, the plant was relocated to a building on Alexander Avenue that later expanded to become the Heavy Goods Warehouse. It was here that thousands of copies of the catalogues were printed. These included not only the two "Big Books" (the Spring and Summer, and Fall and Winter editions), but numerous smaller catalogues limited to specific kinds of merchandise, such as farm engines, wagons, farm implements, groceries, radios, houses, and barns. By 1945, four catalogues were issued each year by the Winnipeg Mail Order: Spring and Summer, Fall and Winter, Midwinter, and Midsummer.

In 1955, it was decided that of all Eaton's catalogues would be printed in Toronto by the Murray Printing and Gravure Company. Some of the larger presses from Winnipeg were shipped to Toronto and many of the Winnipeg printers were offered jobs in the Murray plant.

Following the downsizing, the Winnipeg printing plant continued to print forms for the Winnipeg store, as well as taking on printing jobs from outside sources, including the telltale brown paper bags used by the Manitoba Liquor Control Commission.

Waiting for the catalogue

THE ARRIVAL OF THE NEW Eaton's catalogue was a much-anticipated event for most families. In some small towns, party lines buzzed when the catalogues arrived at the post office. Some mothers who normally sent other family members to pick up the mail made special trips to be the first to see all the catalogue had to offer. One advantage of having a catalogue was that it was easy to determine the exact price a friend or neighbour had paid for a new outfit.

For children, a Fall catalogue was like Toyland on paper. It provided tacit authorization to begin making lists, dropping hints, and dreaming of what Christmas Day might bring. In late November and well into December, as many as twenty thousand items left the Winnipeg Mail Order each day to find their places under Christmas trees across western Canada.

Out of stock

ORDERING MERCHANDISE FOR each catalogue presented special challenges for mail order staff. Because the contents had to be

2 10-inch plow attachment **114⁹⁹**

4 Tiller attachment **59⁹⁵**

1 Before March 8, 1976 **1,151⁹⁵**

3 ‡Farm price before March 8, 1976 **1,916⁶⁹**

Compact 10-hp model

1 A real brute among compact tractors. Powerful 10-hp Briggs & Stratton synchro balanced engine has 12-volt electric starter/alternator. Three-speed trans-axle transmission has range 3/4 mph to 6 mph (all speeds variable with throttle). Segment and pinion steering for easy turning. Reli-

16-hp model features hydrostatic drive for full power

- Synchro-balanced 16-hp engine helps eliminate vibration for greater comfort
- Automotive-type rack and pinion steering
- Adjustable rear-wheel spacing allows for close-in work stability

3 King of the compacts! Comes with advanced hydrostatic drive that works like an automatic transmission—no shifting, no clutching. Lets you speed up, slow down or back up with a single lever. And, you get full engine power to the attachments regardless of ground speed. Hydraulic power lift makes raising and lowering attach-

OPERATED BY
T. EATON Cº LIMITED

FOODATERIA

OPERATED BY
T. EATON Cº LIMITED

In addition to Catalogue Order Offices, some Manitoba communities had Eaton's food stores or heavy goods stores. Eaton's horses and drivers attended the Portage la Prairie Fair in 1947 and paused for a photo in front of the Portage Foodateria.

finalized many months in advance of publication, decisions about what was to be offered in each book – and the prices – required a great deal of advance planning. Unpopular items would have to be sold later at lower prices, possibly below the company's cost.

If competitors, especially Simpson's, offered the same or similar items at lower prices, there was no way of reducing the price until the next catalogue came out.

If there were insufficient numbers of popular items, potential sales were lost and customers would be disappointed. However, Eaton's practice of supplying substitute merchandise often turned disappointment into delight. Many customers found that the item they received was actually better (and more expensive) than the one they ordered, and were impressed to learn that it was sent to them at the same price as the out-of-stock item. This generous practice was one of the many factors that led to a high level of loyalty among Eaton's customers. It also proved to be very costly for the company.

The Catalogue closes

ON JANUARY 14, 1976, company president Earl Orser delivered a message that caused a collective gasp from British Columbia to Newfoundland – Eaton's was closing its catalogue operation.

Many saw this decision as the obliteration of a cherished part of Canada's history. Public outpourings of emotion, and letters written to the company ranged in mood from sympathetic sadness to outright anger. Thousands shared privately and through the news media what Eaton's catalogue had meant to them and how much of a Canadian institution it had become.

Even Eaton's arch-rival in the catalogue business felt the loss. The Chairman and CEO of Simpsons-Sears Jack Barrow said, "To me it was the equivalent of making an announcement that they had just closed the Anglican Church."

More important in immediate terms was the brutal fact that nearly 9,000 employees, including approximately 1,600 in Winnipeg, were about to find themselves without jobs. Many of these people had worked at Eaton's for decades and had never known another employer. Another cause for concern was the spin-off effect on hundreds of suppliers, as well as the printers, the railways, and the post office. All of them depended heavily on the Eaton's catalogue, and the future of many businesses and their employees were suddenly in jeopardy.

The decision to close the catalogue was the result of a number of factors. The fundamental reality was that the Canada that had been so devoted to Eaton's catalogue no longer existed. In the 1920s, when catalogue sales were the most productive, large numbers of Canadians lived in rural settings and had no way to shop in person. By the 1970s, urban residents found suburban malls (which sometimes included Eaton's stores) to be more satisfying places to select their purchases than the pages of a catalogue. Many rural residents, as well, lived only a short drive from suburban shopping centres.

More important in immediate terms was the brutal fact that nearly 9,000 employees, including approximately 1,600 in Winnipeg were about to find themselves without jobs.

In the weeks preceding the January 14th announcement, the company did all it could to keep the decision a secret until the day it was to be made public.

Stores in shopping malls offered a wider selection of merchandise than could be found in any catalogue, and it had the added advantage of being there to be tried on, and, if purchased, taken home immediately. For big-ticket items, shopping in person provided the opportunity to see more than just a drawing or photograph of a major investment.

Because catalogues had to be finalized so long in advance of their date of issue, clothing offerings tended to be conservative, and limited in variety and style. As styles and trends began to change more rapidly, specialty shops could provide more current selections. In spite of Eaton's efforts to reproduce colour accurately in the pages of its catalogues, seeing a piece of clothing in person was generally preferred to seeing a photograph.

Another factor was that catalogue prices were fixed for the period of time that a catalogue was current. Stores were able to offer sales on short notice that were advertised in newspapers, on television, and on radio, and these sale prices were often more attractive than catalogue prices.

Beginning in the late-1960s, the catalogue operation losses exceeded $40 million. In 1974 alone, the loss was $17 million, and losses for 1975 were projected to be more than $30 million. Ironically, one of the main contributors to this situation was the very policy that customers most admired in dealing with Eaton's. The company's dogged adherence to its "goods satisfactory or money refunded" promise cost the company not only the price of items that could not be re-sold,

but also the shipping costs in both directions. In addition, the practice of substituting better quality, more expensive merchandise for out-of-stock items became very costly.

As revenue fell, the cost of printing and distribution became prohibitive. Nonetheless, the catalogue remained profitable in the area served by Winnipeg. Manitoba Eatonians were very aware of this fact, and it only served to aggravate their anger and frustration at seeing well over a thousand of their colleagues receive termination notices.

In a last-minute effort to rescue the catalogue, Eaton's attempted to negotiate a joint-venture deal with the U.S. department store J.C. Penney. Just as its competitor Simpson's had merged with the U.S.-based Sears, Eaton's courted J.C. Penney to see if joint ownership of the Catalogue operation could be arranged. However Penney declined the offer as well as the opportunity to purchase some of Eaton's smaller and less profitable stores. This sealed the fate of the Catalogue.

In the weeks preceding the January 14th announcement, the company did all it could to keep the decision a secret until the day it was to be made public. Managers from across Canada met at a hotel in Toronto in early January to be briefed on how to deliver the news to employees. They were provided with carefully worded scripts which they were expected to follow as they made the announcements.

In Winnipeg, managers were closeted in the Charterhouse Hotel, just a few blocks away from the store and Catalogue. Well into the night of

January 13th, they received a crash course on conducting exit interviews.

The announcement in Winnipeg came as a complete shock to most. The secret was so well kept that a five-year lease was signed on the Catalogue Order Store in Selkirk, Manitoba one week before the announcement was made. The closing of the rural stores had a major impact on many rural communities in Manitoba, not only because they meant job losses in a very limited job market, but also because of the loss of income that local businesses enjoyed from shoppers who came to towns from outlying areas to place catalogue orders.

David McFetridge, a 44-year Eatonian who was a manager in the Winnipeg Catalogue, says that in retrospect there were some clues that it was not business as usual. "In 1975, the usual call for a budget didn't come. I wondered about that, but I just figured maybe they had some change in plans. I knew there was something different, but no one thought of them closing it."

Personnel manager Ken Gibson wondered why he was asked to leave a telephone number where he could be reached before he left for a holiday in California around the tenth of January. A few days later he received a phone call telling him that the announcement had been made and that he should catch the first flight back to Winnipeg. "They had expected the worst – people jumping out of windows or damaging stuff on purpose," he comments, "but it didn't happen. Interviews were set up with every single person and four months pay was guaranteed."

A NAVEL BATTLE

ASTUTE READERS OF the 1967 Spring and Summer catalogue spotted something unusual about models who were shown wearing bikinis, lingerie, and other tummy-baring attire. They had no navels. The result of this air-brushing exercise was a barrage of outraged letters and telephone calls to Eaton's protesting this less-than-natural depiction of the models. In the next edition of the catalogue, navels returned.

Managers were allotted forty-five minutes to deal with each employee in a private interview. Employees with more than three months of service were given sixteen weeks notice to allow time for the final catalogue to be completed and for them to find alternate jobs. Many older employees with long service received severance pay and early retirement packages. Although a considerable number of employees were terminated, some were placed in positions within the store operation.

Managers were advised in advance of the announcement about precautions they should take for the safety of themselves and their families. They were encouraged to arrange for unlisted home telephone numbers, to make sure that they had deadbolts on their doors, and to develop contingency plans for the safety of their family members. ∎

In 1942, members of the "War Contingent" (with a "V" for Victory on each rig) lined up on Hargrave Street.

ON WHEELS

The horses arrive

ON JUNE 6, 1905, THIRTY-TWO horses were guided into railway cars in Toronto to travel to their new home in Winnipeg. Thirty of them were needed to work as an essential part of the Eaton delivery service in Winnipeg. The other two were show horses for store manager A.A. Gilroy, an avid horse-lover.

The T. Eaton Company home delivery system, which began in Toronto in 1877 with one small wagon and a mare named Maggie, had grown tremendously in that city. Transplanted residents of Toronto were pleased to see the familiar Eaton delivery wagons now making their way through the streets of Winnipeg. The distinctive rigs, with their large spoked white wheels, dark blue bodies, and red wire mesh cages, had been designed by Edward Young Eaton, the eldest son of Timothy and Margaret. Before his premature death from Bright's disease at the age of thirty-seven in 1900, "E.Y." had risen to the position of vice-president, and had carefully crafted the company's efficient delivery system. Prior to John Craig, he was the heir-apparent.

Initially, the Winnipeg fleet consisted of twelve wagons and sleighs. Not long after the store opened, the high demand for home delivery necessitated the addition of twenty horses and eight wagons. Eventually, there would be as many as 300 horses in the Eaton's stables.

By 1910, there were fifty routes in Winnipeg, offering three deliveries each day. In the 1920s, the delivery service included eighteen heavy goods and cartage wagons, fifty-two horse-drawn rigs, and two inspector rigs. Arthur W. Newman was in charge of the stables in 1905 and remained in this position for many years, never without a pocketful of loaf sugar. He was succeeded by Herb Steen.

In 1905, the spacious stables (17,500 square feet) were located on the same lot as the store. They included individual stalls for the horses, each personalized with the name of its equine occupant. The horses were curried on a daily basis and received regular clippings and shampoos. The stable was washed daily and completely scrubbed twice a week.

In 1905, the spacious stables (17,500 square feet) were located on the same lot as the store.

Chapter 3

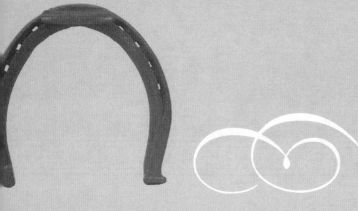

OLD BRIT

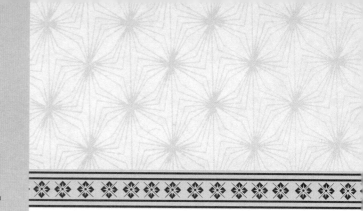

ONE OF THE MOST HEART-WARMING examples of the devotion of Eatonians to their horses is the story of Old Brit. After arriving at the Eaton stables in 1909 at the age of four, Brit became one of the company's most award-winning show horses. Besides picking up many ribbons at fairs across the Prairie provinces and in the northern United States, the handsome dappled grey was given the privilege of making deliveries on prestigious routes to downtown hotels and the railway stations.

But the years passed, Brit's hair turned white, and his once-strong legs became too weak and shaky to pull a fully loaded wagon.

Like some of his human counterparts, Brit did not appear to welcome the idea of retirement. Other horses were moved to carefully selected farms to graze out their twilight years, but this proud animal seemed to want to continue to earn his keep. He appeared to dislike being left behind when the other horses went to do their daily jobs.

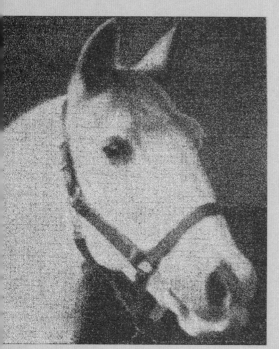

The stablemen decided to find a way to keep Brit as an active and contributing member of the delivery team, despite his reduced capabilities. Each morning he was harnessed up in the same way as the other horses and driven the one-block distance from the stable to the store. His rig was loaded with boxes and parcels that needed to be taken to the Mail Order Building (where the stables were located), and this became his daily morning delivery routine.

This arrangement seemed to satisfy Brit, and he spent the rest of each day at the stables, where he enjoyed treats of sugar and affectionate ear-pulls from the stable manager and the stablemen.

Brit lived in the Eaton's stables until he died on May 25th, 1927.

Because of the ongoing expansion of the Big Store, the stables were later relocated to another area of the same site. When Mail Order Building Number Three was completed, the stables moved to that building; the floors were connected by ramps to facilitate the movement of horses from one level to another.

Although other retailers used horses for home delivery of bread, milk, ice, and other commodities, they didn't attract the same attention, especially from children, as the Eaton's horses. While the horses used by other businesses were usually heavy-set and were often carelessly groomed, most of the high-stepping Eaton's horses used for home deliveries were slim and athletic in appearance, with glossy coats. Many of the Eaton's horses were hackneys, which explains their slim, handsome appearance and their high-stepping gait. Eaton's horses resembled race horses; those of other businesses looked more like plough horses. Matched with the always-immaculate wagons and the clean-cut, uniformed drivers, these ambassadors of Eaton's never failed to be noticed.

In the 1930s there were two home deliveries daily, and sometimes three to local hotels. If an order was placed before noon, delivery was guaranteed that same afternoon. The company owned more than 150 horses. In one year alone, 1933, the Eaton's stables used 4,670 horseshoes — a total weight of 3 $\frac{1}{2}$ tons.

In addition to their daily delivery rounds, Eaton's horses and rigs toured the fair circuit in Winnipeg and rural Manitoba, sometimes to compete in judged competitions, sometimes for

To celebrate the 1942 Birthday Sale, this two horse rig proudly made its way down Portage Avenue.

In 1913, members of the Winnipeg Shipping and Delivery department were ready for another busy day.

Children were especially fascinated by the Eaton's horses, and many knew the name of the particular horse that delivered on their street.

public relations purposes, and always to be admired by people who appreciated fine horses. The ribbons that they won were proudly displayed in the driver's recreation room in the stable building.

The spectacle of the horses

THE DEPARTURES OF THE EATON'S wagons from the downtown stables were events that often drew large crowds. The horses were hitched to their loaded wagons and lined up inside the building. When all were ready to depart, the signal was given, the stable door was opened, and the proud drivers and horses paraded single file into the street. Sometimes the drama of the pageant was heightened by a traffic policeman who stood in the intersection to ensure that other traffic yielded to the emerging Eaton's cavalcade.

Children were especially fascinated by the Eaton's horses, and many knew the name of the particular horse that delivered on their street. Despite frequent requests from neighbourhood children, riders were not allowed on the Eaton's rigs. However, this prohibition did not prevent children from offering the horses sugar lumps, apples, carrots, and other treats while the drivers were carrying parcels to houses. The stables were frequently open to the public, and many children were able to visit "their" Eaton's horse at home.

Adult customers also showed a special interest in the horses, sometimes displaying more concern for them than they did for the drivers. If a horse became lame on a route, concerned customers often phoned the stables to complain before the driver had an opportunity to deal with the problem. During hail storms, the horses and drivers were offered refuge inside empty garages. Many of the horses quickly figured out which customers were likely to offer candies and other goodies.

Hoofbeats was distributed to employees in 1943 to celebrate the return of the horses.

The horses leave — but not for long

ON FEBRUARY 23, 1939, the horses and drivers left the downtown stable for their two o'clock deliveries. This was expected to be their final journey together. The age of motorized transportation had gradually made inroads into the Eaton's delivery system, particularly in the suburban areas of Winnipeg, and for the delivery of large and heavy items. Beginning with a dark blue panel truck that resembled a hearse, the number of trucks in the Eaton's fleet had gradually increased.

The decision was finally made to eliminate horse-powered deliveries. After ensuring that they would be going to good homes, the horses were sold. Their many admirers in Winnipeg sadly said farewell.

Delivery rigs for heavy goods (in this case furniture and carpets in 1911) were pulled by two horses. Most home deliveries were carried out by one-horse wagons.

ONE SMART **HORSE**

IN APRIL, 1947 STEVE KIZ was looking for a temporary job with Eaton's before returning to school that September. Eaton's was short of drivers, and being a junior employee, Steve was told he would be driving a horse and wagon at a salary of twenty-five dollars a week. He did this for two years before being "promoted to a truck." This "temporary" job would last for more than forty-three years and see him rise to the rank of transportation manager for the western region.

Steve and his horse Gunner did their daily deliveries on Number 5 Route in the River Park area, including Churchill Drive and Jubilee. At that time, Eaton's offered one home delivery each day, and this meant that the wagons were often loaded right to their roofs with parcels when they left Mail Order Building Number Three in the morning.

Steve describes Gunner as "one smart horse" because of his ability to understand traffic signals. "I had one traffic light, on Pembina at Jubilee. When it was red, he'd come to a stop, and then when it turned green he knew when to go." Gunner did, however, find the amber light somewhat confusing.

Like many other Eaton's horses, Gunner knew his route and he recognized the homes of regular customers. When Steve stepped off the rig to deliver a parcel, Gunner would automatically stop. When Steve finished that delivery and returned to the wagon, Gunner would move on and stop in front of the home of the next customer.

When Eaton's horses visited local fairs, they enjoyed
first-class accommodations.

A fresh coat of white paint and some creative landscaping resulted in park-like surroundings for the Eaton's stables on Pembina Highway. While this new site was not as convenient to the store as the Mail Order location, it had the advantage of providing much more outdoor space, and allowed the horses the luxury of spending some of their non-working hours enjoying fresh air and sunshine.

In making the decision to discontinue horse-drawn deliveries, the company pointed out that one truck could do the work of twenty horses. In addition, the safety of the drivers and horses in the busy motorized traffic of Winnipeg was a major consideration.

The outbreak of World War Two soon brought a welcome encore for the horses and the rigs. The need to ration gasoline and rubber to aid the war effort led Eaton's, in 1942, to reinstate some of the horse-drawn wagons. By 1945, twenty-three horses were again operating in Winnipeg, and were known as "the War Contingent." Eventually thirty-two horses were called into service.

Many of the horses that recruited to join the War Contingent were given names appropriate for the times. Some of the stallion's names were Churchill, Gunner, Ack Ack, Sailor, Pilot, and Wings. Their mare team members included WAVE, WAAC, and WREN.

The wagons had been sold when horse delivery was stopped in 1939, and many of them were dismantled by the purchasers. The top of one wagon was found on a farm west of Winnipeg serving as a chicken coop, while the gear was located hauling firewood near Selkirk. Various parts of the retired wagons were retrieved to be fitted together by Eaton's garage staff. The newly assembled rigs required fresh coats of paint in the truck-painting department to overcome three years of exposure to the Manitoba elements. At first, the wagons continued to have wooden-spoked steel wheels, but when the rubber supply improved, the wagons were equipped with car wheels and tires.

The stable facilities in Mail Order Building Number Three had been taken over for warehouse purposes. New accommodations had to be found, and a building at 416 Pembina Highway (at Garwood), was chosen as the location. Although it had previously been a

PEACOCK

APPROPRIATELY, THE FIRST HORSE to join the War Contingent was Peacock, a bay bred from fine hackney stock and raised in the Eaton's stable. Like the other horses, Peacock had been sold, but he was retrieved and returned to active service. Because sugar was rationed, and horses were definitely not considered eligible for sugar ration cards, Peacock appeared content with candies as periodic treats. He also enjoyed chewing plugs of tobacco and the occasional cigar. Peacock continued his work for Eaton's, along with his driver Alf Goodall, on a route that included Mulvey, Jessie, and Warsaw Avenues until 1948. Peacock was retired at the age of 23, and spent the remainder of his years nibbling grass in a pasture and enjoying periodic visits from the drivers he had come to know. If horses are capable of reminiscing, perhaps Peacock thought about the time he led the Santa Claus Parade with a burly policeman on his back, or the many times he was admired by visitors to the stable.

"Hoofbeats"

"Consider, then, that spirit and ardour are in the temper of a horse, what passion is in the mind of men."
—Xenophon,
Treatise on Horsemanship.

This publication is designed primarily to assist in arriving at a good understanding between the horses and the men who drive or look after them.

That is why Churchill, one of the "downtown" horses, is taking time to give us his side of the story.

After reading his comments, so full of real horse sense, we are going to be sporty enough to pay close attention to his various requests and meet them in a spirit of true co-operation.

Evidences of this co-operation are contained in the reply of the drivers and stablemen in this our first issue.
—C.T.

riding academy, the building was being used as a chicken hatchery when Eaton's decided to purchase it. The stalls, hay racks and mangers had been removed and needed to be quickly reconstructed by Eaton's carpenters.

As in the past, Eaton's horses received the best of treatment. Whole oats were purchased, rather than the more convenient crushed form. This enabled stable staff to inspect the food carefully for quality and impurities before crushing it in a specially-acquired power crusher. The stable staff used a hay cutter so the horses could be fed fresh hay, and often supplemented it with salt and linseed. While on the road, horses were provided with nose-bag lunches, and after a busy day, hot cooked meals were a special treat. Their shoes were inspected every day. Harnesses were custom-fitted to each horse. Each horse was weighed once a month, and a veterinary dentist visited the stables regularly for check-ups. Devoted grooming, of course, was a regular routine. To provide non-human companionship for the horses and keep unwelcome company away, two rat terriers were added to the stable staff. The return of the horses enabled Eaton's to continue its participation in summer fairs throughout Manitoba. In addition, the Pembina stables became the site of annual horse shows. The 1947 show drew a record crowd of five thousand spectators to the stables on a warm August evening.

Shoes are OPTIONAL

THE ONLY EATON'S DRIVER in a Manitoba town knocked on the unlocked screen door of a regular customer and heard a cheery "come on in." As he walked into the house, he saw that the customer, a rather large woman, was sitting alone at the kitchen table painting her fingernails and wearing nothing but a pair of red high-heeled shoes. He quickly backed out of the house and fled to the safety of his truck.

Women drive the trucks

AS IN MOST OTHER DEPARTMENTS of Eaton's and other companies, the recruitment of male employees into the armed services resulted in labour shortages. This necessitated the assignment of women to jobs that were traditionally done by men. Eaton's drivers, because of their skills and experience, were considered to be especially valuable for military transport purposes, so women employees needed to be called into service to replace them. This early experiment in equality of the sexes was somewhat controversial. Public perception at the time was that women were not nearly as capable of driving motor vehicles as men. In addition, delivering often involved having to carry heavy parcels not only from a truck to a residence, but sometimes up several flights of stairs to customers' apartments.

Initially six women were recruited to become truck drivers on a trial basis, and eventually forty women worked at various times as drivers. One male driver still speaks with admiration, almost fifty years later, of a particular female driver who "could handle a hundred pounds of sugar like nothing." Despite their efforts to gain acceptance, one of the women who served as a driver during that period recalls that she and her female colleagues never came to feel that that they were seen as equals by most male employees.

As was the case in other areas of work, the women drivers continued to perform their new tasks capably until the war ended and the men who had previously filled these positions returned.

(Right) Winnipeg-manufactured four-cylinder White trucks were the most typical means of suburban delivery between 1911 and 1927. The boxes of these vehicles were very similar in appearance to the horse-drawn rigs, and their high clearance enabled them to open up snow-clogged roads for other vehicles in an era before snow ploughs were common. The truck shown here was restored in 1970 by Eaton's Winnipeg transportation department.

(Below) The wagons designed by Edward Young Eaton rode on spoked wooden wheels. Later versions used rubber-tired automobile wheels.

The women then went back to their former jobs, which usually paid significantly less than the traditionally male-only positions.

The horses leave forever

THE HORSE-DRAWN RIGS WERE now used on a year-round basis, unlike the earlier days when sleighs were utilized during the winter. Drivers were issued winter uniforms (including heavy wool grey pea jackets, lined leather mitts, and felt boots), and the horses were provided with blankets (windproof grey wool, with a monogrammed red diamond "E").

After the war, horse-drawn deliveries in Winnipeg continued to decline until they were finally phased out in 1950. Some of the horses were retired to spend their senior years in pastures, while others were sold to carefully-screened farmers and riding academies.

The only other time that an Eaton's rig and horses made an appearance on the streets of Winnipeg was in Canada's centennial year, 1967.

Two double teams made deliveries to hotels and other downtown locations to commemorate this phase of Winnipeg history. The wagon used for this occasion was made from the cannibalized parts of two wagons, one found in some bushes off Shaftesbury Boulevard, and the other recovered in St. Boniface.

The era of horse-drawn deliveries had come to an end. After almost fifty years of faithful service, the familiar red, white, and blue rigs and the sleek horses would no longer capture the admiration of Winnipeggers of all ages. Motorized vehicles had won out, but they would never match the thrill of seeing an Eaton's delivery wagon rolling down the street

Ambassadors on wheels

THE ERA OF THE HORSE WAS OVER, but Eaton's delivery service continued to flourish. An Eaton's advertisement in Winnipeg's daily newspapers in 1966 featured a full-page tribute to the seventy regular parcel delivery men, with an average of nineteen years of service, and included a group photograph and the names of the drivers. The heading of the advertisement was "the friendliest thing on wheels."

Eaton's drivers were familiar and trusted figures in Winnipeg's neighbourhoods. Many were given keys to customers' homes and apartments so parcels could be left indoors when no one was home. It was not uncommon for snacks to be left for the drivers.

There was a common belief among customers that any item, no matter how small and inexpensive, could be ordered from Eaton's, and it would be cheerfully delivered to their homes at no extra charge. Driver Steve Kiz remembers a Selkirk customer (in fact he remembers her name and address) who ordered a loaf of salt-free bread once a week. He delivered this thirteen-cent item every Friday.

Although delivery service from the Big Store was primarily within the city, customers in nearby rural communities also received this service. During the summer, cottagers at Lake Winnipeg resorts enjoyed the daily delivery of groceries as well as anything else they chose to purchase at Eaton's. Refrigerated boxes installed in the trucks ensured the safe arrival of perishables.

Acts of special kindness and consideration by the drivers often received tributes from the recipients. Many customers ordered by telephone, and their only personal contact with Eaton's was provided by the driver in their neighbourhood. To them, the driver represented the entire company. During World War Two, when many households had no adult males, the Eaton's drivers went out of their way to be helpful to mothers and children.

Letters from customers expressed appreciation for such courtesies as returning lost money and keys, chopping wood, plugging in frozen cars, adjusting smoking coal-burning furnaces, and regularly checking on customers who were ill or elderly. Many simply praised the never-failing friendly and courteous attitude of their drivers.

Acts of special kindness and consideration by the drivers often received tributes from the recipients.

MOST CITY DELIVERIES in the fifties and sixties were made by Metro vans, but this Mercedes-Benz diesel model was introduced in 1960 on the Selkirk, Manitoba, route because it offered better fuel economy.

Huge semi-trailer units were modern
replacements for two-horse rigs.

Although company policy prohibited riders in Eaton's vehicles, drivers sometimes encountered emergencies which justified making exceptions. Remarkably, two such incidents involved a beach delivery driver named Jenner in 1937. In the first one, he noticed that a car that had overturned in the ditch and he drove two unconscious victims to the nearest hospital. The second incident involved a tearful young boy he saw by the side of the highway. The boy's mother had died in a Winnipeg hospital and, unable to afford train fare, he had completed only part of his sad journey home by bicycle before one of his tires went flat. The sympathetic driver gave the boy a ride to his destination.

The company stressed safe driving and road courtesy to its drivers. As early as 1945, defensive driving techniques were instituted. Annual dinners were held to present cash awards and buttons in recognition of accident-free driving. At the 1951 dinner, 980,000 miles of driving without personal injury were recognized, and 228 drivers shared $2,741 in cash awards.

Drivers received bonuses during special company promotions. The annual fall Bulb Contest saw drivers reminding householders to replace burned-out light bulbs and to stock up on extra ones. In the spring, drivers encouraged customers to let them take their fur coats for storage in Eaton's vaults.

Because many orders were COD, drivers often collected as much as $2,000 in one day. For several decades, the drivers felt safe carrying large amounts of cash and leaving their trucks unlocked while they were making deliveries. In the late 1970s, one of them was robbed by two men, driven to the outskirts of the city, and abandoned. After that, lockable steel strong boxes were installed in every delivery van for the safekeeping of cash, and the truck doors were fitted with locks.

The numbers of routes, trucks, and drivers fluctuated with the volume of business. In 1941, Eaton's had a fleet of 135 trucks. By 1951, there were 185 trucks and 88 routes. The delivery staff peaked between 1955 and 1960 with 133 parcel delivery drivers and 46 heavy goods drivers and their helpers on the payroll.

The completion in the 1960s of the massive service building at Wellington Avenue and Berry Street resulted in the relocation of all of Eaton's transportation services to that facility. At that point, there were 73 parcel trucks and 28 furniture delivery trucks, which handled an average of 14,500 parcels and 1,100 pieces of furniture a day. On one day during the 1967 Birthday Sale, drivers delivered 28,000 parcels. By 1987, as Eaton's business in Winnipeg declined, there were only 12 parcel trucks and two deliveries a week. Eventually, Eaton's deliveries were contracted out. ∎

For unexcelled entertainment we rec\
talking to his horse, a real Manitobs\
Can't blame the horse for laughing

Young Jim Roberts was heard\
of his customary Christmas g

Because many orders were COD, drivers often collected as much as $2,000 in one day. For several decades, the drivers felt safe carrying large amounts of cash and leaving their trucks unlocked while they were making deliveries.

Sir John (front row, second from the right) in 1915
with officers of the Eaton Machine Gun Battery.

OF WAR

Keeping the faith

ONE OF THE FACTORS that strengthened the dedication of Eatonians to the company was the respect that their employer showed to them when war broke out. The company not only made every effort to ensure that Eaton's employees who enlisted in the military felt that they remained part of the Eaton's family, it also continued to pay them.

The T. Eaton Company's practice of paying employees while they were members of the military during wartime began during the Boer War of 1899 to 1902. Four male employees who fought in South Africa with the Canadian Contingent continued to receive their full Eaton's wages during their absence. Their return was celebrated with a special employee-sponsored concert at Toronto's Massey Hall, and the presentation of gold watches by Margaret Eaton on behalf of her husband Timothy.

World War I

THE BOER WAR PRECEDENT was followed up on a much larger scale in World War I. In that conflict, more than 3,000 male Eatonians enlisted, with 1,100 of these from Winnipeg. Married men who volunteered for active service continued to receive full pay from Eaton's in addition to their military pay. Single men received half their Eaton's wages. By October 1919, the salaries paid out totalled $2.2 million.

The company's support of its overseas employees went beyond providing income. To demonstrate that these Eatonians were not forgotten, their individual photographs were displayed in the Winnipeg and Toronto stores. The company's buying offices in London and Paris served as banks where servicemen on leave could make withdrawals from the wages they were continuing to receive from the company. These offices also provided brief refuges of Canadian hospitality in cities far from home.

The family yacht, Florence.

Winnipeg drivers raised vegetables in a Victory Garden, a twelve-acre plot in the sparsely-populated Silver Heights area. Proceeds from sales of these vegetables were donated to the Red Cross.

Returning soldiers were provided with special assistance through a Soldiers' Settlement Department in the store.

To aid the war effort, more than 16,600 employees subscribed $2.2 million to the 1918 Victory Loan campaign. This was supplemented by pledges of $350,000 from the company directors and slightly more than $2 million from the company.

Returning soldiers were provided with special assistance through a Soldiers' Settlement Department in the store. For those who were interested in becoming farmers under the Soldiers' Land Settlement Scheme, Eaton's published a booklet with detailed information.

On May 8, 1920, the returning Winnipeg veterans were recognized with the presentation by Sir John Eaton of gold medals featuring the Eaton coat of arms.

Some of the Great War veterans were no longer able to work as a result of war injuries, but of the 2,021 men who returned to Canada by 1919, 1,375 were back on the job with Eaton's in

Parcels from fellow Eatonians to servicemen on the front included such welcome items as coffee, chocolate, and hand-made woolen mittens and socks. At Christmas, each serviceman received a box of treats courtesy of Sir John and Lady Eaton and Eaton's employees, plus a box of cigarettes from Lady Eaton. The forty-one Eatonians who were captured as prisoners of war received monthly packages of food and tobacco that were sent by the company office in Zurich.

Comfort
AND CHEER

FOR CUSTOMERS WHO WANTED to send "Special Gift Cases of Comfort and Cheer" to troops during World War I, Eaton's Mail Order advertised assortments of non-perishable food items in 1916. Ranging in price from $1 to $4.75, and sturdily packed in tin or cardboard boxes, these double-wrapped packages could be sent directly to the war front from Winnipeg or shipped to the purchaser for forwarding. Typical items included tea, candies, chocolate, chewing gum, and beef cubes. The headline of the advertisement read "The Big Store's Service Reaches the Boys in the Training Camps, Trenches and Hospitals just as surely and satisfactorily as it does the folks at home."

Winnipeg and Toronto. In situations where their former jobs were no longer available, some employees were moved to jobs of equal value. In addition, the company hired 1,465 returning soldiers who had not previously worked for Eaton's.

World War II

WHEN WORLD WAR II broke out, management had concerns that the company could not afford to provide full pay for absent employees. Instead, it was decided that Eaton's would supplement the military wages of enlisted married employees to maintain their total income at the same level as it was prior to the war. Single men received a company supplement to bring their total wages up to two-thirds of their previous income. This income was not sent directly to the service personnel, but was banked by the company on their behalf at an interest rate of ten percent. This money could be left in the account until the recipient returned home, or it could be withdrawn in person at the London Buying Office. These subsidies cost the company approximately $4 million.

Many Eatonians received promotions that brought their military pay to a figure that was actually higher than their Eaton's salary, and the subsidy from the company should have been discontinued. In at least some of these cases, however, Eaton's continued to pay them.

The London office served once again as a hospitality centre for Canadian troops. D-Day veteran David McFetridge remembers being

NYLONLAND

ONE OF THE FASHION HARDSHIPS experienced by women during World War II was that nylon stockings were no longer available. Because nylon was needed to make parachutes (one parachute required the fabric that would otherwise create twenty dozen pairs of stockings), most women accepted the fact that they would have to do without new nylon stockings until the war was over. As a stop-gap measure, customers with runs or snags in their stockings visited the eighth floor Hosiery Repair Shop where runs in nylon stocking were repaired for a few cents.

February 19, 1946 was declared Nylon Day across Canada – the day when limited numbers of the fashionable stockings would once again be available for sale. In Winnipeg, an estimated 20,000 women began lining up well before 8 a.m.. By the time the doors opened, women stood four deep from the south Hargrave entrance, all across the Portage Avenue frontage, and down Donald to the south entrance on that street.

Careful planning by Eaton's management not only avoided the stampedes that took place in other cities, it resulted in each customer having her single new pair of stockings in her hands and paid for within an estimated two to five minutes after entering the store.

Customers and the media later expressed their admiration for the efficiency of this plan, which was devised weeks in advance. The coveted stockings were laid out on ten large circular counters across the main floor of the store (an area dubbed "Nylonland"). Two hundred and fifty extra salespeople and thirty-seven additional cashiers were pressed into service to supplement the regular hosiery staff. Barriers were erected, doors were carefully watched, and elevator and escalator service in the area were curtailed. By 10:30 a.m., the crowds were gone and Nylon Day was over.

Not wanting to deprive their female employees of the opportunity to purchase nylons, special arrangements by Eaton's were made for women to leave their workplaces at staggered pre-assigned times to report to the time office. In this carefully orchestrated plan, 4,000 Winnipeg Eatonians were able to obtain their allocation of one pair each.

John David Eaton chatted with veteran Jim Maltby from Regina (in wheelchair) at the luncheon.

(Centre) The large numbers in attendance at the Winnipeg war victory event necessitated the use of both the concert hall and the ballroom of the Fort Garry Hotel, with an executive from the company in each room. The rooms were decorated with the flags and shields of the army, navy, and air force, and huge blue and white banners proclaimed "Welcome Home Eatonians." A public address system was used to broadcast key aspects of the ceremony to both rooms.

A STORE LIKE NO OTHER · EATON'S OF WINNIPEG

To demonstrate the importance of the event to the Eatons, several family members were in attendance. Pictured here are John David, Lady Flora, Gilbert, and Robert Young (back row left to right). In the front row are wives Signy, Marjorie, and Hazel.

The United Services Centre in the Donald Annex was visited by an estimated three million service men and women from various nations. The usual sign on the Annex read "TOYS WHEEL GOODS AUTO ACCESSORIES"

Contacts solemnly included information and photos of Eatonians who were killed, wounded, missing in action, or taken prisoner.

Supporting the war effort

IN KEEPING WITH SIR JOHN'S decision to refuse to profit from the manufacture of war materials in World War I, Eaton's returned to the government all profits that resulted from producing war materials in World War II.

One of the ways that Eatonians helped the war effort at home was through their involvement in the Eaton Employees' War Auxiliary. This organization, with Lady Eaton as the Honourary President, was responsible for a number of supportive endeavours, usually outside of the members' regular working hours.

Some of the employees' efforts were in support of the Red Cross. Several campaigns were held where employees voluntarily donated blood to be sent overseas. Winnipeg Eatonians formed sewing and knitting groups to contribute hand-made socks, scarves, gloves, and socks to the Red Cross drive. In 1944, donations to the Red Cross were valued at close to $30,000.

Efforts to conserve materials in short supply were aided by employee support. A "Salvage on Parade" display in the Annex in 1942 educated customers on the proper techniques of recycling paper, rubber, glass, metal, and even bones and fats. To conserve gasoline during World War II, many Eatonians cycled to work, and the company provided supervised and roofed bicycle racks on the Carlton Street employee parking lot where more than three hundred bicycles could be locked.

One of the most ambitious programs in support of war efforts was the United Services Centre. In 1942, Toyland was moved from the Donald Annex to be replaced by a social and

welcomed there with tea and biscuits and looking over a guest book to see the names of other Winnipeggers who had dropped in.

As had been the case during World War I, ongoing communication with Eatonians involved in the war let them know that they were still very much part of the extended Eaton's family. More than 1,300 men and women from the Winnipeg store continued to receive *Contacts*, the company magazine. Besides providing information about people and activities "back home," the magazines included photographs of "Eatonians now serving the Empire," information about those who were decorated or mentioned in dispatches, and messages of support and encouragement. As the war progressed, *Contacts* solemnly included information and photos of Eatonians who were killed, wounded, missing in action, or taken prisoner. Eatonians serving in the armed forces also received Christmas parcels and cards on behalf of the company and the employees. These contained knitted items of clothing and non-perishable foods.

Returning
TO EATON'S

WHEN WORLD WAR II began, no formal guarantee was given that veterans would be returning to Eaton's. Some, however, recall being assured privately by their department managers that, "if they made it back," their jobs would be waiting for them. Partly because of the attitude of loyalty of the company towards its employees and partly as a result of the 1942 Reinstatement in Employment Act, virtually every Eatonian who wanted to return to his or her previous position was placed in the same (or an equivalent) job at comparable pay. Many had received promotions within the military, and, for at least some veterans, this kind of achievement resulted in being given positions of greater responsibility with Eaton's than they had held prior to the war. Others who had received injuries that prevented them from performing their previous tasks were assigned tasks they were able to handle. A man who lost an arm might become an elevator operator or escalator attendant. One man who lost both legs in the war was reassigned as a typewriter repairman.

recreational canteen. The facilities, along with $17,000 worth of renovations that included a mezzanine, a bandstand, and a kitchen, were donated by Eaton's. During the years it was open, the centre was staffed by more than six thousand volunteers. The United Services Centre was a place where Canadian and other Allied personnel who were far from home could purchase meals, snacks, and refreshments (non-alcoholic, of course) at very reasonable prices, play cards or pool, listen to music, and dance.

It was this latter activity that proved especially attractive to many young female Eatonians, because it provided an opportunity to meet and dance with an almost limitless number of handsome young men in uniform. Supervisors, however, hovered on the dance floor to ensure that hostesses and service personnel were dancing a respectable distance apart. A group known as the "Trumpet Call Revue," made up mainly of Eatonians, completed its 65th performance in 1942. In total it entertained almost 55,000 service men and women. The United Services Centre remained open until 1946.

Eaton's employees and the company also contributed generously to the annual Victory Loan campaigns. In 1944, Eatonians across Canada contributed more than 2.3 million dollars, and the T. Eaton Company added another seven million dollars. In Winnipeg, employees' pledges exceeded half a million dollars, with many departments achieving their projected goals within the first week of the campaign.

Eaton's obtained a special postal permit that allowed the company to send packages directly to prisoners of war. Although these packages were limited to such items as books, sheet music, playing cards, and small pieces of sports equipment, many letters of thanks were received expressing appreciation for them. A caution for Eatonians writing letters to prisoners of war was included in the Christmas, 1942 edition of *Contacts:* "There should be no reference to any naval, military, political or economic matter. A seemingly innocent remark can lead to a train of valuable information, with disastrous results to our cause."

Returning in glory

A GALA "WELCOME HOME Luncheon" was held at the Fort Garry Hotel on September 30, 1946, to honour more than nine hundred men and women from Eaton's in Manitoba and Northwestern Ontario who served in World War II. This was one of six similar functions held across Canada.

Because of the large number of veterans being honoured, token presentations were made in each location to six individuals (one man and one woman representing each of the three military services) by the company president, John David Eaton. Each veteran received a ten-karat gold signet ring especially designed by company director Ivor Lewis. Each ring featured a military service crest superimposed on the letter "E," and was engraved on the inside with the name of the recipient. Almost sixty years later, some of these

veterans continue to wear their rings with undiminished pride.

For a number of years following the war, Eaton's held a special pre-Christmas dinner for veterans of both world wars, and the employees' lunchroom was packed for these events. In 1983, a group of Eatonians revived the idea of an annual Veterans' Dinner, and for the first few years well over a hundred men and women attended. That tradition continues today, organized by the Eaton's Retirement Club. Naturally, the membership of the Eaton's Vets' Club has dwindled with time. At the 2003 dinner, fewer than thirty were present.

Some did not return

AT THE END OF WORLD WAR I, the company had three large bronze plaques created to honour the memory of the 315 Eatonians who died in that war. One was unveiled in each of the three stores – Toronto, Montreal, and Winnipeg.

On November 10, 1948, a similar plaque was unveiled by Gilbert Eaton in a solemn Remembrance Day service on the main floor of the Winnipeg store. Activities in the store paused as veterans of both wars and family members stood in silence. This plaque bore the names of the 263 Eatonians who fought and died in the Second World War. The plaque that was unveiled that day appeared almost identical to its earlier counterpart, but was actually a replica constructed by Eaton's craftsmen of plastic and glass, a move necessitated by wartime metal shortages. It was later replaced by a permanent bronze version.

Both plaques stood in a place of honour flanking the statue of Timothy Eaton on the main floor of the downtown store until the store was scheduled for demolition. They were then placed in temporary storage by the group responsible for the construction of the downtown sports and entertainment complex on the former site of the Big Store until they could rejoin the statue in the Eaton's display in the entertainment complex. ■

DURING WORLD WAR I, John Craig Eaton personally donated $100,000 to establish the Eaton Machine Gun Battery, which was equipped with Vickers-Maxim guns and fifteen armoured vehicles. As well, the family yacht *Florence* was modified for military use and donated to the war cause. It was subsequently sunk near Trinidad. As a further and extremely generous show of support, the company declined to profit from the manufacture of war materials. To assist Canadian manufacturers, Eaton's sold Canadian-made goods at no profit one month each year during the war. It was these gestures that resulted in the knighting of Sir John Craig Eaton in 1915. Flora became Lady Flora McCrea Eaton.

Winnipeg's

The Winnipeg parade took various routes over the years, but it always ended precisely at 11:00 a.m. at the Big Store. In an annual ritual reminiscent of the first parade, Santa climbed a ladder to the roof of the annex, where a mock chimney awaited. This symbolically announced that Santa had arrived and was ready to receive visitors. So many spectators crowded the streets to watch Santa's ascent that there was often barely room for the floats to move down Graham Avenue. One year, the extra Santa prematurely exited the secret compartment of the float and sauntered down Portage Avenue while the other Santa was waving from the annex roof. This undoubtedly necessitated some hastily improvised explanations by some parents to their confused children.

The Christmas season

ALTHOUGH EVENTS LIKE Trans-Canada Sales and Birthday Sales attracted throngs of shoppers to the Eaton's stores in Winnipeg, the longest sustained busy periods for Eaton's were the weeks leading up to Christmas.

The T. Eaton Company essentially declared when the Winnipeg Christmas season was to begin. Eaton's Santa Claus Parade and the subsequent arrival of Santa in Toyland was a signal to other retailers that the commercial aspect of Christmas was officially underway. Having been given this notification by Eaton's, they would launch their own Yuletide displays and promotions (including their own versions of Santa Claus) at the same time.

Frenzied buying required the hiring of thousands of temporary employees each year. Many university students and housewives looked forward to the extra Christmas money that resulted from becoming a seasonal Eatonian. During the 1950 Christmas season, the total number of Winnipeg employees was 12,500.

The Santa Claus Parade

EATON'S FIRST SANTA CLAUS Parade in Winnipeg, on the morning of Saturday, December 2, 1905, was a modest effort, but it was received with a level of excitement that foreshadowed the decades that followed. After arriving by train at the Canadian Pacific depot on Higgins Avenue, Santa took his seat in a large tally-ho sleigh pulled by four horses and accompanied by a trumpeter. The plan was for Santa to ride slowly down Portage Avenue throwing bags of candies to children along the way. However, the enthusiasm of the throngs of eager youngsters was so overwhelming that he was unable to keep up with the demand. A.A. Gilroy and George Graham, the toy department manager, hopped up on the sleigh and helped Santa Claus toss candies. This first parade concluded when Santa climbed a ladder to a canopy over the Hargrave Street entrance, and disappeared through a second floor window. He reappeared to receive visitors in a log house and workshop on the fifth floor the following Monday morning.

...the enthusiasm of the throngs of eager youngsters was so overwhelming that Santa was unable to keep up with the demand.

Chapter **5**

The 1914 Santa Claus Parade began "miles out" on Portage Avenue in St James. The entire parade is shown here. It consisted of two buglers, two floats, and eight horses.

The numbers of spectators also grew over the years. In 1947, it was estimated that 75,000 people watched the parade.

By 1920, the parade had grown to eight floats, accompanied by a number of decorated motorcars. In 1930, the number of floats had again increased, and a larger marshalling point near the Redwood Bridge was chosen. In the early 1950s, the McGregor Street Armoury became the starting point of the parade. The hundreds of people who were to march in the parade and ride on the floats donned their costumes at H.M.C.S. Chippawa before being hauled in Eaton's furniture vans to the armoury. Display Manager Lorne Cameron recalls, "It used to scare the hell out of me that we were going to lose a bunch of them."

As years went on, the parade grew larger and more elaborate. It generally took an hour to pass a given point and was precisely spaced and timed, with enough distance between floats to allow spectators to enjoy the impact of each one. The route was often planned to pass children's

hospitals, where it would pause to allow Santa to wave to young patients. In the days preceding the parade, radio broadcasts featured interviews with Santa, who gave verbal previews of the event.

Children were captivated by the eye-catching floats, which generally featured storybook favourites, and were carefully designed to ensure that even the youngest and most sensitive would not be frightened. The slow-moving floats were accompanied by marching characters, clowns, and bands.

The numbers of spectators also grew over the years. In 1947, it was estimated that 75,000 people watched the parade. In addition to Winnipeg families, rural residents would flock to the city to see the event, and, in many instances, to shop at Eaton's when the parade was over. Eaton's would also charter buses to transport orphans to the parade. After watching the parade, these youngsters were treated to lunch in

Displays offered ideas on wardrobe combinations.

the Employees' Cafeteria and given bags of candies and other treats.

Originally, the floats were built in the stable area of the mail order buildings. In later years, Eaton's rented a hangar from the R.C.A.F. at the end of Ellice Avenue. In the mid 1950s, Eaton's erected a prefabricated Butler building on Duncan Avenue near the Alexander Avenue warehouse, and it became appropriately known as the "Parade Building." Although the majority of floats were re-used in subsequent parades, each year a few were refurbished with new displays to ensure that spectators would delight to new and different sights and sounds.

Floats were always moved to the parade marshalling area in the dead of night to avoid tarnishing the magic for children. The workers responsible for the floats sometimes put in shifts that ran from 8:00 a.m. the day before the parade until the following 3:00 a.m.. They took a brief break, and then returned an hour or two later to be ready for the parade to start.

In earlier years, wagons rented from farmers were used as the foundations of floats. Eaton's delivery trucks, creatively disguised to blend in with the themes, were used to pull floats built on trailers. Later, some floats were self-propelled, using Volkswagen engines. Because some of the floats were extremely large, corners had to be turned very skillfully to avoid running over spectators.

Preparation for a parade began almost immediately after the previous year's event. A succession of display personnel and carpenters were responsible for designing and constructing the dozens of floats. Two of the chief designers in the 1950s and 1960s were Neil Cooper and Kenneth Cox. During his tenure as display manager, Herman Carson annually demonstrated the satisfaction Eatonians took in a job well done by proudly marching alone along the entire parade route behind Santa's float.

OVER THE YEARS, DIFFERENT ROUTES were utlilized as the parade made its way to the store. Although Portage Avenue was used sometimes, this 1932 parade saw Santa pass through Broadway and Osborne.

PLANNING FOR THE EXTENSIVE Christmas decorations that were used throughout the store began almost a year in advance, and often involved visiting shows in places like New York in April or May to purchase some of the necessary baubles. In the seventies, Christmas decorations were displayed right after November 11th, and display manager Giles Bugailiskis and his staff often had to work all day on Remembrance Day to have everything ready in the main areas of the store for the following day. Thousands of gift-wrapped empty boxes were stored from year to year to be used in Christmas displays, and one year the store itself was wrapped in a gigantic red ribbon to become an enormous gift box. Live poinsettias by the thousands were purchased each year and appeared on counters and merchandise bunks on the main floor, while colourful garlands were wrapped around the store's pillars. Panels of cardboard were silk-screened red, and taped to display cases to add to the festive touch.

Like the floats, the costumes used in the parade were never rented from outside suppliers, but were artfully created by Winnipeg Eatonians. For many years Louise Williams not only designed the costumes, but took on the task of actually sewing them. Each year, the costumes for two marching units of twenty or thirty people each were retired and replaced by new ones. This ensured that spectators would see something new and different in every parade.

The highlight of each parade was the Santa Claus float, which travelled at the end of the procession with its red-suited superstar seated in a large sleigh. "Pulling" the sleigh was a team of large-as-life reindeer whose legs moved when the float was travelling and became motionless when the float stopped. This effect was achieved by having two strong-legged high school boys hidden under the floor of the float, taking turns in operating a mechanism of bicycle pedals and chains.

Only a few people closely involved with the event were privy to the fact that there were actually two Santas in each parade. One was prominently seated in the final float, waving to cheering children along the route. The second Santa, fully-costumed, was stowed in a secret compartment – under a trap door in the floor just in front of Santa's sleigh – ready to take over on a moment's notice.

Although there is no definitive record of how often the spare Santa was actually needed, the risk of Santa's voice giving out (or of his beard blowing off in strong winter gusts) was always a possibility. There were also occasions when snowballs were thrown by mischievous on-lookers. John Paterson, a 33-year Eatonian who worked in the display warehouses, was the hidden Santa during one parade when a Santa was knocked unconscious. As John attempted to take his place on the sleigh, he found that he couldn't open the trap door because the comatose Santa was lying on top of it. Luckily,

Eaton's employees served as parade marshals, making sure that participants and spectators were safe.

Although there is no definitive record of how often the spare Santa was actually needed, the risk of Santa's voice giving out (or of his beard blowing off in strong winter gusts) was always a possibility.

PUNKINHEAD

EATON'S "SAD LITTLE BEAR" Punkinhead was designed by cartoonist and graphic artist Charles Thorson, whose colourful and troubled life is chronicled in the biography *Cartoon Charlie*. In the late 1920s and early 1930s, Thorson worked as an artist for Brigden's of Winnipeg, the company responsible for the production of both the eastern and western versions of Eaton's catalogue. In that pre-photographic era, catalogue illustrations were hand-drawn.

According to his biographer Gene Walz, Thorson designed and built a papier mache gnome for the 1931 Eaton's Santa Claus Parade in Winnipeg and chose to name it "Punkinhead," his pet name for his young son Steve. That name was to be resurrected almost two decades later for a very different character.

In 1934, the impulsive Thorson (at the age of 44) left Winnipeg for Los Angeles, determined to impress Walt Disney with his portfolio of drawings and cartoons. He managed to arrange an interview with Disney and was hired immediately.

In his two years with the Disney organization, Thorson provided character designs for a number of cartoons, most notably Snow White and the Seven Dwarfs. He was later to tell Winnipeg friends that he modeled Snow White on his Icelandic-Canadian girlfriend.

Thorson left Disney in a snit, feeling he did not receive appropriate recognition for his work, and worked for MGM and Warner Brothers studios. Although the claims have been disputed, many credit Thorson with creating such famous cartoon characters as Bugs Bunny and Elmer Fudd. Despite the fact that he was incredibly talented, Thorson's tenure with all of his employers was brief, mainly because of his fiery temper, which was aggravated by extensive drinking and womanizing. By the mid-1940s, the ever-restless Charlie left his cartoon animation career behind and began illustrating children's books.

After returning to Winnipeg, Charlie decided that Eaton's should have a unique mascot for its Santa Claus parades, something to rival Montgomery-Ward's Rudolph the Red-Nosed Reindeer. Beginning with some drawings from a children's book he had illustrated, Thorson created a bear with a distinctive and unruly top-knot of orangey-yellow hair. Originally this character was christened "Fuzzy-top," then "Carrot-top," and then "Carrot-head," but the name that was finally adopted was "Punkinhead".

A fur and papier-mâché Punkinhead made his first appearance in Eaton's Toronto Parade in 1947. The mascot proved to be very popular with children, and Eaton's decided to publish Punkinhead booklets illustrated by Thorson. The first of three booklets, *Punkinhead the Sad Little Bear*, was given to children along the parade route (and handed out by Santa to his young visitors in the stores) in 1948. Early in 1949, Charlie was paid one dollar by Eaton's for the copyright to Punkinhead. Two subsequent booklets, *Punkinhead and the Snow Fairy* and *Punkinhead in Santa's Workshop* were also illustrated by Thorson.

Charlie's career with Eaton's abruptly ended at a cocktail party at the Fort Garry Hotel. Although the party was in his honour, Charlie had too much to drink, was offended by a remark, and knocked out an Eaton's executive (whose name has never been publicly revealed) with one punch.

Punkinhead became the Christmas mascot of Eaton's and was prominently featured on his own float in numerous Santa Claus Parades, as well as in displays in Toyland. Eaton-produced radio programs co-starred Santa and Punkinhead.

Punkinhead enjoyed fabulous popularity (not only during the Christmas season), and a wide range of merchandise bearing his image and name included children's plates and bowls, lamps, watches, colouring books, games, clothing, furniture, and masks. These items continue to be very collectible, and Punkinhead teddy bears from the 1950s (originally a five-dollar item) now sell for several thousand dollars. Punkinhead was popularized in song by Canadian country singer Wilf Carter (who was known in the USA as Montana Slim) with a song titled *Punkinhead (The Little Bear)*.

In 1997, Eaton's re-launched Punkinhead across Canada to a whole new generation of children. This newer model differed somewhat in appearance from the original, and the topknot was no longer the dramatic orangey-yellow. Although this retro version experienced some success, it contributed little to restoring the previous popularity of the fading business.

a parade marshal was able to push the unconscious Santa aside.

Another reality, despite the official attitude of the company on liquor consumption, was overindulgence in whisky by some Santas. Fortunately, no Winnipeg Santa is known to have reached the stage of intoxication of a Toronto counterpart who shouted "Merry Christmas, you little bastards!" at young onlookers. On one occasion, however, when the Winnipeg parade visited Brandon for an encore presentation, the Santa of the day was so inebriated he could barely sit upright in the float as he joyfully flung toys into the crowd.

It is worth noting that there was very little actual advertising in the parades. Santa's float included a sign that read "To Eaton's Toyland." As well, Punkinhead – who was clearly identified with Eaton's – was prominently featured, but most of the floats and characters represented fairy-tale and Christmas themes with no advertising of specific merchandise.

In the pre-television era, radio broadcasts both before and during the parade brought the excitement into homes in Winnipeg and rural Manitoba. The 1954 parade was the first to be televised in Winnipeg. Although CBC Winnipeg lacked the mobile equipment necessary for a live outdoor broadcast, Eaton's and CBC executives found a simple solution. The parade route was arranged to travel down Portage Avenue past the CBC building, and a 400-foot cable was snaked out of the building and connected to a camera normally used in indoor studios. From this sidewalk vantage point, the camera caught all of

the action for home viewers. Eaton's also provided television sets to the children's wards of local hospitals.

In later years, the Toronto parade was televised nationally, and by CBS in the USA, where it attracted an estimated twenty-five million viewers. Ironically, this development was a contributing factor in the decision to cancel the Winnipeg parade.

By the 1960s the parade included more than thirty floats and as many as a thousand marchers. Many employees looked forward to their part in the annual event, for which they received some extra pay and a meal. Their ranks were supplemented by students from almost every Winnipeg high school, who were chosen as much for their ability to fit into the costumes as for any particular talent. In addition to the fun and prestige of participating in the parade, the youngsters received five dollars and were treated to lunch in the company cafeteria.

In 1966 Eaton's Santa Claus Parade made its final journey through the streets of Winnipeg. A statement from D. S. McGiverin, the General Manager of Eaton's Western Division, in February 1967 said, "The magic of the Winnipeg Santa Claus parade which prevailed in times past has been lessened by the exposure the children of today have to so many things not available to their mothers and fathers," and went on to refer to the ability of television to transport children – in living colour – to distant places. The gigantic Toronto parade was televised nationally, and could be viewed by families across Canada in the comfort of their homes. Undoubtedly, another

By the 1960s the parade included more than thirty floats and as many as a thousand marchers.

To help excited children to get into the Christmas spirit at Breakfast with Santa, reindeer antler hats were given out.

BREAKFAST **WITH SANTA**

EVEN THOUGH THE SANTA CLAUS parade disappeared in 1966, Winnipeg children had an opportunity to see Santa in another setting. "Breakfast with Santa" became an annual tradition with many families and was almost always sold out. On three Saturday mornings prior to Christmas, parents lined up at the Hargrave entrance as early as 7 a.m. (often with children sleeping in their arms), hoping to get the best seats in the Valley Room before the fun began at 8 a.m.. To avoid stampedes, store personnel escorted the families in groups of twelve though the still-closed store to the fifth floor.

The standard menu was a stack of pancakes with syrup, white or chocolate milk, and an orange. Costumed characters strolled among the tables, greeting the guests and pausing for photo opportunities. In addition to notables from well-known Christmas stories and carols, Disney characters such as Aladdin, Mickey Mouse, and Minnie Mouse delighted the breakfasting children. The entertainment that followed included magicians, clowns, bands, and a tailor named Angelo from the exclusive men's main floor clothing shop the Pine Room, who played his accordion. To intensify the syrup-fuelled excitement of the youngsters, the final act of the morning was a casual stroll through the Valley Room by Santa Claus himself.

After the families left to make their way up to the seventh floor to see Santa's Village and to sit on the knee of the great man, store employees remained behind to try to restore the Valley Room to its normal condition. The display department's Bruce Meisner was one of them: "There was syrup everywhere. You had to wear rubber gloves and a plastic apron to clean up." But, as Bruce observes, Breakfast with Santa was something many employees looked forward to. "It was great. Seeing all the little kids kept Christmas real for a lot of employees."

factor was the cost of the parade, which some reports estimated at $100,000 annually. None of the Winnipeg employees involved in preparations for the parade lost their jobs as a result of the decision. In 1982, the Toronto parade (with an estimated annual cost of $250,000) was cancelled, a victim of recession, reduced customer spending and staff layoffs.

At first, the Winnipeg Firefighters Club and then the Winnipeg Chamber of Commerce made an effort to continue the parades. These later efforts were often blatantly commercial, and in the view of many lacked the magic of the Eaton's parades. In 1976, the Junior Chamber of Commerce took over the sponsorship and organizing of the event. Eaton's had donated the Santa float to the firefighters, and it was subsequently passed on the Jaycees. When the Jaycees were refurbishing the Santa float in 1993, they found that the floor boards under the reindeer were actually old wooden Eaton's signs.

The Christmas windows

FOR MANY WINNIPEG FAMILIES, a visit to the main floor display windows displays was a much-awaited Christmas event. The display department pulled out all the stops to create panoramas that attracted crowds of parents and children who stood transfixed in sub-zero December weather, dazzled by the mechanized occupants of the Portage Avenue windows. Parents would bring children more than once each December. Although the displays were created primarily to appeal to youngsters, adults were also enthralled by them.

A number of mechanical story-book figures were purchased from Dayton's in Minneapolis during the seventies, and some were incorporated in Christmas window displays.

The displays were changed each year to feature different themes, often including fairy tale characters. The 1941 windows featured a "Circus in December" theme, including a miniature ferris wheel, roller coaster, and merry-go-round with teddy bears and clowns. The highlight was a mechanical monkey performing a high-wire bicycle act. In 1948, the centre windows on Portage Avenue brought seven Mother Goose rhymes to life.

In an era that preceded images created by technology, the figures in the Christmas displays captivated onlookers. Constructed primarily of chicken wire and papier-mâché, these colourful characters were designed and built by local Eaton's artists and craftsmen. One of the people responsible for designing the characters was Neil Cooper, who was a Lancaster bomber pilot in World War II. From his wartime experience he knew how electric motors were used in aircraft to open flaps and doors. Neil arranged to have Eaton's purchase some of these small motors as war surplus and these enabled the display characters to move their arms and heads, much to the fascination of the children. To complete the effect, recorded music was piped out into the frigid Portage Avenue air.

One of the most memorable displays was known as "Santa's Village." A number of mechanical story-book figures were purchased from Dayton's in Minneapolis during the seventies, and some were incorporated in Christmas window displays. When Santa began to hold court in the seventh-floor Assembly Hall, all of these characters were put in simulated windows in a medieval Lithuanian village

setting. After the seventh floor was closed to the public, this display was set up on the third floor in the space previously occupied by the Char Bar restaurant. The area was bordered by wooden partitions and used only during the Christmas season.

During the process of closing in 1999, Eaton's generously donated the entire "Santa's Village" display to the Manitoba Children's Museum at The Forks. After a cumbersome moving job, and some refurbishing, the fifteen windows of fairy tale stories were placed on permanent display. For most of the year, the area served as a story-telling gallery. The mechanical figures were kept motionless to preserve the aging motors. But, as Christmas approached, the display was adorned with Christmas trees, lights and

Parents could purchase photographs of their children with Santa, and these have become part of countless family albums.

Until the 1970s, the most prominent window, at the corner of Portage and Hargrave, was converted from a nursery rhyme display to a nativity scene two weeks before Christmas. This later became a family Christmas scene.

decorations, and the magical figures of Snow White, Cinderella, and many other timeless favourites again sprang to life. Museum staff members report that the displays that thrilled earlier generations still hold a degree of appeal for 21st century children. The greatest enthusiasm, however, is seen on the faces of parents and grandparents who joyfully announce "Hey, I remember that!"

Toyland

THE DONALD STREET ANNEX served a variety of purposes, but one of the most memorable was that it was the location of the Toy Department, or, as it was known for many years, Toyland. During the year, the annex displayed a variety of items that changed with the seasons, including paints, hardware, sporting goods, boats, and even snowmobiles. Toys usually occupied only about one-third of the space. But in November the toys took over the entire annex.

Although the kinds of toys children wanted for Christmas changed from year to year, the magic of Toyland remained the same. Excited children, their often-reluctant parents in tow, would scurry up and down the aisles in wide-eyed wonderment. As an additional enticement, employees often demonstrated the latest toys.

To add to the crowds and the excitement, Toyland was for many years the home of Santa Claus, and long lines of anxious and eager youngsters silently rehearsed what they would say when one of Santa's helpers helped them up to Santa's knee.

It was estimated that he had met more than half a million children, and many of the youngsters who once sat on his knee had in turn become parents who brought their own children to visit him in Toyland.

The Real Santa

IN THE MINDS OF GENERATIONS of Winnipeg children there was no doubt where Santa Claus was at Christmas. He was in the downtown Eaton's store, which advertisements christened "Santa's Store." The role of Santa Claus was usually played by Eaton's employees who were allowed to leave their regular responsibilities to don the familiar red suit and white beard. In 1944, Eatonian Joseph Dancy retired after spending seventeen Christmas seasons as Santa. It was estimated that he had met more than half a million children, and many of the youngsters who once sat on his knee had in turn become parents who brought their own children to visit him in Toyland.

Another Eatonian, furniture salesman Lloyd Jones, played the role of Santa for more than thirty years. John Paterson was recruited when a regular Santa was ill. He enjoyed it so much that he did it for four years, and then he returned for two more after he retired. One particularly busy day just before Christmas, he was visited by 1,500 children.

Santas were given strict instructions on how to hold children on their laps, not always an easy task when they were wearing slippery snowsuits. The job had its own special hazards, including the possibility of over-excited or frightened children wetting their pants. One older girl, not pleased with what she had received the previous year, threatened to punch a Santa out. The combination of the heavy suit, the full beard, and the photographers' lights made the job very hot

work, so some Santas stripped to their underwear before donning the costume.

Usually Santa was assisted by green-suited high-school-student elves and Mrs. Claus, who wore an outfit very similar to her spouse, including the regulation wire-rimmed spectacles. Because Santa was basically confined to his throne, the elves, under the direction of Mrs. Claus, took care of crowd control, as well as handing out the candy that each child received.

As the opening hours of the store expanded, several Santas were needed to spell each other off. In fact, in an effort to reduce waiting times, there were sometimes two Santas in the same area. The routing of the line-ups was carefully designed so children would not realize that there was a nearby duplicate. There was so much demand to visit Santa in the 1940s that children's hands were stamped after they left to discourage them from going to the back of the line for second visits.

In addition to thousands of visitors in person each Christmas season, the Eaton's Santa was deluged by letters. Because it was universally accepted that the Santa Claus at Eaton's was the genuine article, the post office delivered envelopes addressed to "Santa Claus, North Pole" to Eaton's downtown store. The letters received handwritten personalized responses composed by temporary employees. ∎

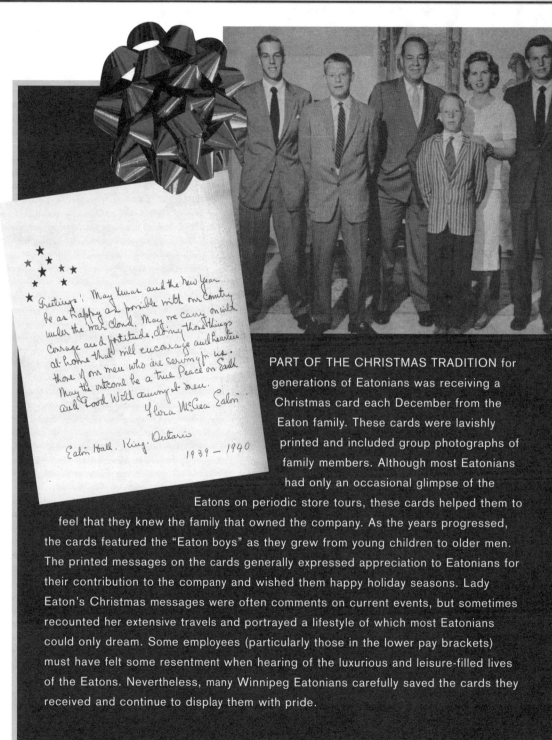

PART OF THE CHRISTMAS TRADITION for generations of Eatonians was receiving a Christmas card each December from the Eaton family. These cards were lavishly printed and included group photographs of family members. Although most Eatonians had only an occasional glimpse of the Eatons on periodic store tours, these cards helped them to feel that they knew the family that owned the company. As the years progressed, the cards featured the "Eaton boys" as they grew from young children to older men. The printed messages on the cards generally expressed appreciation to Eatonians for their contribution to the company and wished them happy holiday seasons. Lady Eaton's Christmas messages were often comments on current events, but sometimes recounted her extensive travels and portrayed a lifestyle of which most Eatonians could only dream. Some employees (particularly those in the lower pay brackets) must have felt some resentment when hearing of the luxurious and leisure-filled lives of the Eatons. Nevertheless, many Winnipeg Eatonians carefully saved the cards they received and continue to display them with pride.

Goods well

The Bonspiel Fair included a miniature version of
Buckingham Palace (1954).

DISPLAYED

Display windows

TIMOTHY EATON'S FIRST store, at 178 Yonge Street in Toronto, opened on December 6, 1869. It had a frontage of only twenty-four feet, and just two show windows. Because of these space limitations, merchandise was often displayed using the simple practice known as "door dressing." This meant choosing attractively-priced items and placing them on the sidewalk in front of the store, or even in the doorway.

In 1883, the T. Eaton Company's only store was relocated to 190 Yonge Street. The new building's frontage of fifty-two feet included several large display windows. This was in keeping with one of the premises upon which the company operated: "goods well-displayed are half-sold."

The use of plate-glass show windows to display merchandise and to entice passersby to decide to go into stores and make impulse purchases had become increasingly popular since the mid-1800's, and the pastime of "window-shopping" was particularly fashionable among working-class people, and especially young women.

The design of the Winnipeg store incorporated forty-two large display windows at the sidewalk level. When the store was first built, each window was furnished with two panes of glass divided by a vertical reinforcing centre bar. In 1927, a $100,000 plan to refurbish the street-level façade included teakwood doors with bronze grills and the extensive use of tyndall stone and black marble. As well, the relatively thin panes of the display windows were replaced with much thicker single panes of heavy glass, and bronze frames were added.

Although the interior of the store featured electric lighting from the first day, this was originally supplemented by natural light from the windows. The main floor display window areas were separated from the inside of the store by waist-high walls These delineated the window displays from the customer service areas, but still allowed a considerable amount of outside light to illuminate the store during the daytime hours.

> *"The use of plate-glass show windows to display merchandise and to entice passersby to decide to go into stores and make impulse purchases had become increasingly popular since the mid-1800s, and the pastime of "window-shopping" was particularly fashionable among working-class people, and especially young women."*

Chapter 6

Eaton's Store Winnipeg

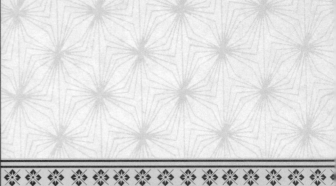

An added advantage to this arrangement was that the displays were visible to customers from inside the store as well as from the sidewalk.

Eventually these half-walls were replaced by full-height "sandstone" walls that hid the displays from within the store and provided an attractive backdrop from the outside. Although the "sandstone" appeared to be authentic, it was actually made of plaster of Paris and baking soda, artistically painted by Eaton's craftsmen to give the illusion of stone blocks.

Eaton's was renowned for its window displays, fashioned by creative members of the display department. At times, the windows fronting Portage Avenue were changed daily, and usually featured items at special sale prices. The "centre seven" windows facing Portage Avenue between the two entrances were used as fashion windows to show particularly stylish and attractive items. "Shadowbox" windows hid most of the inside area to show small items such as jewellery or cosmetics in a small space at eye level and very close to the glass.

In addition to making efforts to ensure that the displays were creative and attractive, care was also taken, particularly in the earlier years, to avoid offending viewers. A fine line had to be defined between displaying items such as women's lingerie in an eye-catching manner and incurring the anger of easily offended customers. Allowing unclad (or even semi-clad) mannequins to be seen by the public while clothing changes were underway was strictly prohibited.

In the 1970s, many Eaton's displays took a new and bolder direction that reflected the spirit

STRONG **TEACUPS**

A WINDOW DISPLAY THAT MANY Winnipeggers remembered from the 1960s was designed to show the durability of a line of British-made china. A Jaguar automobile was put inside the windows at the corner of Portage and Hargrave, no small feat in itself when it's considered that it took several men to remove one of the heavy panes to allow the car to be moved into the display area. The Jaguar was lifted on jacks and then carefully lowered onto four delicate upside-down teacups. It remained there for a month with no damage to the cups. What amazed passersby didn't know was that the engine and other heavy components had previously been removed from the car in what has to be one of the few instances of deception in Eaton's advertising.

of a concept called NED (which stood for "New Exciting and Different"). Newly-appointed display manager Giles Bugailiskis saw it as his mandate to create displays that would move away from Eaton's staid image. Topless female mannequins with their backs to the windows were one of the results.

Until the 1950s, incorporating cocktail glasses or any items related to smoking in displays was contrary to Eaton's policy. This might have been in part to avoid offending customers, but it was probably more a reflection of company policy dating back to the founder and reflecting his personal and religious views.

Similarly, the custom of drawing heavy beige drapes to conceal window displays from public view on Sundays clearly conformed to Timothy Eaton's belief that Sunday was a day for church-going and religious reflection, not a time to be considering purchases. The drapes were closed each Saturday before midnight and re-opened on Monday morning at 7:30 a.m. This practice continued at the Winnipeg store until 1968.

During the first Pan-American Games in 1967, the "centre seven" windows were turned into street-front shops for visitors. To allow entrance to these unique boutiques, each

massive (and extremely heavy) pane of glass was carefully removed by ten men at a cost of approximately $3,000 per pane.

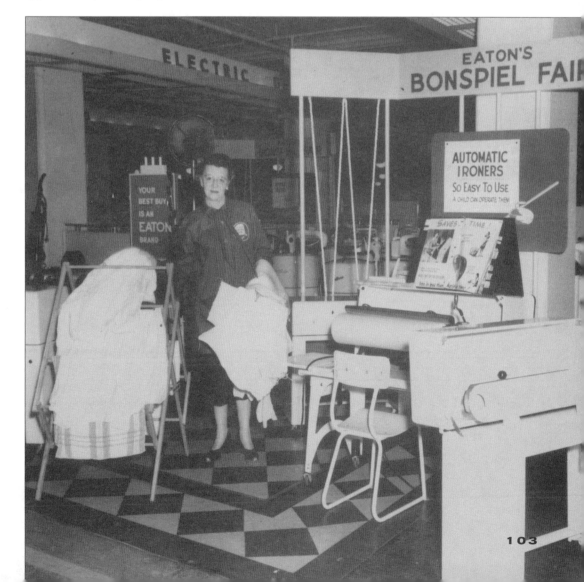

Spring arrived in February for Eaton's shoppers who visited the store to enjoy the
annual arrival of fresh flowers.

The mannequins

AN ESSENTIAL PART OF DISPLAYS, both in the windows and throughout the store, were hundreds of mannequins. These silent salespeople were utilized to model a wide range of clothing, often while appearing to enjoy motionless golfing, skiing, and other activities.

In earlier days, mannequins were made of plaster of Paris or slabs of wood, often weighing more than ninety pounds. Later, papier-mâché became the material of choice to construct mannequins that weighed only thirty or forty pounds. By the 1960s, much lighter models were made of fiberglass and polyester resins. The later mannequins were much more realistic in appearance and had less-visible joins at the shoulders and wrists where the arms and hands were connected.

Unlike the mannequins in most other Winnipeg stores, the Eaton's window mannequins were not supported by metal "bum rods." Each had a toggle bolt screwed into its head (hidden by a wig) and was kept standing by very thin metal fish line running from the bolt to the grids in the ceiling.

The fashions of different eras were also reflected in the bodies of mannequins. From the pigeon-toed look for women of the 1930s to the broad-shouldered, well-muscled look for men of the 1940s to the waifishly slim look that many women tried in vain to achieve in the 1960s, mannequins were designed to reflect prevailing notions of what constituted chic. Some were created to resemble celebrities,

Temperature EXTREMES

SETTING UP AND TAKING DOWN displays presented challenges that went beyond devising ways to make them attractive. The display windows at the Big Store were sealed off from the store and were not heated or air-conditioned. This meant the show areas could be stiflingly hot in the summer and bitterly cold in the winter. As a result, display personnel wore shorts in the summer and layers of warm clothing in the winter while they worked on displays hidden from public view. Some merchandise faded quickly from heat and direct sunlight and had to be replaced frequently. Although the twenty-one windows along Portage Avenue were quite spacious, some windows along Hargrave and Donald Streets had display areas only about two feet deep. This limitation presented special challenges in finding items that could fit in the available space. It also meant that only relatively slim display workers were able to work in those areas.

HIDDEN MESSAGES

DURING THE 1970S, THE WINNIPEG display staff had an off-the-wall collective sense of humour. When setting up the traditional family dinner scene in the windows at the corner of Portage and Hargrave, they sometimes included a private joke in the seemingly normal portrayal of a happy family enjoying their Christmas dinner. Sometimes it was a drunken relative lying under the festive table. Other times it was a funny uncle engaged in inappropriate touching. These bizarre touches were done so subtly that a viewer would have had to know what to look for in order to spot them. The general public never caught on, so no complaints were received.

SHOWING THE FASHIONS

FOR SEVERAL DECADES, Eaton's was the supplier of the most exclusive imported ready-to-wear women's fashions in Winnipeg. In the late 1950s, Lillian Vadeboncoeur succeeded Wilma Blocher as Eaton's fashion director and took over the coordination of the store's renowned fashion shows. These formal shows, generally held in the Grill Room, were regularly attended by women who were interested in the latest fashions selected by Eaton's buyers (primarily in Paris) and were able to pay the price. Other shows took place in the departments that sold women's fashions. For teenage buyers interested in fashions, a partnership between Eaton's and Seventeen magazine saw such celebrities as Twiggy and Mary Quant make appearances in Winnipeg.

There were, of course, creative and attractive displays of merchandise within the various departments of the store, just as there were in the display windows.

including Audrey Hepburn, Jacqueline Kennedy, Joan Collins, and Cher.

Displays in the store

LIKE THE EXTERIOR, the interior of the Big Store was deliberately designed to project an image of uncluttered simplicity. This facilitated the use of a wide range of displays that attracted the attention of shoppers with no visual interference from the permanent features of the store or the fixtures.

There were, of course, creative and attractive displays of merchandise within the various departments of the store, just as there were in the display windows. These were changed frequently to showcase the latest in fashions and technology. The most memorable displays, however, were those that were part of a store-wide theme.

For several years, the Manitoba Bonspiel was a week-long event, attracting thousands of curlers, spectators, and their families to Winnipeg. One of the traditions associated with this event was Eaton's Bonspiel Fair, which

began in 1951 and featured a variety of displays and exhibits on every floor, along with a full range of spring merchandise. During the first fair, visitors to the main floor could see belt-making, glove-making, and jewellery-engraving. The Donald Annex included boat-building as well as a magician. On other floors, the exhibits ranged from pancake-making and a power tool demonstration on the third, to ladies' garment-making and Eaton's Research Bureau fabric-testing on the fourth. Music lovers who rode to the seventh floor were treated to a demonstration of the latest development in recorded music – RCA Victor's 45 rpm records. The 1954 Fair included a preview (on Viking television sets of course) of what Winnipeggers could expect to see when the CBC began Winnipeg's first broadcasts later that spring.

When the Manitoba Bonspiel became a weekend-only event, the Bonspiel Fair was replaced each February by a spectacular annual display of flowers and spring merchandise. In a 1995 article in the Eaton's Retirement Club newsletter, long-time display department member Mildred Hamilton recalled how more than thirty thousand flowers appeared overnight in the store in February 1959. Flowers from Hawaii and several southern states were especially flown in, trucked to the Donald Annex, arranged by an assembly line of display department members, and put in place by a crew of Eatonians. The next morning, the dreary winter was brightened by fresh flowers that hung from the main-floor pillars, adorned countertops, and filled the fashion floor. The spring-like fragrance of the flowers was enhanced by the songs of tropical birds and soft

One of the most publicized Eaton's fashion shows was a fundraiser held at the Centennial Concert Hall for the Manitoba Theatre Centre in 1969. It featured Pierre Cardin (inset: shown chatting with Lillian Vadeboncoeur) and his newest fashions.

Because of the open design and the spaciousness of the store, mannequins had plenty of room to model the latest fashions.

One of the most popular (and unusual) highlights of the "Uncrate the Sun" promotions in the eighties was a simulated airplane flight. The fuselage of an actual aircraft was put together in the Assembly Hall, and customers were treated to most of the sensations of an actual flight. Air Canada flight attendants served food on airline trays as passengers watched videos about their "destination" on overhead television monitors. To add to the realism, recordings of revving engines and the sounds of taking off and landing were piped over speakers. The passengers sat in assigned seats and were expected to observe the seat belt warning lights.

background music. Occasionally some birds escaped from their cages, and a few made their way to the third floor, perhaps looking for friends in the pet department.

Promotions featuring faraway places were regular events at Eaton's. Some of the most popular theme countries were Britain, Italy, Iceland, and Jamaica, and most themes were repeated every few years. "Uncrate the Sun" was a major campaign used for several years to spotlight sunny places like Florida and California during the winter. Merchandise and display staff had the pleasant task of visiting the various locations during the planning phase of each promotion in search of ideas, props, and special goods to be featured.

The 1958 Festival of British Imports highlighted the range of British merchandise available at Eaton's. The displays included sparkling replicas of the Crown Jewels, icing sugar models of British landmarks, and the latest models of English automobiles. During one of these festivals, costumed bell-ringers from Britain performed their unusual music from a stage built at the second-floor level overhanging Portage Avenue.

A 1966 "Jamaica Journey" event saw a team including display manager Herman Carson, fashion coordinator Lillian Vadeboncoeur, and fashion buyer Mary Ripley journey to Jamaica to view, photograph, and purchase fashions. In addition to exciting new merchandise, the

Merchandise and display staff had the pleasant task of visiting the various locations during the planning phase of each promotion in search of ideas, props, and special goods to be featured.

A display of tropical fish in the Donald Street Annex in 1951 had an estimated 100,000 visitors in a two-week period.

promotion featured a calypso band and a tropical menu in the Grill Room. John Mainella, a buyer, remembers a trip he and two other Eatonians took to Italy in the 1970s in preparation for a "Ciao Italia" promotion. "We spent four weeks over there, going right from one end of Italy to the other. We spent about twelve thousand dollars on costumes."

Celebrities were often brought to Winnipeg to participate in special events. One of the Icelandic promotions included the Mayor of Reykjavik and an Icelandic pony. One British event saw the Pearly King and Queen in their traditional Cockney costumes bedecked with mother-of-pearl buttons, flown to Winnipeg to mingle with Eaton's Shoppers. On another occasion, Chuck Eisenmann, the owner and trainer involved with the television series *The Littlest Hobo*, entertained families with the four different dogs that portrayed the heroic canine.

Some events were not store-wide, but nonetheless attracted wide attention. In the late 1940s, a miniature CPR train journeyed through a realistic rural landscape created by Eaton's carpenters and painters. Each time it was set up in the store it carried an estimated total of 50,000 to 60,000 excited children. A display of tropical fish in the Donald Street Annex in 1951 had an estimated 100,000 visitors in a two-week period. Perhaps the most bizarre event was a dead five-hundred pound beluga whale brought in from Churchill in the late fifties. It was placed on display, but had a much shorter stay. The odour of the whale became so overwhelming after a few days that it had to be removed.

Eaton's was a place to be entertained as well as to shop. Teenagers flocked to see and hear Chad Allan and the Expressions, predecessors of The Guess Who (upper photo), as well as Ray St. Germain and Wayne Finucan (lower photo).

Even a minor disaster could be turned into a display opportunity by Eaton's. After the roof of the Eaton's Curling Club on Mayfair Avenue collapsed in the infamous March 4, 1966 blizzard, the ice-making equipment was removed from the building and temporarily reinstalled by Eaton's engineers in the Donald Street Annex. After an indoor skating rink was built by Eaton's construction department, the annex was ready for a fashion show on ice. Most of the skaters and models in the show came from the Winnipeg Winter Club, but arrangements were made with Ice Capades to fly in some of their skaters. Engineer Gord Bailey was responsible for maintaining the ice and comments that the professional performers "were pretty fussy on how hard the ice should be." Between the fashion shows, the entertainment included figure skating demonstrations, a barrel-jumper, and an adagio team. When the rink was dismantled, the ice was taken outside to melt overnight into street sewers, and the ice-making equipment was donated by Eaton's to the curling club in Dauphin, which happened to have an Eaton's store.

The use of store facilities for community events also attracted throngs of visitors. More than 20,000 women reportedly attended a one-week show of budget fashions in the Hall of Science in April, 1934. The 43rd Annual Poultry Show in 1935 attracted more than 10,000 visitors in one week. With dog shows, beautiful baby contests, automobile displays, model aircraft shows, cooking and sewing demonstrations, musical events, fashion shows, and a myriad of other events taking place in the Big Store, it is not surprising that it became popular as a centre of free entertainment.

As a result of these, and many more events, Eaton's became a place to go and not just as a place to shop. Long before the term "destination" became a marketing buzz-word, Eaton's profile in Winnipeg was similar to that of The Forks, or the West Edmonton Mall. ■

A titillating DISPLAY

ONE OF THE MOST unusual window displays in the seventies featured pantyhose. Display staff hung a curtain that ended about three feet from the floor, so all that was visible from the Portage Avenue sidewalk was the legs of several pantyhose-clad mannequins standing behind the curtain. Some of the more mischievous display people decided to go a step further, put a brassiere on each mannequin, and cut out the centre portion of each bra cup to expose the mannequins' nipples. The effect was brothel-like, but only display workers were aware of the prank. They did, however, have some concerns when a male passerby was spotted lying flat on the sidewalk looking up behind the curtain. Although it was likely that he was able to see the provocative brassieres, no complaint was ever received.

The cabbage PATCH EXPLOSION

DURING THE CABBAGE PATCH Kids doll craze in the early eighties, Eaton's staff members were virtually mobbed by eager shoppers as they moved the popular dolls onto the sales floor. The display department's Bruce Meisner tells how a display of the figures in the Portage and Hargrave windows elicited dozens of phone calls from frustrated customers who couldn't understand how there could be no dolls available for sale when the window area was full of them. "We were actually fearful that they were going to smash the windows to get those dolls out. What people didn't know was that all the dolls were actually defective. They were missing body parts or labels, and part of the agreement with the supplier was that we weren't able to sell them."

ROASTED
CHICKENS

Shoppers on their way to retrieve their cars could pause at the Grill Room Products area, located on the third floor by the Hargrave Avenue overpass to the Parkade. Large glass display counters tempted passersby with battered fish, huge beef meatballs swimming in gravy and fried onions, spicy shepherd's pies topped with creamy mashed potatoes and a sprinkling of paprika and, of course, the trademark chicken pot pies. There were dozens of cold meats, Eaton's superb potato salad, and tangy oil and vinegar coleslaw.

The Grill Room

MANY OF THE FONDEST memories of Eaton's for Manitobans are associated with the Grill Room. This elegant dining room, with its arched tyndall-stone entrance and an oil painting of the store's first manager A. A. Gilroy to welcome guests, was a favourite dining place for several generations of Winnipeggers.

The Grill Room first opened in 1907, sharing the name of a similar restaurant (also on the fifth floor) in the Toronto store. The Grill Room was the place for a leisurely luncheon or dinner, graciously served on Minton bone china and silver cutlery, by waitresses in distinctive black uniforms and crisp white aprons. Some of these waitresses spent their entire careers in the Grill Room, and had the honour of serving successive generations of the same family. In the early part of the century, a full-course meal in the Grill Room (including cream of corn soup, baked whitefish with creole sauce, potatoes, butter beans, and apple sponge with whipped cream, as well as tea, coffee, or milk) cost twenty-five cents.

Although fine dining could be enjoyed in many restaurants and hotels in Winnipeg, many insisted that Winnipeg's best restaurant was located in a department store. For customers with modest incomes, the Grill Room provided an opportunity to step into a world of luxury, into a room with beautiful oak paneling and exposed beams, stained glass windows and wrought iron chandeliers. It was a place where women felt comfortable dining alone and enjoying service that made them feel like royalty. It was a room where afternoon tea was served in a leisurely, almost regal style. During the 1930s, a string quartet serenaded luncheon guests. Notable diners in the Grill Room included John Diefenbaker, Harry Belafonte, Nana Mouskouri, and Roger Whittaker.

Probably the most popular menu item was the distinctive chicken pot pie – succulent pieces of chicken in a unique sauce, topped with a flaky crust, and served in an oval green bowl. The Georgian Room in the Toronto store also served chicken pot pie, and some lamented the eventual

For customers with modest incomes, the Grill Room provided an opportunity to step into a world of luxury, into a room with beautiful oak paneling and exposed beams, stained glass windows and wrought iron chandeliers.

THE GHOST OF THE
GRILL ROOM

THE EXPERIENCE OF ONE FAMILY of four who strolled through the deserted dining room resulted in more than just memories of the past.

While her father, mother, and brother wandered off to explore the private dining area, the fourteen-year-old daughter decided to see what the kitchen looked like. As she peered through the circular window in a swinging door, she saw something that sent her running back to her family saying "We need to get out of here." She told them that she had just seen a ghost.

The father, knowing his daughter had an active imagination (and not at all sharing her belief in the supernatural) saw this as an opportunity to teach her the difference between fantasy and reality. He did what he could to calm her down, rationally explained that she had simply seen an Eaton's employee, and suggested that he and his daughter go back to the kitchen to see who was really there.

The dad went through the swinging door into the kitchen first, hesitantly followed by his daughter. He clearly recalls seeing the figure of a man, standing behind some boxes stacked on the floor, dressed all in white, and wearing a white chef's hat. His daughter, now eighteen, describes the sight as something she will never forget. She can still visualize the exceptionally pale face of this figure, recalls that he was "not fat but a bit pudgy," and says "he had a body, but it wasn't really a body because you could see through it." Both father and daughter quickly backed out of the kitchen, and the whole family left the Grill Room to let it return to its silence.

Fashion shows in the Grill Room were designed to attract people of all ages.

replacement of the carefully hand-cut potato balls with potato chunks bought in bulk. Potatoes, however, were never an issue in the Winnipeg pies because they contained only a few peas and grated carrots, plenty of chicken, and the delicate sauce – but never a potato.

A close second was toasted asparagus and cheese rolls, which could be enjoyed as a light lunch, a snack, or at afternoon tea. In some years, more than thirty thousand of these simple delicacies were served. A plate of three rolls was accompanied by a generous serving of Eaton's own Thousand Islands dressing in a silver sauce boat. Former Winnipeg mayor Bill Norrie remembers that a favourite Saturday afternoon activity for his mother and sister was a trip to the Grill Room to enjoy toasted asparagus and cheese rolls – an occasion that merited wearing hats and gloves.

For some, oysters and cream served in silver bowls was a particular delicacy. Other diners favoured beef and kidney pie, Lobster Newburg, or fresh halibut. During special promotions in the store, the Grill Room menu featured appropriate ethnic dishes, including Icelandic, German,

British, and Italian cuisine. Eventually, and despite the views of the company's founder on the consumption of liquor, the Grill Room even became licensed to serve drinks with meals.

A separate private dining area adjacent to the main dining area was used for directors' meetings and later as a managers' dining room. When newly promoted Eaton's managers were first admitted to this exclusive enclave, they felt they had really arrived. The room could also be reserved for special occasions such as birthday parties.

As the number of customers in the store declined and competition increased, the Grill Room's hours were reduced in the early 1990s. Only a small number of loyal customers, mostly older women, continued to make the Grill Room their restaurant of choice. It became increasingly impractical to continue to operate an elegant dining room with a seating capacity of 225 in a department store. At the end of January 1996, the Grill Room was closed to the public.

During the final weeks of the Big Store's life, one of the main destinations for

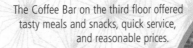

The Coffee Bar on the third floor offered tasty meals and snacks, quick service, and reasonable prices.

Winnipeggers saying their farewells was the now-empty Grill Room.

The Hostess Shop

FOR THOSE WHO PREFERRED to enjoy Eaton's foods at home, the Hostess Shop, a culinary boutique located next to the entrance of the Grill Room, offered a wide range of take-home choices.

One of the services that the Hostess Shop provided was to prepare casseroles in the customer's own cookware. Hosts could engage in a little harmless deception by bringing casserole dishes from home, and return later to pick them up filled with ready-to-serve Eaton's specialties. Hunting enthusiasts often brought game meat to the Hostess Shop to have it made (in their own pans) into delicious pies, often baked with generous lacings of apricot brandy that oozed through the crust.

For teas, showers, and other special occasions, there was a wide selection of fancy sandwiches and dainties that could be ordered in advance. Tiny and delectable sandwiches, including egg salad and salmon salad, made on crustless fresh bread from Eaton's Bakeshop, were carefully wrapped in waxed paper and packed in prestigious Hostess Shop boxes.

Places to eat

WHILE THE GRILL ROOM was the main restaurant in the Big Store, it was by no means the only place to eat. The names, themes, and menus of the restaurants changed frequently over the years, but there was always an abundance of places to enjoy a cup of tea or coffee, a snack, or a complete meal.

In 1911, the various restaurants could seat a thousand people and served approximately five thousand meals each day. At that time, lunch in the Grill Room cost twenty-five cents, while in the more economical cafeteria it was only fifteen cents.

The third-floor Donald Coffee Bar, opened in 1938, featured mostly made-in-Winnipeg equipment, including chromium-based stools with genuine leather seats, pale blue Formica counters, and even a dishwashing machine. The opening lunch special was a hot turkey sandwich with mashed potatoes, gravy, green peas, ice cream and tea coffee or milk for thirty cents.

By 1945, there were ten choices to meet the appetites and budgets of most customers. The fifth floor offered the Grill Room, the Restaurant Bar and the Cafeteria. The third floor featured the Coffee Bar and the Health Bar. On the main floor, there was the Coffee Corner. In the basement customers could find the Luncheonette, the Hot Dog Counter, the Malted Milk, and the Pop Counter.

As consumer tastes and dietary preferences shifted, the restaurant sites were periodically transformed to feature different names, decors, and menu themes. In November 1969, the 151-seat Char Bar opened on the third floor, with charcoal-broiled hamburgers as their specialty. One aspect of this restaurant proved to be far ahead of its time – it was smoke-free. Although health issues might have been part of the

A TABLE FOR ONE

AFTER THE GRILL ROOM CLOSED, it was used for the monthly coffee parties of the Eaton's Retirement Club. Club executive member Joyce Howe recalls that one day she was sitting at the registration table and an older gentleman approached her to request a table for one. After Joyce explained that the restaurant was no longer in operation, he left in disappointment, telling Joyce that he had come all the way from Ontario and was looking forward to asparagus cheese rolls..

Eaton's of Winnipeg boasted the longest meat counter in North America, stretching across the entire back of the third floor from Donald to Hargrave. Behind this 220 foot counter, glass refrigerator doors displayed row after row of hanging sides of beef stamped with diamond "E's." This choice beef was aged a minimum of twenty-four days, and orders were often shipped to Vancouver, Ottawa, and Toronto. Some local restaurants, including Rae and Jerry's, in the early days, relied on Eaton's for first-class steaks and roasts. Many Winnipeggers purchased all of their meat at Eaton's from butchers like George Thomson and a colleague known simply as "Nick the Butcher" who seemed to know the names and meat preferences of all of their regular customers. The Sausage Room in the Cooked Meats Kitchens prepared a wide variety of distinctive Eatonia sausages. Haggis was available at Eaton's on a year-round basis.

rationale for this policy, the main motivation was to serve more customers. A study that Eaton's did in similar restaurants determined that smoking patrons generally occupied seats an average of ten minutes longer than non-smokers.

In the 1970s, the Deli served up mouth-stretching sandwiches, with hot corned beef or pastrami piled high on Kaiser Rolls. The Soup Kettle offered a choice of three hearty made-from-scratch soups, accompanied by fresh fruit, crackers and cheese, and a variety of desserts. Another popular restaurant was the twenty-seat Euphoria, which was located near the women's wear department. It specialized in salads and proved especially appealing to diet-conscious women.

The fifth floor Valley Room opened in 1958, and immediately proved to be one of the most popular eating places for Eaton's customers. Eaton's distinctive fish and chips, and rice pudding were two Valley Room favourites.

The Hash House

ALTHOUGH THE EMPLOYEES' cafeteria was not open to the public, countless Winnipeggers were familiar with it – and its affectionate though somewhat derogatory nickname – as a result of temporary or part-time employment with Eaton's. Located on the second floor of the Annex, this no-frills cafeteria offered Eatonians good basic food at bargain prices. One of the simple attractions of the Hash House was toast made on a large conveyor belt type of toaster using bread from the store bakery. For many employees, a cup of coffee and a couple of pieces of this memorable toast became an essential part of their morning routine.

The Hash House was the melting pot where Eatonians of all ranks and departments came together for coffee breaks and meals. Sweethearts used the cafeteria as a rendezvous point, and the buzz of conversation in the room included all the latest gossip. When the Hash House closed, some

In the late 1970s, the Valley Room served more than six thousand meals daily.

One of the simple attractions of the Hash House was toast made on a large conveyor belt type of toaster using bread from the store bakery.

The crusty French bread was baked in a special oven imported from France.

Eatonians wore black arm bands to mourn the loss of their gathering place. To provide some consolation, a section of the Valley Room was set aside as an employee cafeteria.

The Bakeshop

THE BAKESHOP WAS ORIGINALLY located on the fifth floor of the store, and utilized coal-burning stoves that had to be stoked early each morning in preparation for the day's baking. They were eventually replaced by electric ovens. As demand for baked goods increased, the bakery operation was moved to the catalogue building, and in later years the bakery was situated in the underground tunnel area beneath Graham Avenue. In 1965, an average of 4,000 pounds of flour and 1,500 pounds of sugar were used each day to turn out a huge range of baked items. Bakers were on the job virtually around the clock.

Most of the recipes used butter and had a minimum of additives or preservatives. With more than twenty-five varieties of fresh-baked bread, there was something for virtually every taste. The crusty French bread was baked in a special oven imported from France. When the Royal Alexandra Hotel closed, the oven used to bake their trademark crusty rolls was moved to Eaton's. The moist and dark Icelandic bread baked by Eaton's carefully followed a recipe entrusted to them by the mother of food services manager Alan Finnbogason. She would occasionally buy a loaf to make sure her standards were being met.

Those with a sweet tooth found a huge array of goodies to entice them. Tasty tortes in numerous flavours could be purchased by the whole or the half. Decadent Neapolitan cakes consisted of layers of dark chocolate cake interspersed with real whipped cream. Donut lovers could visit the third floor counter to watch spicy cake donuts parade through a special machine as they were fried to golden perfection.

For many, the most memorable dessert at Eaton's was the distinctive red velvet cake. Despite health-related concerns about consuming red food colouring, this chocolate cake with a difference was highly popular.

In the mid-1960s, fourteen different kinds of pie were offered. On one $1.49 Day sale, more than 5,000 were snapped up. An estimated 45,000 pounds of fruit cake were baked each year for the Christmas season, as well as vast quantities of mincemeat pies.

When the store's ovens died of old age in the early 1990s, the cost of replacement was judged to be prohibitive. Eaton's bakery closed and baked goods were contracted out.

The fish counter

FOR MANY YEARS, the third-floor fish counter was one of the few places in Winnipeg where fresh fish could be found on a year-round basis. In addition to Manitoba species, a wide variety of imported fish was available. Many Winnipeggers had their first taste of the internationally renowned smoked Lake Winnipeg goldeye from Eaton's fish

ONE OF THE ORIGINAL PLANS for this book was to include a variety of recipes for the many foods that were associated with Eaton's. The theory was that readers could then prepare for themselves some of their Eaton's favourites and reminiscence in their palates as well as in their minds. The task of locating recipes turned out to be much more of a challenge that originally anticipated.

The methods of creating Eaton's specialties were considered the property of the company, and the few food services personnel who knew them were sworn to secrecy. Even today, with the company no longer in existence, some of these Eatonians continue to honour the oath they took several decades ago. They occasionally prepare Eaton's foods for friends and family, but they refuse to share the recipes.

As a result, only a few recipes could be obtained. Fortunately these include three of the most popular items Eaton's had to offer. There is no guarantee that these are exactly the same recipes that Eaton's of Winnipeg used, but they have been declared by the people who provided them to be very close to the originals, and delicious reminders of the tastes of Eaton's.

RED VELVET CAKE

This recipe was provided by Ann McGregor and has also appeared more than once in Ilana Simon's Winnipeg Free Press Recipe Swap *column.*

INGREDIENTS
1/2 cup (125 ml) shortening
1 1/2 cups (375 ml) white sugar
2 eggs
2 ounces (60 ml) red food colouring
2 tbsp (25 ml) cocoa
1 tsp (5 ml) salt
2 1/2 cups (625 ml) cake flour
1 tsp (5 ml) vanilla
1 cup (250 ml) buttermilk
1 tsp (5 ml) baking soda
1 tbsp (15 ml) vinegar

Frosting:
5 tablespoons (75 ml) flour
1 cup (250 ml) milk
1 cup (250 ml) butter
1 cup (250 ml) icing sugar
1 tsp (5 ml) vanilla

METHOD

Cake: Cream shortening, add sugar gradually, and beat until light and fluffy. Add eggs one at a time, beating after each addition. Make a paste of red food colouring, cocoa, and salt. Add to shortening mixture. Sift cake flour. Mix vanilla with buttermilk. Dissolve baking soda in vinegar and add to buttermilk. Add flour alternately with buttermilk mixture to shortening, starting and ending with flour. Mix until smooth and pour into three 9-inch round pans or one 9 by 13-inch pan, well greased. Bake in 350F oven for 35 to 40 minutes or until done.

Frosting: Make a paste with flour and a little bit of milk. Add remainder of milk gradually, mixing until smooth. Cook on stove at medium heat until thick. Let cool. Cream butter with icing sugar and vanilla. Beat until fluffy. Add cooled flour mixture one spoon at a time, beating well between additions.

CHICKEN POT PIE SAUCE

This recipe comes directly from food services manager Alan Finnbogason, he has declared it authentic, and it is printed exactly as he provided it.

INGREDIENTS

1/3 cup margarine
1 – 1 1/2 tbsp chicken base
4 cups water
1/4 cup corn starch (or a little more)
3/4 cup carrots
3/4 cup onions
3/4 cup celery
3/4 cup green peas
1/2 tsp salt
1/2 tsp pepper
1/4 tsp savoury
1/4 tsp basil

METHOD

1. Heat the margarine in a kettle.
2. Add first three vegetables.
3. Add flour and mix.
4. Add heated chicken stock or water with chicken base.
5. Bring to a boil.
6. Finish off with seasoning and green peas.
7. If modified starch for frozen pies is being used, go from step 2 to step 4, mix starch with some of the chicken stock and add to kettle.

Place cooked chicken in ramekins or large casserole. Cover with sauce, mix, then top with raw pastry. Bake at 350F until pastry browned and contents heated. (Six servings)

TOASTED ASPARAGUS AND CHEESE ROLLS

This recipe was provided by Alan Finnbogason and has been tested (with very satisfactory results) by Lee Major (of the PBS television series Two Grumpy Guys in the Kitchen). These are relatively simple to prepare and some Eatonians have devised their own variations. One recommended the addition of a bit of garlic for extra flavour. Others insisted that sandwich bread is preferable to regular loaves. More convenient approaches would be to use processed cheese spread or canned asparagus, but those ingredients would be further from the original Grill Room version than this recipe.

METHOD

Cut the crusts from one large fresh loaf of bread and cut into 3/4 inch slices. Spread good quality cheddar cheese (sliced thin) on each slice of bread and place some butter and a fresh asparagus spear in the centre of the bread. Roll each bread slice and hold it together with a toothpick. Add a bit of melted butter on the top and place under a broiler for about 2 minutes until golden brown. Remove toothpick. Spritzel with lemon (or accompany with thousand islands dressing) and serve.

EATON'S

GROCERY F

ORDER FROM WINNIPEG ONLY

THIS FOLDER IN EFFECT F

ALMOND ICING, Honeysuckle Brand, 1-lb. tin....50c

Baking Powder

Eatonia, per 1-lb. tin....25c
Per 5-lb. tin....1.05
SUNGLO, per 1-lb. tin....19c
Per 3-lb. tin....50c
MAGIC, per 12-oz. tin....23c
Per 1-lb. tin....28c
Per 2½-lb. tin....65c

Baking Soda

BULK, per 5 lbs....27c
COW BRAND, per ½ lb....6c
Per 1 lb....10c

Bird Seed

BROCK'S, per 10-oz. pkg....12c
BIRD GRAVEL, per 1½-lb. pkg....9c
BRUCE'S, per 10-oz. pkg....12c

Biscuits

SODA BISCUITS, 12-lb. box....1.85
CHRISTIE'S PREMIUM SODAS, per 2-lb. pkg....39c
WESTON'S CREAMY SODAS, per 2-lb. pkg....37c

Bisto (Gravy Maker)

BISTO, per medium-sized pkg....22c
Per large-sized pkg....42c
SYMINGTON, per tin....18c

Blue

KEEN'S OXFORD, three pkgs....25c

SPECIAL NOTICE

Due to uncertain conditions, we reserve the right to vary the
articles if the occasion demands and to limit the quantity of
sold to a customer and to alter the terms and conditions subj
goods are now advertised for sale. We have endeavoured to en
plies of Catalogue articles. However, should our stock of good
before the Catalogue expires, suitable substitutions will be made

Canned Meats

BONELESS CHICKEN, Mephisto, 7-oz. tin....29c
CORNED BEEF, two No. 1 tins....45c
LUNCH TONGUE, York, per tin....29c
POTTED MEATS, Clark's, all kinds, six ¼ tins....47c
SAUSAGE, York, per No. 1 tin....27c
VEAL LOAF, Libby's, 2 medium tins....33c

Canned Pork and Beans

CLARK'S, six 15-oz. tins....49c
HEINZ, Baked, two medium tins....29c
YORK, six 15-oz. tins....47c
LIBBY'S, six 15-oz. tins....47c

Canned Milk

CONDENSED, Eagl...
EVAPORATED, St. Char
Six 1-lb. tall tins....
Case of 48 tins....
POWDERED, C.M.P., Ski
Per 10-lb. tin....
KLIM, Whole Milk, per 5-
BORDEN'S CHOCOLAT
per 1-lb. tin....

EATON'S Delicious C

Are Pure and Always Freshly Roas

Whole or Ground—State Which You Require

Expertly Blended for

STRENGTH — FLAVOR — RI

EATON Coffee Values are in the

EATON'S MAYFAIR BLEND PURE COFFEE.
Our finest Coffee.
3-lb. pkg....1.78
5-lb. pkg....2.90

EATON'S PALAWAN BL
3-lb. pkg....
5-lb. pkg....
10-lb. pkg....

THE BASEMENT FOODATERIA was a complete supermarket with a full range of groceries at competitive prices, as well as specialty items found only at Eaton's. Foodateria customers who parked in the parkade had their groceries sent there through an underground tunnel for convenient pickup. Even when the large grocery chains appeared, many Winnipeggers continued to do all their shopping at the Foodateria. Bill Norrie recalls that, when he was a child, his mother would walk from their home on Banning Street to shop in the Foodateria, then carry the groceries home. When Eaton's supermarkets in other cities were closed due to declining business, the Winnipeg Foodateria continued to operate as a viable department, and remained open until the store itself was closed.

counter. In the 1950's, Fridays were especially busy days at the fish counter. By special arrangement, fish from Vancouver docks were rushed each Thursday by overnight express train to Winnipeg and offered for sale the next morning at Eaton's.

The cheese counter

EATON'S OFFERED MORE than a hundred and sixty varieties of cheeses from around the world at its third-floor cheese counter. After spending the requisite period of time in the store's refrigerated cheese aging room, these delights were stored in marble-faced refrigerators and displayed in the thirty-two-foot marble counter. While customers looked on, their choices would be cut from blocks or rounds, then carefully wrapped in waxed brown butcher's paper. There was no precutting or prepackaging. Orders of even a couple of slices were as welcome as much larger requests.

Eaton's Candy Kitchen

EATON'S CANDY FACTORY was on the ninth floor of the Mail Order Building and specialized in Pandora Chocolates. These premium chocolates were individually hand-dipped by nimble-fingered women in a room where the temperature was kept at a chilly 65 degrees Fahrenheit. The employees who packed the chocolates in their distinctive boxes were so fastidious in artistically arranging them that one packer would complete only forty boxes in a day. An Eaton's joke is that the company had to stop making Pandora chocolates when the two little old ladies who hand-dipped them retired. They couldn't find replacements with sufficiently cold hands.

Fifteen hundred pound batches of gumdrops were kept for forty-eight hours in a room heated to 140 degrees Fahrenheit to bring them to the correct level of moistness. Marble-topped tables that measured twelve feet by three feet were used to prepare 400-pound slabs of peanut fudge. During the pre-Christmas season, candy canes were made by hand by a team of five people. Each day, 3,600 canes came from one huge striped cane that started out one foot in diameter, and was pulled and rolled until it was only half an inch thick. The last two workers cut the single canes off at nine-inch intervals and gave each its characteristic curl.

The most popular brand of candy was Cottage Sweets. The ingredients included ginger from China, cinnamon from Hong Kong, chocolate from West Africa, and maple sugar from Quebec. In the late 1960s, the factory used forty-five tons of sugar, fifty thousand pounds of chocolate, and nineteen tons of nuts annually. A pre-Christmas project each year was to make up bags of assorted Eaton's candies for Santa Claus to give to his visitors. In 1969, 35,000 of these were packed. ■

The employees who packed the chocolates in their distinctive boxes were so fastidious in artistically arranging them that one packer would complete only forty boxes in a day.

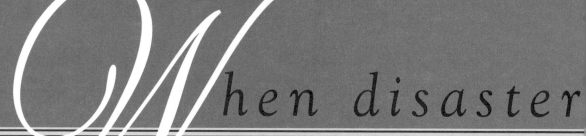

More than 10,000 Winnipeg homes were flooded and an estimated 80,000 Winnipeggers were forced to flee the city.

STRIKES

THE FLOOD OF 1950

The Flood of the Century

ALTHOUGH THE FLOOD that took place in the spring of 1997 was dubbed "the Flood of the Century," many believe that this title should be reserved for the 1950 flood. At that time, the Red River Floodway had not been constructed, so the damage within the City of Winnipeg was much greater. With approximately one-eighth of Winnipeg covered by flood waters in 1950, more than 10,000 Winnipeg homes were flooded and an estimated 80,000 Winnipeggers (out of a population of 300,000) were forced to flee the city.

Eaton's set up an emergency Flood Relief Centre in the Hargrave Street Annex to coordinate the various disaster relief activities in which the company and its employees were involved. This was a particularly useful location for one of the services provided by Eaton's to flood workers – supplying coffee, sandwiches, and

hot soup. These were prepared in the employees' cafeteria on a twenty-four hour a day basis, and then sent down to the main floor in a dumb waiter. Eaton's trucks took care of the deliveries. Eaton's drivers also delivered food to dike workers on behalf of the Red Cross. In the first seven days of the flood, 7,850 gallons of coffee and 54,174 sandwiches were provided.

Assisting Eatonians in need

RECOGNIZING THAT THE HOMES of many Eatonians were threatened by flood waters, the company undertook to store their furniture in a safe and dry place. To achieve this, a temporary mezzanine was constructed on the second floor of Mail Order Building Number Two.

Eaton's drivers, electricians, and other able-bodied personnel were placed on standby. Some slept overnight on display beds and carpets in the Hargrave Annex so emergencies could be

In the first seven days of the flood, 7,850 gallons of coffee and 54,174 sandwiches were provided.

Chapter 8

170 Patients Taken From Hospital

By KEN BOTWRIGHT

(newspaper body text largely illegible)

THE WINNIPEG TRIBUNE

The Weather

WINNIPEG, SATURDAY, MAY 6, 1950   50 PAGES   NO. 108

RED SURGES INTO CITY STREETS; WILDWOOD ORDERED EVACUATED

300 Fort Garry Families Flee; Main Dike Holding

Compulsory evacuation of all families in the Wildwood Park area was ordered at 4.30 a.m. Saturday.

More than 300 families were to be taken from the district in cars donated by citizens of other families.

This included more than 250 families ordered evacuated earlier Friday night.

Flood May Top

Come again

FLOOD BULLETINS

US Sees 4 Years To Arm

Workers Vainly Fight for Dikes

By DAVE ADAMS

Full destructive force of the rain-threatened Red River exploded this morning on Greater Winnipeg, driving hundreds of persons out of their homes and two hospitals, and leaving a trail of broken dikes in its wake.

---

handled at any hour. When employees telephoned to report that their homes were in immediate danger, furniture delivery trucks were dispatched. Electricians disconnected appliances while drivers and their helpers hauled furniture to the trucks. These items were marked and put into storage until they could be returned. Approximately 225 homes were emptied in this way. In approximately 60 homes, carpets were removed by Eaton's carpet installers and moved to the Mail Order Building for storage. Employees were paid their regular wages while involved in these activities, and many put in a considerable number of unpaid extra hours as

volunteers. In some cases, furniture from neighbours' homes was also rescued and stored.

In other situations, furniture was moved to upper storeys of houses by Eaton's personnel. Mel Jenkins, one of the employees involved in these rescue efforts, remembers that a piano that was too difficult to move out of a house was lifted almost to the ceiling on wooden blocks, and remained there until the flood subsided.

Carpenter supervisor Len Rogers recalls that a wood lathe in their shop was busy sixteen hours a day turning out wooden sewer plugs that were given to Eatonians whose basements were at risk

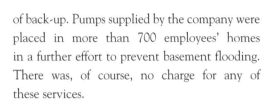

of back-up. Pumps supplied by the company were placed in more than 700 employees' homes in a further effort to prevent basement flooding. There was, of course, no charge for any of these services.

Eatonians in other provinces opened their homes to Winnipeg employees who were forced to leave Manitoba. The Winnipeg store made travel arrangements for the families of more than 100 Eatonians to as far away as St. Stephen, New Brunswick, and Vancouver.

Alex Kapitany, an American citizen who had just begun working with Eaton's as an electrician, had just accepted a very attractive job with General Electric in Flint, Michigan. He was so impressed by the way Eaton's treated its employees during the flood that he decided he would rather remain an Eatonian (and he stayed for thirty years).

Assisting the flood effort

IN ADDITION TO COORDINATING activities to assist Eatonians threatened by the flood, the Flood Relief Centre coordinated a number of activities on behalf of the Red Cross to benefit the community in general. Telephone lines were kept open twenty-four hours a day.

Four booths were set up in the downtown store to collect donations for the Manitoba Flood Relief Fund. Special "Flood Editions" of the *Winnipeg Tribune* and the *Winnipeg Free Press* were sold by Eaton's staff members, with all proceeds going to the fund. Thousands of copies were sent to Eaton's stores across Canada.

Eaton's employees were actively involved in building dikes in various parts of the city, while others used boats to transport stranded families to safety.

A BOAC aircraft filled with donated Red Cross supplies arrived from Britain at the Stevenson Field, as the Winnipeg airport was then called, on June 2nd. To assist the Red Cross, Eaton's donated two shiny new furniture vans and uniformed drivers to help unload and transport the 731 "Bundles from Britain."

University of Manitoba Campus lies under water.

The only Eaton's building that was threatened by the flood was the Alexander Avenue Warehouse. As the Red River overflowed its banks, Eaton's engineers – at times assisted by as many as 100 employee volunteers – laboured day and night with sandbags and pumps to hold three feet of water at bay. The basement remained dry, and the printing plant bindery located in the building continued to operate.

The largest financial donation received by the Manitoba Flood Relief Fund, more than $300,000, came from Eaton's. More than $150,000 of this was raised by 40,000 Eaton's employees across Canada, and their contribution was matched by the company. The collection of this money was accomplished in just six days, with employees simply donating cash from their pockets. Some Winnipeg Eatonians whose homes were high and dry donated their entire pay envelopes. One older woman contributed the money she had received as a Mother's Day gift. The Winnipeg receiving and caretaking staffs cancelled their annual picnic and donated the hundred dollars normally given out as prizes.

Eaton's delivery service to Winnipeg Beach, normally offered only during the summer, began on May 15th to accommodate many evacuees from the city who had moved to cottages during the crisis.

Many performed these services as volunteers outside of their working hours, but some were allowed to assist with flood efforts on company time and received their regular pay. A small mountain of sandbags filled by Eatonians was stockpiled in the customer parking lot. Virtually all of the company's trucks were made available to transport food, pumps, and volunteers.

Cleaning up

WHEN THE FLOOD WATERS finally subsided, Eatonians were kept busy returning furniture and reconnecting electrical appliances.

For those who weren't so fortunate, a large area of the Mail Order became a Flood Repair Centre. An assembly line of technicians was set

By 6:00 a.m., the Time Building and the Dismorr Building were fully ablaze.

up to clean and repair household items that had been submerged during the flood, including furniture, electric ranges, refrigerators, and washing machines. Everything from rusted bicycles to delicate chinaware was moved from flooded homes by six Eaton's furniture trucks, cleaned and restored to good-as-new condition, and returned.

Operating manager Alan Finnbogason was loaned at no charge by Eaton's to the Flood Relief Fund for a period of ten months. During that time, his salary was paid by the company. Personnel from the furniture department were also made available at no charge to assist in evaluating losses. Other employees were paid by Eaton's to type up flood damage claim forms at the City Dairy offices on Notre Dame Avenue after their regular work days.

WINNIPEG'S BIGGEST FIRE

The fire begins

THE TIME BUILDING FIRE of 1954 is considered to be the largest fire in Winnipeg's history. The problem began at approximately 1:00 a.m. on Tuesday, June 8, 1954 in the wiring behind a neon sign above the J. J. H. McLean music store in the Time Building at 333 Portage Avenue, at the northwest corner of Portage and Hargrave. The first alarm was called in at 1:18 a.m., and after the third alarm at 5:33 a.m., all available firefighters and pieces of firefighting equipment were at the scene of the blaze. The severity of

As a number of Eatonians manned hoses on the roof of the store, they watched the flames devour the buildings across the street. Their efforts probably saved many Portage Avenue structures from destruction.

An offer
IS DECLINED

the fire was aggravated by hurricane-strength westerly winds of more than seventy miles per hour.

By the time the fire was brought under control, much of the northeast and northwest corners of Portage and Hargrave had been devastated. The seven-storey Time Building was totally destroyed, as were the Dismorr Block at 327 Portage Avenue and the Edwards Block at 325 Portage Avenue. In addition, serious damage was incurred by the Affleck Block at 317 Portage Avenue and the Norlynn Building at 309 Hargrave Street. All of these were primarily office buildings with retail outlets at the street level. The total damage was estimated at more than a million and a half dollars.

Because the fire began in the early morning hours, there was no loss of life, and there were only minor injuries to firefighters. Had it begun during the day when the area would have been crowded with workers and shoppers, the human impact could have been much more serious.

The store is threatened

THE FIRE BLAZED JUST 150 FEET from the Eaton's store, and the combination of searing heat and vicious winds posed a genuine threat to the store. Although the outer walls were brick, the window frames and sills above the first floor were made of wood, and some of these were beginning to smolder. On many floors, the outer perimeters served as storage areas for merchandise, hidden from the view of customers by plaster board partitions that defined the boundaries of the public areas of the store. If the strong west winds had begun to blow from a more northerly direction, or if the intense heat from the burning buildings across the street had penetrated openings created by broken windows,

THE ARRIVAL OF THE FIRST fire trucks aroused the curiosity of a number of Eaton's electricians who were working a late shift to upgrade wiring in the store. Alex Kapitany recalls that he and some of his co-workers walked across Portage Avenue at around 1:30 a.m. and saw sparks in the area of a large neon sign on the Time Building. Alex approached one of the firefighters to discuss what appeared at the time to be a relatively minor problem. Alex identified himself to the fireman as a qualified journeyman electrician and showed proof of his qualifications. He offered to bring his wire cutters from the store and to cut the BX cable that supplied power to the sign.

Although the conversation took place half a century ago, Alex still clearly recalls what was said. The fireman told them that he could not authorize Alex to cut the cable. The fireman indicated that there had been a similar problem with the same sign the previous year. On that occasion the fire department arranged for the cable to be cut and was subsequently held responsible for the cost of repairs.

The electrical workers accepted this decision and continued to watch as the sparks from the cable worked their way into the walls of the Time Building and the fire quickly spread beyond control.

FIRE IN
MINNESOTA

THE INVOLVEMENT OF EATON'S OF WINNIPEG in disaster relief began only a few years after the store opened. In 1910 a raging bush fire virtually devastated the town of Baudette, Minnesota, killing 168 people and leaving hundreds of others homeless. Only half an hour after reports of this tragedy reached Winnipeg, Eaton's arranged for a railway car to transport relief supplies to what was left of the community. The car was filled with merchandise from the store, including tents, blankets, canned food, lanterns, and sheepskin-lined coats.

"Black Tuesday
A LOOK
BACKWARD"

IN A BROADCAST EDITORIAL that was aired on July 5, 1954, radio station CJOB declared the downtown fire large enough to be classified as a conflagration and credited the Eaton's firefighters with saving much more than the department store. "Winnipeg may never know the debt it owes to the T. Eaton Company Limited for getting its own private fire-fighting forces into action, using twenty hose lines to spray water from its own pressure system. For in saving itself, Eaton's may have saved a city, because Eaton's men covered their store front with a vertical water-blanket for three hours. Scores of city firefighters were then free to check, and to spray many other buildings in the area – some of them a block away from the main fire centre, but still in extreme danger."

the fire could have made a dramatic entry into the store by igniting merchandise in the stock rooms. Once inside the building, with its false walls and ceilings and wooden floors – as well as acres of flammable merchandise and furnishings – an inferno could have erupted that no fire-fighting effort would have been able to overcome.

Senior managers of Eaton's in Winnipeg had company-installed bells and special telephones in their homes to notify them of emergencies in the store. They were also issued police passes for their cars which entitled them to exceed the speed limit on their way to emergencies. The bells rang at around 7:00 that morning to alert managers to the fact that there was a serious problem at the store. After racing downtown, the managers discovered that there was virtually no pressure in the main water lines because of the firefighting efforts across the street, so the store's own well water system was turned on.

"When you want a big job done, ask Eatonians to do it"

EATON'S HAD ITS OWN VOLUNTEER fire brigade to deal with emergencies, but this one required tactics that never could have been anticipated. Their challenge that morning was to create a constant curtain of water on the outer walls of the store to protect the building from the heat. Some Eatonians manned hoses at street level while others leaned out of windows to spray water both above and below. Even at the height of the crisis, a few found time for humour as they spotted

fellow employees at windows on other floors and aimed their hoses at them.

Most of the Eatonians were wearing ordinary clothing rather than special firefighting gear. As these firefighters became soaked, they went into various departments of the store to find complete changes of clothing and footwear. Some needed to do this several times, and their discarded clothes were left scattered in soggy piles on the floor throughout the store. There was no suggestion that the firefighters should pay for the clothing they appropriated.

Several volunteer firefighters manned hoses on the roof of the store. Some lay face-down on the cornice and aimed fire hoses downward. One especially courageous Eatonian was Phil Marr, who worked in the mechanical engineering department. Phil was a diminutive but adventurous man who volunteered to hang upside down from the cornice to spray water down the walls of the store. Two of his colleagues lay on the cornice, their ankles held by four other Eatonians behind them. These two men grasped Phil's ankles and he hung head-down eight storeys above Portage Avenue. He held a hose until he became so light-headed that he had to be pulled back up to the roof. After a short break, Phil once again allowed himself to be dangled over the edge to resume his perilous task.

Despite the vicious wind, the intense heat, and the broken hydro wires that snapped and sizzled on Portage Avenue, the exhausted, smoke-stained volunteers continued to shield the store from the blaze with a wall of cold water.

By the time the blaze across Portage Avenue was brought under control, most of the display windows facing Portage Avenue and Hargrave

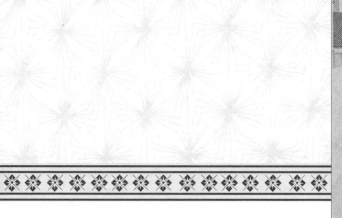

The windows closest to the fire cracked from the intense heat...

Street had broken. The windows closest to the fire cracked from the intense heat, and the windows near Donald Street cracked as the brass frames holding them in place expanded in the heat. The next day, with the store closed, employees used two-by-fours to knock the remains of the broken panes outside to the sidewalks, and the chunks of glass were hauled away by dump trucks. These huge panels were made of special glass which had to be imported from Belgium, and the replacement process took two years to complete. In the meantime, thinner panes were used.

Many of the windows in the upper storeys were also broken and had to be replaced, along with singed wooden window sills and frames. The red brick walls were blackened by smoke, with some bricks charred to a depth of an inch or more, but the store was largely unscathed.

A few weeks later, the Executive Committee of the Western Canada Insurance Underwriters' Association unanimously commended the management and staff of Eaton's for their outstanding efforts. Their letter observed "it is seldom that a private fire brigade is called upon to perform the duties which this brigade did."

The company provided new clothing for some of the volunteers who fought the fire, and others recall receiving an envelope a few days later containing a ten dollar bill as a thank-you for their efforts.

Cars were buried in snow and the transit system was paralyzed.

THE BIG BLIZZARD

A snowy morning

WHEN WINNIPEGGERS AWOKE on the morning of Friday, March 4, 1966, one glance outside made it clear that winter was still around. Snow had begun to fall the previous evening, and by morning several inches blanketed the ground. Radio stations were warning their listeners that a major storm was developing. But this was Winnipeg, and people were not about to let a bit of snow change their plans.

Alan Finnbogason got up at the usual time, and, until his phone rang at seven o'clock, was preparing for another routine day as operating manager of Eaton's. It was suggested that he look

Display furniture provided comfort (but not much privacy).

outside. After a bit of searching, he found his old air force parka and flight boots to wear to work and packed his suit in a plastic bag. He didn't realize that by the end of the day he would be managing a makeshift hotel.

Alan made it as far as Berry Street, then managed to flag down an Eaton's truck to take him the rest of the way. Pharmacist John Mainella was able to hitch a ride from St James on a Royal Mail truck until its transmission gave out at Donald and Ellice; he walked the rest of the way. Shipping supervisor Cliff Nichol caught the last bus out of Windsor Park.

A nucleus of regular customers arrived at the store when it opened each morning, regardless of the weather, for their morning coffee. Today was no exception. As weather conditions worsened, more people came into the store to escape the blowing snow.

The managers who were able to make their way to the store that morning realized that this was not to be a normal day of business, and asked staff members who made it in to try to contact others who were still at home and tell them not to come to work. As the day progressed, employees who were able to walk home or to make arrangements to stay at the nearby homes of friends or relatives were encouraged to leave.

Heavy snow continued to fall, and furious winds reduced visibility to zero. Some staff members braved the storm to locate stranded Winnipeggers at bus stops and invite them to take shelter in the store.

By late morning, the people of Winnipeg realized that they had to stay wherever they were.

City officials announced at 11:00 a.m. that all roads were closed. Buses stopped running, mail delivery was suspended, schools were closed, and transportation in and out of the city by air, rail, and bus was cancelled. Mayor Stephen Juba advised all citizens to stay home. The Winnipeg Grain Exchange closed early for the first time in sixty years.

Eaton's drivers had gone out that morning to attempt their city deliveries, but by nine o'clock, radio stations were carrying a message from the company asking them to return. Because the trucks had no radios, customers passed the message on to their drivers.

Stranded in the store

BY EARLY AFTERNOON, the downtown Eaton's store housed an estimated 1,482 people. There were 1,100 employees (approximately 700 women and 400 men) as well as more than 300 customers (mostly women). Although some of the customers originally came to the store with plans of shopping, most had simply come in to seek shelter from the ever-worsening conditions.

There were similar situations elsewhere in the downtown area. The Hudson's Bay store harboured several hundred stranded employees and customers, as well as providing meals for people unable to leave the nearby Law Courts and Norquay Building. As blinding winds swept across the parking lot, Simpsons-Sears at Polo Park readied beds in the furniture department for female employees and gathered sleeping bags in

As weather conditions worsened, more people came into the store to escape the blowing snow.

All it takes is bad weather for Manitobans to pull together, or in this case, push together.

the sporting goods department for male employees. At the bus depot, 150 passengers waited on benches, while at the Canadian Pacific Railway station, six sleeping cars were prepared to accommodate stranded staff members.

An emergency planning committee of approximately thirty Eaton's employees was quickly organized in the store. This group met every two hours to improvise and review plans for accommodating, feeding, and entertaining the stranded employees and customers, as well as ensuring that security and fire prevention measures were kept in place.

Because the store was not equipped with a public address system, printed bulletins were delivered to department staff or posted on bulletin boards. A decision had been made in the morning to close the store at 3:30 p.m.. This was quickly revised to 2:30, and by mid-morning a bulletin announced that the store would close

immediately. Customers were encouraged "to proceed home at your earliest convenience." This bulletin acknowledged, however, that transit service had stopped, and optimistically suggested that hotel accommodations be arranged. It concluded by stating that, if hotel arrangements proved to be impossible, customers would be allowed to stay in the store. By then, all of the downtown hotels were fully booked.

A bulletin issued in the early afternoon recognized the realities of the situation, and requested that customers who wished to remain in the store proceed to the Grill Room, where "refreshments and reading material will be provided for your convenience." Five television sets were moved to the Grill Room, and magazines and playing cards were provided.

A staff bulletin requested that all employees remain on their floors until the designated supper hours, and discouraged "roaming around the store" and non-emergency phone calls. It also advised staff that the sixth floor magazine counters and the main floor toiletry counters would be open from 6:00 p.m. to 7:00 p.m.. Eaton's telephone operators managed to keep cheerful and upbeat as they kept the overtaxed switchboard open. Chalkboards were used to provide messages to employees and customers from anxious friends and family members.

Because of security concerns, managers were assigned to supervise all areas of the store on a rotating schedule that continued though the night. Watch repair manager Jim Thomson recalls being told to "Keep walking around here and make sure nobody steals anything." He laughs as he wonders in retrospect, "If they stole anything, where the hell were they going to go?"

Several adventurous managers made their way across Portage to the Clarendon Hotel, where they found that the bar was open. After more than a few drinks, they returned to the store in no condition to be meeting the public and made their way to the basement floor. A quick-thinking colleague hollowed out a space in a towering display of blue jeans so his inebriated friends could crawl inside to sleep off their overindulgence.

Starting at 5:30 p.m., customers and staff were provided with supper in the Valley Room. This meal, as well as coffee during the day and breakfast the following morning, was provided at no charge. In total, an estimated 3,000 meals were prepared, despite limited kitchen staff and the fact that food supplies were running low.

Even though the meals were free and it was obvious that there was a shortage of serving personnel, some customers complained that service at the Saturday breakfast was too slow.

Spending the night

THAT NIGHT, FEMALE EMPLOYEES were accommodated in the seventh floor furniture department. Some slept on hideaway

Messages from concerned friends and relatives were passed on to people stranded in the store.

beds, but others were able to move in to the stylish bedroom displays that showed off the latest in Spanish, Colonial, and Danish bedroom suites. Mindful of future sales prospects for these furnishings, employees carefully laid kraft paper on the mattresses. Male employees had less luxurious surroundings as they prepared to bed down on cots and upholstered chairs in the ninth floor staff lounge.

Many managers and building maintenance people had little or no sleep as they continued their security patrols overnight, in part to ensure that the employees maintained a discreet two-storey distance. Some Eatonians are now willing to acknowledge that, despite their efforts, some co-ed sleeping did take place. Recognizing that the Winnipeg Fire Department would be unable to respond to a fire alarm, some engineering staff members walked the floors of the store in two-hour shifts. Gordon Bailey volunteered for this duty. "It was either go on fire duty or sit and play cards." He walked the floors with a flashlight, occasionally being startled when he suddenly saw himself in a mirrored pillar.

Along with the employees, some captive customers played cards or read books and magazines from the book department, which had been opened for their convenience that evening. Others chuckled at Maxwell Smart on the popular sit-com *Get Smart* or were thrilled by *The Maltese Falcon* on the thoughtfully-provided televisions. The customers spent the night on a variety of makeshift beds, including piles of carpets, cots, couches and lounge chairs. Blankets were taken from stock to keep the staff members and employees warm. Two nurses kept watch on people with health problems during the night, and electrical maintenance men made sure that the power remained on. Any needed prescriptions were filled by the pharmacy.

They didn't want to leave

BY THE TIME THE TWENTY-HOUR BLIZZARD subsided, a total of fourteen inches of snow had fallen. Winds of fifty miles per hour buried cars and trapped people inside their homes. The city was effectively paralyzed for three days.

On Saturday morning, March 5th, the City of Winnipeg undertook a massive cleanup that would cost almost $700,000. The Greater Winnipeg Safety Council established "Operation Snowbound" to provide assistance to the elderly and others who needed help. This was headquartered in the Catalogue Building, and Eaton's later received a plaque from the Safety Council in recognition of the company's assistance.

Alan Finnbogason recalls that he needed to make an announcement to the customers on Saturday morning. "I had to get up and ask them to leave. They were having such a good time." ■

Some Eatonians are now willing to acknowledge that, despite their efforts, some co-ed sleeping did take place.

This display of bunk beds proved to be a comfortable place to spend the night.

Canada's greatest

OPERATED BY T. EATON C° LIMITED | **EATON GROCETERIA** | **OPERATED T. EATON**

An Eaton's Groceteria opened in Transcona on September 14, 1927. Paved roads came later.

STORE

The greatest good

TIMOTHY EATON'S FIRST STORE, which opened in 1869 at Yonge and Queen in Toronto, was the birthplace of a philosophy that guided the T. Eaton Company throughout its 130 years of business.

Because the practices that arose from this philosophy were so closely associated with Eaton's, it has often been assumed that they were originated by Timothy Eaton. That assumption is debatable, but there is little doubt that Eaton's popularized an approach to business that placed a high priority on customer and employee satisfaction, and the business philosophy of Timothy Eaton had a lasting impact on retail practices.

The most basic statement of Timothy Eaton's vision of how a business should conduct itself is summarized in a phrase that draws on the philosophical writings of Jeremy Bentham: "the greatest good to the greatest number." This phrase, which appeared periodically in Eaton's advertisements, can be seen as the foundation of many policies that were designed to benefit the customers and employees of the company.

Dealing with honesty

ON SATURDAY, JULY 15, 1905, the first day the Winnipeg store was opened to the public, a large newspaper advertisement appeared under the heading "Eaton's Daily Store News." Besides listing some of the opening sale items, including the Eaton Special Hat for $1.00, and 368 pairs of Ladies' Oxfords for $1.50 each, the advertisement declared "One of the principles of our business is honesty in advertising. We sell everything we advertise and everything is just as represented."

This approach was markedly different from that of some other merchants at that time, whose advertisements presented merchandise in exaggerated and misleading terms, and who offered items that were not available in order to lure customers inside their doors. Outright lying was considered an acceptable business practice by some entrepreneurs.

Winnipeggers quickly came to appreciate the integrity of the T. Eaton Company. They knew that an Eaton's advertisement described merchandise honestly and directly. Eaton's was scrupulously forthright in telling customers if

Winnipeggers quickly came to appreciate the integrity of the T. Eaton Company. They knew that an Eaton's advertisement described merchandise honestly and directly. Eaton's was scrupulously forthright in telling customers if items were available only in limited quantities, or if only certain sizes or colours were in stock.

Chapter 9

SOAPS AND CLEANERS

Unless cake is a size generally known, it is advisable to state weight of cake, as "approximately 4-oz. cake," etc.
If claims are made for any therapeutic effects, the soap comes under the Cosmetic Section of the Food and Drugs Act.

DIAMONDS

The word "Perfect" is not to be used in advertising diamonds. Instead of this word, when referring to what would be known in the trade as a "Perfect" diamond, use the word "Flawless." Whenever diamond or other rings are illustrated larger than actual size in advertisements, this fact must be so stated in the advertisement.

FEATHERS

When feathers are used for fillings, the name of the feathers used should be given, such as duck, goose, chicken, etc., in the order of their respective amounts, the largest percentage being named first.

Down is properly used to describe the undercoat of the water fowl. Products described as "down-filled" should be filled only with "down," except for a permissible small tolerance of small feathers, impracticable to eliminate in separation. If mixed with feathers, correct phrasing would be "down and feather filled," providing at least 50% is down.

Feather-Down

A mixture of fine feathers and down; must contain at least 25% down.

All merchandise containing the above must be labelled according to the requirements of existing Provincial Bedding Regulations.

46

GLASS AND CHINAWARE

Crystal

Crystal or Full Crystal is glass containing at least 30% lead oxide and the alkali must be almost entirely potash. Half Crystal Glass must contain a minimum of 15% lead oxide.

Cut Glass

Cut Glass should not be advertised as such unless the design is entirely made by a cutting wheel, or other cutting instruments. If the design was first pressed then finished on the cutting wheel, this should not be advertised as cut glass, but as pressed and cut.

Mirrors

When advertising mirrors whether sold as part of set or separately, they should be described as being made either of plate glass, or sheet glass. The so-called "Crystal" mirror glass is a heavy weight of sheet glass.

Pottery and Chinaware

This should be classified as Porcelain, China, Semi-Porcelain, and Earthenware.
"PORCELAIN"—is a very high grade vitreous china made from special clays. The body is translucent and non-absorbent.
"CHINA"—Is a vitreous pottery, which has a translucent and very white body.
"Bone China" is a superior quality of china and should be reserved for material with not less than 40% bone content.
"SEMI-PORCELAIN"—Is an inaccurate term used to describe a partially-vitrified earthenware. Its use should be severely restricted. It is preferable to refer to this as "fine pottery."
"EARTHENWARE"—Is opaque pottery even though glazed. The body is opaque and porous. So called "semi-porcelain" is a better-grade earthenware.

Open-Stock

Sets should not be advertised as such unless the Department is in a position to supply for a period of two years from date of last advertisement or Department Display.
It is permissible to qualify chinaware which is made in imitation of a certain type by the addition of the word "pattern" e.g. "Dresden Pattern Chinaware."

47

The Guide for Eaton Advertising proclaimed "The Confidence of the Public is our Company's greatest heritage." The company insisted on scrupulous honesty in its advertising practices.

items were available only in limited quantities, or if only certain sizes or colours were in stock.

A small booklet published in the 1950s titled *A Guide for Eaton Advertising* outlined the strict requirements the company enforced in all of its advertising. The booklet included detailed descriptions of various fabrics and materials, and warned against using any references that might be misleading. The common names of furs were allowed, but needed to be followed in brackets by the sometimes less attractive realities of their sources, as in "Alaska Sable (dyed skunk)" or "Manchurian Wolf (dyed Chinese dog). The

word "antique" was not to be used unless the item being described was at least 100 years old, "of good design," and "substantially of the original materials."

The use of comparative pricing was discouraged, and its occasional use was strictly regulated. An alphabetical listing of twenty-five forbidden words and phrases began with "amazing," "astounding," and "colossal" and ended with "worth much more" and "worth several times the price."

Tom Lenton, a manager and buyer during his thirty-four-year career, recalls how advertising copy drafted by department managers had to be scrutinized by a compliance officer in the advertising department before it could appear in print "to make sure that no Eaton's ad told an untruth."

Similarly, sales personnel, no matter how eager they might be to make sales, were expected not to misrepresent merchandise in any way. This insistence on honesty is often illustrated by the perhaps apocryphal story of an early incident that took place in the Toronto store. Timothy Eaton overheard a clerk telling a customer that a garment was "all wool." Mr. Eaton intervened and said "No, madam, that is half wool and half cotton." In keeping with one of Timothy's original principles that "no one is importuned to buy," salesclerks were expected to show merchandise and to provide information, but not to "pester" customers to make purchases.

One fixed price for all

WHEN TIMOTHY EATON entered retailing, it was common practice for prices to be negotiated between customers and merchants through the process of bargaining. Storekeepers initially asked inflated prices, knowing that customers would offer much less, and the final price of a transaction was often determined after a lengthy series of offers and counter-offers. In that kind of atmosphere, shopping was a stressful experience, a game where only the skillful and experienced had a chance of success, and where buyers often left a store wondering if someone else could buy the same item for a lower price.

Eaton's, in contrast, publicized its policy of "one fixed price for all – no haggling." To dramatize how much of a pleasant departure this policy was from the dickering atmosphere, the company declared "a child can safely shop in this store."

This was a particularly attractive and comforting message for women. In the social climate of the early 1900s, it was generally assumed that only men possessed the skills and the aggressive nature to emerge victorious from a bout of bargaining. The implementation of a firm

Many major bus routes delivered shoppers directly to Eaton's.

As more shoppers chose to drive to the store rather than using public transportation, Eaton's parking lots and the parkade became busier.

one-price-for-all policy placed all shoppers on a level playing field. The timing was very appropriate because it coincided with the beginning of a period where more women had their own incomes and were achieving some degree of independence.

Similarly, new Canadians with limited English skills could go to the Big Store knowing that the clearly marked prices they saw were the ones they would pay. No discussion was needed. Again, this was an example of good timing because of the wave of immigration to Manitoba during that period.

Cash only

THE WINNIPEG NEWSPAPER advertisements placed by Eaton's on July 15th, 1905, included the sentence, "We sell for cash…and no one is compelled to bear any part of the losses from bad debts that occur of necessity whenever the credit system is in vogue."

This policy had benefits for both the company and its customers. The extension of credit, common with many other businesses, was a risky practice, and merchants generally had to write off significant amounts of money when

Introducing
PENNIES

MANY ACCOUNTS OF THE OPENING of Eaton's in Winnipeg have told how the company introduced the one-cent coin to Manitoba. According to these reports, prices in Winnipeg stores until then had always been rounded off to the nearest nickel (as in $1.90 or 65 cents) and the one-cent coin was virtually unknown. In Eaton's Toronto store, it was common practice to price items to end in a seven, eight or nine (as in $1.89 or 67 cents). To assist with the introduction of the same pricing policy in the new Winnipeg store, Eaton's ordered a consignment of $500 in pennies (or "coppers" as they were called at the time) to be shipped from Ottawa. At first, customers receiving the unwanted coins in their change were reported to have left them in the counter or deposited them in charity boxes that were provided for that purpose. Newspapers, which went for five cents on the street, were sold for two cents at the store entrances to give customers an outlet for the coins. Ironically, almost all of the prices in the Eaton's ads for Saturday, July 15th and Monday, July 17th, 1905 (the two opening days of the store) ended in either zero or five.

Moving
THE MONEY

BECAUSE SO MUCH of Eaton's business was done in cash, the store and Catalogue routinely dealt with huge amounts of money. When drivers cashed in on sales days, hundreds of thousands of dollars had to be counted. Until bank deposits could be made up, cash was stored in a large vault located in an underground tunnel beneath Graham Avenue between the store and the Catalogue. Inside the vault was a safe, so the money locked in the safe had double security.

"Money wagons" were used to deliver large quantities of cash from the Mail Order to the cash office on the eighth floor of the store. One employee would push a cart carrying a large locked cash box, accompanied by a guard. After passing through the tunnel under Graham Avenue, the cart would travel non-stop to the eighth floor by freight elevator.

Cash was taken to and from banks in an imposing blue Chrysler Imperial sedan, complete with bulletproof glass and an armed guard. For security reasons, the car made its trips at different times each day and randomly used different routes.

debts could not be collected. Waiting for customers to pay their bills also meant that retailers either had to borrow money to pay their suppliers or had to pay interest. The end result was that the prices of goods were marked up to anticipate these expenses.

To accommodate customers who preferred not to carry cash, the Deposit Account program was introduced in 1904. Popularly known as the D. A., this was actually the opposite of credit buying because customers deposited money in their Eaton's accounts in advance. When they made purchases, the amounts of the transactions were deducted from their balances, and itemized statements were mailed out at the end of each month. The Eaton's D.A. was an early version of debit card transactions, except, instead of the money being deposited with a financial institution, it was placed in an account with Eaton's. All deposits were matched by government securities to safeguard the depositors, and interest was paid monthly to depositors on their unused balances. The interest rates were sufficiently attractive that many customers used their Deposit Accounts as savings accounts, and the company had the assurance that virtually all of the money on deposit would end up being spent at Eaton's.

The first concession to the realities of the expanding credit economy occurred in the mid-1930s. Eaton's customers were allowed to delay

payments on purchases, but only for one month. Eventually a formal Deferred Payment plan was introduced, and then, to keep up with the competition Eaton's finally offered its own credit card. The credit card business became so profitable for Eaton's that it was only in the early 1980s that the company reluctantly agreed to allow customers to use American Express, Visa, and MasterCard.

Providing exceptional service

THE WATCH REPAIR: In December 1912, Bob Mugford, from the tiny village of Lintlaw, Saskatchewan, was on his way to visit family members in England. While on a stopover in Winnipeg, he dropped into Eaton's hoping to have his pocket watch repaired before he left the next day on his journey. The watchmaker informed Bob that the work would take a few days, and he was given a repair ticket so he could pick up the watch on his way home. When he returned to Canada, Bob was short of money, so he decided to wait until he had enough cash before retrieving the watch. Years passed, and finally in 1950, he wrote a letter to Eaton's inquiring about his watch. Eaton's reply informed him that there was a watch in the department that had gone unclaimed for many years, and asked

him to send the repair ticket. A few days later, Bob's watch arrived in the mail.

The church curtains: Not long after the Winnipeg store and Catalogue opened, the Ladies Aid of a church in a tiny and not-very-prosperous community in the Riding Mountain area of Manitoba began a fund-raising campaign to purchase curtains for their building. The church consisted of only one room, and the women wanted drapes to separate the Sunday school class from the regular service. They held a fowl supper, which virtually everyone in town attended, and they sold hand-made patchwork quilts. When the women reached what they believed to be the limit the townsfolk could contribute, they wrote a letter to Eaton's saying that their original hope was to purchase heavy maroon plush material, but their limited proceeds dictated that they order much plainer material, and only enough to meet their basic needs. They enclosed a money order as payment. When the parcel from Eaton's arrived, the women were astounded to find it contained dozens of yards of the best maroon plush, matching thread, and hundreds of curtain rings. An envelope was attached to the luxurious fabric, and inside was the money order the group had sent to pay for their purchase. It was endorsed back to the Ladies Aid.

The Christmas gifts: During the Dirty Thirties, the doctor in a small Saskatchewan town wrote a frank letter to Eaton's in Winnipeg. Christmas was approaching, and the children of several families in the town were likely to receive no Christmas gifts from anyone. In his letter the

On April 14, 1912, Winnipeg Eatonian George Graham, on a buying trip to purchase toys, sat down to dinner with his tablemates aboard the HMS Titanic and they autographed the menu as a souvenir of the occasion. A few hours later, the ship struck an iceberg and sank. After Graham's body was recovered, the Winnipeg store was closed for a half day to mourn his loss. In 1915, three other Eaton's buyers and a niece of Sir John drowned when the Lusitania was torpedoed near Ireland. After that, a company rule did not allow more than three buyers to travel together on any form of public transportation.

doctor described the impoverished situation and made it very clear that, while these families would appreciate anything their children might receive, they were not likely ever to have the money to become regular customers of Eaton's. The packages that arrived just before Christmas contained candies, nuts, Christmas crackers, and presents for all of the children.

The paint delivery: One day in 1933, a man who lived in a town fifty miles outside of

Winnipeg arrived in the Big Store's paint department at 5:40 p.m.. There were no other customers left in the area, and several salesmen were already tallying their cash. This customer wanted to purchase $81.00 worth of paint (all in one colour), he needed to use it the next day, and he had to board a train home in a few minutes. He wondered if Eaton's could help him. A resourceful salesman cheerfully took the order – and then used his own Ford to deliver the paint to the customer.

The angora wool: A woman visited the store one day in 1935 intending to buy a ball of black angora wool. The clerk (identified only as Number 50) informed the customer that this item was out of stock and that it might not be available for a while. When the customer explained that she was hoping to use it to complete a pair of mitts, the clerk told her she had some of that wool at home and would be happy to give it to her. The clerk brought the wool when she came to work the next day, and the customer was able to finish the mitts.

The new stove: A customer purchased a new stove in 1952 from salesman Hilary Shane, but the delivery was delayed and the family had already disposed of their old stove. Realizing that they were temporarily left without anything to cook on, Mr. Shane delivered an electric hot plate to the home.

The Eaton Guarantee

IF THERE IS ONE POLICY THAT is indelibly identified with the T. Eaton Company, it is the famous Eaton Guarantee of "goods satisfactory or money refunded." This commitment, first made in 1870, was a sharp departure from the "buyer beware" climate that existed at the time. Eaton's made a pledge that if a customer had a change of mind about a purchase, if it turned out not to be exactly what it was represented to be, or if it wore, tore, or broke before it should, then an exchange would be made or a refund would be given. Unlike many other merchants of the time, Timothy Eaton did not believe that his responsibility for merchandise ended the moment it left the store.

These five words had an amazing impact on retailing by bringing about a fundamental change in the expectations of customers. Other businesses were forced to liberalize their policies

COMMENTS ON THE EATON GUARANTEE

DAVID MCFETRIDGE:
"People would send back boots that were in the same condition as when they left the barn. Some people would return winter clothing in the spring for a refund. They would buy clothing for a wedding and send it back afterwards."

ANN MCGREGOR:
"They always exchanged. There was no question, even though it was unreasonable at times."

GARY FILMON:
"They were the only ones who ultimately took the merchandise back no questions asked. People kept on shopping there because they always knew that nowhere else would they get the same treatment."

SYLVIA COULOMBE:
"One gentleman used to come in and buy his children shoes. Three months later he'd bring them back in and say there was something wrong with them so we'd give him another pair. Three months later he'd be getting another pair. He was getting free shoes for a year. Another would steal baby shoes and bring them back and say he bought them. We'd give him the money for them when we knew darn well he probably stole them in the first place. We finally caught on after he'd done it about three times."

JOYCE HOWE:
"A gentlemen brought back a lot of underwear because his wife had died. It was a couple of years old and never used. They took it back and never questioned it."

MEL JENKINS:
"The biggest exchanges in the Catalogue were in women's wear."

KEN GIBSON:
"It's hard to imagine any other store that would tolerate what Eaton's put up with."

An Eaton's Groceteria on north Main Street preceded the arrival of most major supermarkets in Winnipeg.

The hazards OF TRAVEL

AS MUCH AS BEING an Eaton's buyer provided storybook opportunities to visit faraway places and to accumulate experiences and memories to last a lifetime, the job could be stressful, exhausting, and sometimes dangerous. Buyers knew that they had the authority to make purchasing decisions that cost the company many thousands of dollars. If the decisions resulted in merchandise that sold well, the buyer could take satisfaction in a job well done. On the other hand, if merchandise proved to be inferior to what it was represented to be, if it was overpriced, or if it simply didn't appeal to Canadian consumers, the buyer could be out of a job.

Buying trips meant spending weeks, often months, far away from family and friends. They meant long days, paperwork evenings, and adjusting to local languages, customs, and ways of doing business.

Sometimes nature conspired to make the job even more difficult. Buyers were usually on tight schedules, and searing heat, bone-chilling cold, rain storms, and blizzards couldn't be allowed to interfere with their purchasing missions. In 1923, the Yokohama office was destroyed by fire after a devastating earthquake and thirteen staff members were killed.

on refunds and exchanges, although few ever went as far as Eaton's.

The Eaton Guarantee was extremely simple and had no fine print. There were no qualifying statements that imposed time limits. It went far beyond a warranty to cover manufacturers' defects. Refunds were given in the same form as the original payment, which in many cases was cash, rather than vouchers to be used for future purchases.

In an early advertisement, Timothy Eaton declared that "we esteem goodwill more than profit," and this appears to have been the justification for the policy for the entire life of the company. The rationale for honouring the guarantee even when it was clearly being abused was almost naively simple: a satisfied customer will make more purchases; a dissatisfied customer will not return.

It was estimated in the 1960s that fourteen items out of every one hundred purchased were returned, and that half of these came back not because they were defective or didn't fit, but simply because customers changed their minds. One manager estimates that there was an eighty percent return rate on dresses from the Catalogue. Some women would order five or six hats, keep one, and send the rest back. A blacklist was kept of customers who made a habit of abusing the policy ("red cards" were assigned to them), but it was often ignored. Ann McGregor, who worked in the Mail Order exchange department, says "You'd have to really abuse your privileges a lot before you'd get a red card, so we had very few of them."

Although most customers returned items for good reasons, others saw the Eaton Guarantee as a way to take advantage of a generous and trusting business. Ken Gibson remembers hearing of a resort in Northern Manitoba that sent back twelve outboard motors at the end of the season saying "we weren't happy with them." They received a refund. His father John, who worked in the Mail Order women's shoe department from 1914 to 1965, told him of a pair of women's high button boots that were returned from the Yukon.

Signy Eaton, Premier Walter Weir, and Mayor Stephen Juba participated in the opening of the Polo Park Store

MOVING TO **THE MALLS**

I N THE 1950s AND 1960s, more and more families across North America chose to move from the central areas of their cities to the suburbs. In Winnipeg, many older homes in the core area were put up for sale as their occupants purchased new bungalows in East, West, and North Kildonan, Windsor Park, Fort Garry, St. James, and a number of other emerging communities. In tandem with this trend, personal vehicles, rather than public transit, became the preferred method of transportation. Suburban shopping centres began to spring up, and the traditional shopping destinations on Portage Avenue gradually lost their appeal.

Eaton's as a national company was slow to embrace the concept of suburban stores. Traditionally it had been successful with its large, multi-storeyed department stores, and it was only after it saw the success that other retailers were achieving that the move to the suburbs began. Eventually Eaton's opened three suburban stores in Winnipeg. The timing was not good. Winnipeg's population remained static, so having four locations rather than one did not lead to increased sales, but simply spread them out.

One example of the tardiness of Eaton's to diversify its locations can be seen in the case of Winnipeg's Polo Park. In 1959, the Polo Park Shopping Centre, named after the race track it displaced, was opened by Winnipeg Mayor Stephen Juba along with television personality Fred Davis. One of the main attractions that drew thousands of Winnipeggers to this exciting new development in shopping was the brand new store of Eaton's growing competitor, Simpsons-Sears.

It wasn't until May 2, 1968 (which happened to be the birthday of the Bay) that John David Eaton opened the new $5 million Eaton's store at Polo Park. It offered three floors of shopping and was the company's largest suburban store in western Canada.

Eaton executive Tony LaMantia, who was involved in the planning of the Polo Park outlet, describes it as "very successful." The convenient

Most of the staff members in the Polo Park store were experienced Eatonians who came from downtown. Their numbers were supplemented with newly-hired employees, with increasing numbers of them being women who preferred to work part-time. Because of the size of the Polo Park store, it didn't offer the huge range of merchandise and services that were available at 320 Portage Avenue, but it was large enough and attractive enough to attract customers.

150 **A STORE LIKE NO OTHER** · EATON'S OF WINNIPEG

Even though the two-level St. Vital Eaton's store, with a gross area of 138,000 square feet experienced some success, it closed its doors in November 1999. The space was renovated and reopened in September, 2000 as a Sears store.

location of the Polo Park Shopping Centre, the huge (and free) parking lot, and the availability of so many other retailers in the complex made this store more enticing than the downtown location for many shoppers. In 1986, the mall underwent a significant expansion with the addition of a second storey. The luxurious décor of Polo Park only helped to dramatize to shoppers how aging (and almost dingy) the downtown store looked in comparison.

Unfortunately, competition increased, Eaton's fortune across Canada declined, and the Polo Park Eaton's closed on October 17, 1999, just two days before the downtown store.

Eaton's second venture outside of downtown Winnipeg was not a good idea. Located in the relatively small Garden City Shopping Centre in the northwest corner of the city, it joined a Sears store that had opened in

1970. Because it was a single-storey store with a gross area of less than 90,000 square feet (compared to more than 220,000 at Polo Park), the Garden City store had a relatively limited offering of stock and services.

Financially the store was a near-disaster. In the words of Eatonian Debra Jonasson-Young, "Garden City never made a cent – ever. As a matter of fact, from the time it opened until it closed it was losing a million a year." When the company's restructuring plan was implemented, Garden City was among the first to go. It closed on February 28, 1998.

On October 17, 1979, Eaton's joined The Bay, Woolco, Safeway, and 90 other stores for the grand opening of the sprawling St. Vital Centre. By 1998, the mall had grown even larger with the addition of 40 new stores and services, a large Chapter's Book Store, and a ten-screen Famous Players Silver City Cinema.

Although many rural Manitobans visited the Big Store in Winnipeg to shop, Eaton's also provided services in their own communities.

Clockwise from top left: Portage la Prairie heavy goods store (1960), Brandon Catalogue Order Office (1953), Brandon Groceteria and TECO store (1928), Brandon TECO store (1928), Brandon store (1950), Virden Catalogue Order Office (1956),

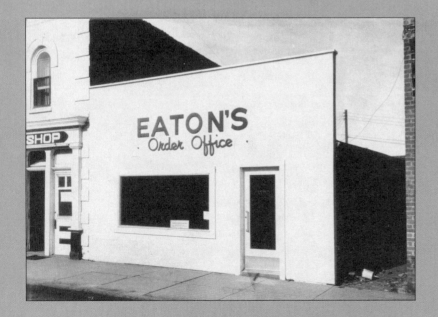

The boots, which were forty or fifty years old, were still in the original box. The customer's wife had died and the boots had sat on a shelf ever since. He was given a refund for the original purchase price.

Dorothy Schell, who worked in the Catalogue exchange department, remembers that large wagons full of returned merchandise would roll in regularly, especially after Christmas. She remembers processing worn-out shoes, wedding veils, and dishes that were returned without even being washed. When asked what she would do when such items were returned she smiles and says "Goods satisfactory or money refunded. They'd get their money back."

Families in some of the city's upscale neighbourhoods had new furniture delivered just in time for a weekend party, and then had the furniture picked up for a refund early the next week. In one instance, a wealthy customer placed a special order for $17,000 worth of living room furnishings. After the furniture was delivered, she decided she didn't like it and returned it for a refund. Because of the price and style of the items, they were placed on the sales floor at half of the original price. The same customer visited the store and tried to re-buy the furniture at the bargain price. In this case, she was refused.

Administering the Eaton Guarantee was sometimes frustrating for salesclerks. They were expected to use their judgement when goods were returned and to deny exchanges or refunds when they believed they weren't justified. Mystery shoppers were used in later years to ensure that clerks turned down unreasonable requests. On the other hand, when customers went to managers or to customer service to appeal refusals, the clerks' decisions were often reversed.

The policy could also be a source of frustration for department managers, who were expected to run profitable operations. Returns cut into their bottom lines. The executive office had a special fund to cover some of these circumstances, and refunds were sometimes charged to that fund instead of a department's budget.

Very often merchandise that was returned was not suitable for resale, even at discounted prices. Sometimes such items were given away, but the company ran the risk of seeing them returned by recipients seeking refunds or exchanges. Although customers were officially expected to produce sales receipts before returns could be authorized, this rule was often not enforced. Sometimes returned merchandise was given, or sold for very low prices, to employees. Sometimes it was simply destroyed.

Eaton's branded lines

IN EARLIER YEARS, the name used on a product was, to some degree, an indication of its pricing and level of quality. TECO was the name assigned to identify merchandise for families with a modest budget. EATONIA was the largest-selling line of merchandise and was attached to good quality merchandise that sold at popular price levels. GLENEATON, on the other hand, identified products that were of

Families in some of the city's upscale neighbourhoods had new furniture delivered just in time for a weekend party, and then had the furniture picked up for a refund early the next week.

The Winnipeg Research Bureau occupied the top floor of Mail Order Building Number Three in the 1940s. It included a temperature and humidity controlled room to test textiles, and a laboratory for chemical testing. Various devices were used to check fabrics for strength and to determine how well they stood up to laundering and dry cleaning.

higher quality and, of course, sold at a higher price. The name EATON was reserved for the best quality merchandise the company sold and was used only for prestigious personal items. Other specialty names were allocated to specific lines of products and often suggested the characteristics of the products that bore them. BULLDOG, for instance, was considered an appropriate name for sporting goods, tires, and car batteries.

It was decided in the early 1950s that brand names would be even more closely identified with specific types of merchandise, and a list of twenty-eight names was announced in 1954. GLENEATON came to be used only for women's accessories. TECO, one of the oldest brand names associated with Eaton's was assigned to hardware, building, farming, and gardening supplies.

VIKING, previously used only for radios, received broader utilization by being applied to household appliances, such as washing machines, stoves, refrigerators, sewing machines, and – the latest introduction – television sets. BERKLEY was adopted for smaller electric appliances.

SOLAR continued to be used for watches and clocks, with a new logo (a stylized sun) added as a distinctive logo. BIRKDALE designated men's clothing, with BIRKDALE JUNIOR applied to boys' wear and BIRKDALE GRAD designating clothing for teenage boys. BELLEFAIR became the name for dresses, suits, and coats for women, misses, and juniors.

In addition, a flurry of new brand names was introduced, some of them invented by Eatonians as a result of a contest. TRULINE was considered an effective name for sporting goods such as golf clubs, fishing equipment, and rifles. OPTIMA was chosen for cameras, binoculars, and other optical products. HADDON HALL, with its implications of classic quality, was assigned to home furnishings.

At the same time these name changes were introduced, a number of packaging innovations came into use. New motifs were designed to showcase the brand names (such as a ship design on Viking appliances to suggest ruggedness). Lettering was bold on heavy goods and men's lines, but more delicate on women's lines.

The name EATON was reserved for the best quality merchandise the company sold and was used only for prestigious personal items.

A wide range of items, including furniture and clothing, was carefully inspected for workmanship and proper sizing.

In 1965, the number of brand names was reduced to sixteen. A uniform, stylized six-sided label was designed and printed in cadet blue with white letters for easy identification. Although each actual brand name continued to appear on the label in a distinctive font, the word "Eaton's" now appeared at the top of each label.

Quality control

THE EATON'S RESEARCH BUREAU in Toronto was established by Sir John Eaton in 1916 and a similar facility later opened in Winnipeg. Few retailers operated testing laboratories, and Eaton's was the oldest and largest in Canada. This department carefully checked products to ensure that Eaton's advertising was properly representing merchandise. It also helped buyers to confirm that suppliers' claims were accurate.

Although many tests were performed using specialized equipment, sometimes the process was based on plain common sense. To check the effective of one type of electric can opener, a Research Bureau employee sat down with a hundred empty sealed cans. He opened each can to see if the tops were removed cleanly and without jagged edges. Dishwashers were tested by using plates covered with dried mixtures of foods and condiments.

The Winnipeg Quality Control Department had the responsibility of ensuring that high standards were maintained in merchandise and deliveries. Inspectors from that department randomly selected parcels from the delivery dispatch conveyor belts. They opened thousands of outgoing packages each week to make sure that customers were receiving exactly what they ordered. This helped to minimize errors in filling orders (as in the case where a customer ordered a douche and was sent a lawn sprinkler) and helped to maintain a high level of customer satisfaction.

Other inspectors carefully scrutinized shipments when they arrived to check for defects. This not only helped to ensure that Eaton's was receiving what it paid its suppliers to provide, it also was an extra precaution to avoid customer dissatisfaction. A wide range of items, including furniture and clothing, was carefully inspected for workmanship and proper sizing.

Sales events

TIMOTHY EATON INTRODUCED the practice of "Friday Bargain Day" in Toronto in 1896 as a way of clearing out unsold merchandise. This event was so popular that other sales events were soon established.

Bargain-savvy Winnipeggers quickly learned that sales at Eaton's were occasions to look forward to. One of the most popular was the Trans-Canada Sale, a semi-annual two-day event that saw merchandise offered at attractive prices on a store-wide basis. This sale offered the same specially-purchased merchandise in all Eaton's stores across Canada and, in most circumstances, at the same bargain prices. During the Trans-Canada Sales, the store was almost as busy as in the Christmas season.

The Service BUILDING

IN 1961, EATON'S OPENED an enormous warehouse building at the corner of Wellington and Berry. Located close to the city's airport, the sprawling building covered eight acres of space when it was completed.

This new facility was designed to consolidate services that were inefficiently scattered through the downtown area in various locations. The Alexander Warehouse, constructed in the mid-1990s, was no longer adequate for the storage and shipment of heavy goods. At different times, overflow from that aging building had to be accommodated in a warehouse on George Street and in another at Princess and Alexander. The new Service Building (which sometimes was called the Heavy Goods Building or the Logistics Building) became the central storage area for furniture, large kitchen appliances, and other merchandise that required considerable space. As well, the

warehouse was the home of Eaton's fleet of trucks and the loading and departure point for deliveries. Alan Finnbogason, who was involved in planning the Service Building, estimates that the savings achieved by centralizing the warehouse and delivery services paid for the building in five years.

In 1967, the Service Building was doubled in size to almost 650,000 square feet, the equivalent of more than nine football fields. By 1990, the building had 37 overhead doors and used 34 million feet of natural gas and nearly 4 million kilowatt hours of electricity annually. In addition to acting as a storage and distribution centre for heavy goods (with as many as ten boxcars being unloaded each day), the centre housed the drapery and picture-framing workrooms and the fur storage facility. A large Mail Order Salesroom was located on the Wellington Avenue side.

EATON'S
Goods Satisfactory or Money Refunded

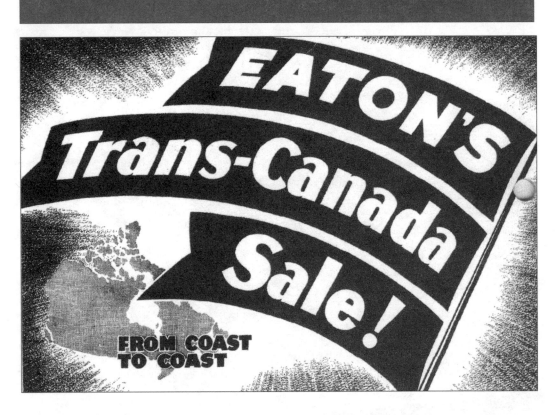

to purchase merchandise directly from manufacturers, rather than dealing with wholesalers. This enabled him to obtain goods at lower prices and to stock unique items that customers could not find in other stores. Timothy himself made the first buying trip outside of Canada by sailing to England in 1870. Although he himself went on several more buying expeditions, he also sent many of his employees abroad to make purchases. Even though women were not appointed to store management positions during that era, Timothy believed that female buyers were able to recognize emerging trends, and he assigned a large number of women to buying positions.

By 1919, Eaton's had established buying offices in London, Leicester, Manchester, Belfast, Paris, Zurich, Yokohama, Kobe, and New York. In later years, additional offices were opened in other European, Asian, and North American cities. The T. Eaton Company quickly established a positive reputation among suppliers in other countries, who were impressed by the ethical way in which the company conducted business and by its policy of making payments promptly. They also respected the company's demand for consistent quality.

Although the actual orders were placed by buyers from Canada, each office had a locally-based staff that was responsible for locating merchandise that might be of interest to Canadian consumers and for cultivating relationships with manufacturers. Local personnel also acted as interpreters and made sure that buyers from Canada were sensitive to local customs and values.

Birthday Sales were also well attended, not only for the bargains they offered, but also because of the special birthday ribbons that were given out. For many Winnipeggers, going to the store to add a ribbon to their collections was an annual event.

Eaton's buying offices

SHORTLY AFTER OPENING the Toronto store, Timothy Eaton realized that it was advantageous to his business

Most buying trips were long and arduous, especially during the days of steamship travel, and many buyers were away from home for two or three months at a stretch, Buyers were expected to conform to numerous company rules. Some of these had their basis in the personal convictions of Timothy Eaton. Trips could not begin on Sundays, nor could business be transacted on Sundays. Others were based on practical considerations – no goods should be purchased after daylight because colours could not be seen as well. Timothy's personal instructions mandated that buyers not allow others to pay for their meals and not visit the homes of suppliers.

Manufacturing facilities

THE T. EATON COMPANY set up its first manufacturing facility in 1890 with eight sewing machines turning out men's shirts and women's underwear. By 1919, Eaton factories in Toronto employed more than 6,400 workers and occupied 19 acres. Additional factories operated in Hamilton and Montreal. The goods produced included virtually every kind of ready-to-wear clothing, as well as school text books, upholstered furniture, and even ice cream.

The ability to manufacture many of the items sold in the stores and through the Mail Order gave definite advantages to Eaton's. In addition to lower costs and better quality control, it enabled Eaton's to offer exclusive lines of merchandise not available to competitors.

Although the company had extensive manufacturing capabilities in Ontario, there were several factories in Winnipeg.

Department 1206 was the drug factory. By the 1930s, more than six hundred products were being manufactured in Winnipeg. This facility turned out millions of ASA tablets, and Eaton's offered their own fruit saline, cod liver oil, and other elixirs designed to preserve or restore good health. One of the most popular tonics was Eaton's Beef, Iron and Wine, which some Eatonians humourously described as being ninety percent cheap sherry, with a rusty nail and an Oxo cube thrown in to provide some colour. Perhaps this explains why there were so many repeat orders. In addition to household remedies, the factory produced perfumes, cold creams, bath salts and talcums on a very large scale.

Eaton's creamery was located for many years in the Alexander Avenue Warehouse. This operation provided all the dairy products for the Big Store, including Sunglo butter and the buttermilk sold in store restaurants for three cents a glass.

The 11,660-square-foot drapery workroom, located on the third floor of Mail Order Building Number One in the late 1940s, was considered the largest and most up-to-date facility of its kind in western Canada.

Coffee-roasting and blending on the ninth floor of the Catalogue building wafted the aroma of Eaton's own Mayfair coffee across Graham Avenue to tantalize customers. The coffee was sold on the third floor of the store, where customers could look on as the whole beans were ground for them. ■

The ability to manufacture many of the items sold in the stores and through the Mail Order gave definite advantages to Eaton's.

One reason many Eatonians felt a personal acquaintance with the Eaton family was the family Christmas card that each employee received annually. Many Eatonians carefully saved these cards and, as one commented, "watched the kids grow up from one year to the next." Some local Eatonians were annoyed when the 1997 card departed from tradition and included newly-appointed CEO George Kosich (seated front right) in the annual family portrait. They only wanted pictures of Eatons.

PLACE TO WORK

The rewards of loyalty

THE CLOSE RELATIONSHIP of the T. Eaton Company and its Winnipeg employees was built on a foundation of mutual loyalty. By providing an array of programs and benefits that supplemented the modest wages, the company earned the life-long dedication of generations of workers. The very name "Eatonian" that employees adopted suggests that they saw themselves as members of an exclusive group. Eatonians, by and large, believed that they had an employer that genuinely cared about them as individuals and was concerned about their welfare in virtually all aspects of their lives. They repaid this concern with a tenacious loyalty that was envied by other employers. Looking back on their experiences, many of them simply say "you'd never find a better place to work."

Two expressions that are commonly used by Eatonians illustrate the kinship they felt to the company. "Once an Eatonian, always an Eatonian" suggests the permanence of the loyalty they felt. "They have diamond 'E's' imprinted on their foreheads" is a more graphic way of expressing Eatonians' devotion to the company.

Something for everyone

EATON'S RECOGNIZED THAT, in order for employees to bond with each other and feel they were an important part of the organization, they needed opportunities to interact outside the work setting. An amazing selection of social and recreational programs was provided that strengthened the relationship between the company and its workers and saw the development of life-long friendships.

Not long after the Big Store opened, John Eaton rented sixteen acres of land along Portage Avenue in an undeveloped area between Winnipeg and St. James. Situated just outside the Winnipeg city limits, this grassy area, bordered by a few trees, would eventually become the location of the Polo Park Shopping Centre. For many years the "Eaton Athletic and Recreation Association Grounds" were the site of baseball, basketball, cricket, tennis, quoits, and football facilities that were used by thousands of

Eaton's recognized that, in order for employees to bond with each other and feel they were an important part of the organization, they needed opportunities to interact outside the work setting.

Chapter

10

EATONIANS
LOOK BACK

"**T**HEY TREATED YOU WELL. Maybe you didn't get as much money as somebody across the street got, but it was offset by the fact that you were content in what you were doing." (*Len Rogers – carpenter, supervisor – 39 years*)

"IT WAS A GREAT PLACE TO WORK. There were a lot of great people there. It was a large enough organization that you could pretty much have careers within your career at Eaton's." (*Tom Lenton – salesperson, manager, buyer, supervisor – 34 years*)

"I HAD TWENTY-SEVEN WONDERFUL YEARS. It gave me a start that I don't think I could have had with many other companies. I had a wonderful opportunity to learn and grow with the company." (*Debra Jonasson-Young - salesperson, manager – 27 years*)

"IT WAS LIKE A BIG HAPPY FAMILY. I don't think any other store could be like that." (*Gloria Sokalski – saleswoman – 37 years*)

"YOU DIDN'T MAKE MUCH MONEY BUT you made friends, and they're true friends to this very day." (*Joyce Howe – parcel girl, saleswoman – 38 years*)

"...IT WAS A WONDERFUL PLACE TO WORK. It was the people. I wasn't making much money then but I loved my job." (*Joan Sneesby – credit office receptionist – 23 years*)

"PEOPLE I CURLED WITH fifty or sixty years ago are still friends of mine." (*Ken Gibson – stock keeper, receiver, personnel manager – 43 years*)

"I HAVE A LOT OF VERY, VERY FOND MEMORIES about Winnipeg, the downtown, Polo Park. I enjoyed it and met a lot of awfully nice people." (*John Craig Eaton – great grandson of Timothy Eaton*)

Eatonians. In addition to competitions among Winnipeg Eatonians, Sir John set up house leagues in several sports that saw teams from Winnipeg and Toronto compete.

By the 1930s, Eaton's offered a dizzying array of sports activities that included rifle shooting, roller skating, table tennis, archery, and even tug-of-war as well as the more traditional activities such as hockey, baseball, and ice-skating.

Most of the activities, including hockey, were open to both men and women, and most teams saw top executives and managers playing side-by-side with stock clerks and salespeople. Eatonians were able to participate in these at little or no cost to themselves, in part because of a generous legacy left by A.A. Gilroy.

Each summer, picnics were held for employees and their families. Some were for specific departments, but on occasion huge store-wide picnics took place. Kim Tronrud remembers the picnics held at La Barriere Park during the 1980s when "they'd bring semi loads of ice cream and hot dogs. Every manager was cooking. Everybody got baseball hats, t-shirts, and as much food and drinks as you wanted. And whatever wasn't eaten, you got to take home."

For those who preferred to spend their leisure time in quieter pursuits, the choices included stamp collecting, bridge, a wartime Red Cross knitting club, and a camera club. Eatonians interested in outdoor activities could join the Eaton Employees' Garden Club. Dog lovers were able to become involved with the Eaton Dog Club and its annual show. A large lending library had more than 7,000 books and was staffed by a

librarian and two assistants. Although the 1937 collection offered many books on self-improvement and career advancement (there were twenty copies of Dale Carnegie's *How to Win Friends and Influence People*), there were numerous titles for leisure reading, including forty copies of *Gone with the Wind*. Hundreds of books were removed from circulation each year and sold for a nominal price in the book department.

Recognizing that many employees had individual hobbies, the Assistants' Association (an organization of assistant managers) sponsored annual Employees Hobby Shows in the spacious seventh-floor Assembly Hall. In 1951, 487 active and retired Eatonians entered 837 exhibits in various categories, including photography, art, and handicrafts. After World War II it became more acceptable for men to become involved in therapeutic activities for injuries to fingers and

hands, so male Eatonians were well represented in crafts like petit-point and cross-stitching.

There were plenty of opportunities for dancing, including a square dance club. Thousands of Eatonians attended annual dances sponsored by the Assistants' Association. The 1947 Spring Dance at the Winnipeg Civic Auditorium was attended by 4,400 employees and their friends. The admission price was fifty cents and music was provided by Eatonian Gar Gillies' Dance Band. The 1951 Valentine's Dance saw more than 2,000 people fill three ballrooms of the stately Royal Alexandra Hotel. Three orchestras, led by Irvin Plumm, Harold Green, and Jimmy Gowler, provided the music. Surplus funds from these dances were used for charitable purposes.

Eaton's drama groups had a high profile in the community. The Winnipeg Masquers, founded in 1932, was acclaimed at the Dominion

Eaton's Bowling LEAGUE

BOWLING BEGAN AS A TEAM activity for Eatonians in 1925 as a ladies league, and the men joined in 1929. By 1958 Eaton's boasted the largest single-company mixed league in western Canada, with more than sixty teams using nearby alleys at the Bowladrome and Wassons. Seasons culminated with huge (and sometimes rambunctious) windups that were often held at the Royal Alexandra Hotel. Some Eaton's teams also participated in business leagues that included other retailers. Dave Hodgson, a 41-year Eatonian, remembers that one year he was pressed into service to become a member of a Hudson's Bay team because Eaton's had more bowlers than they could accommodate and their rival couldn't find enough.

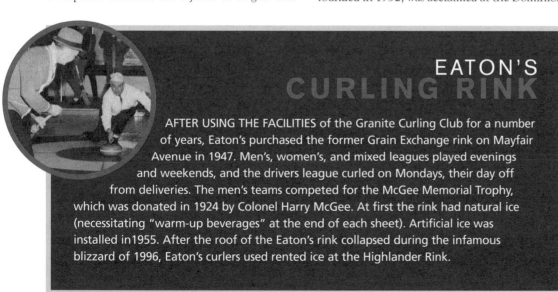

EATON'S CURLING RINK

AFTER USING THE FACILITIES of the Granite Curling Club for a number of years, Eaton's purchased the former Grain Exchange rink on Mayfair Avenue in 1947. Men's, women's, and mixed leagues played evenings and weekends, and the drivers league curled on Mondays, their day off from deliveries. The men's teams competed for the McGee Memorial Trophy, which was donated in 1924 by Colonel Harry McGee. At first the rink had natural ice (necessitating "warm-up beverages" at the end of each sheet). Artificial ice was installed in1955. After the roof of the Eaton's rink collapsed during the infamous blizzard of 1996, Eaton's curlers used rented ice at the Highlander Rink.

THE EATON
ANGLING
CLUB

I N ONE OF THE FEW ACTIVITIES that were restricted on the basis of gender, the Eaton Angling Club arranged weekend getaways in an atmosphere where "men are men and fish are fish and women there are not." In 1934, the club acquired a fishing lodge near Lac du Bonnet that offered a real 'he-man' holiday. It accommodated fifteen men and included four boats, dishes and cutlery, wood and ice, and cots and mattresses. Memberships were available for a small fee, regular bus service from Winnipeg was available, and the men had only to bring their own blankets and food (milk and eggs could be purchased at a neighbouring farm). In later years, the club offered charter bus excursions to fishing spots throughout the province.

Drama Festival. The Dramatic Club made its debut in April 1953 with a production of Heaven Can Wait at the Playhouse Theatre, directed by radio personality Bill Walker. In 1954 the ambitious Eaton Theatre Guild presented A Marriage Proposal and The Dear Departed, with You Can't Take It with You as their major production.

Some Eatonians chose to become involved in helping worthy causes in the community. Many contributed generously to the Eaton's Employees' Charitable Fund, which made donations to a host of local charities, including the Community Chest (the forerunner of the United Way), the Manitoba Divisions of the Canadian Red Cross and the Canadian Cancer Society, the Manitoba Heart Foundation, the March of Dimes, and the Salvation Army. In 1966, the EECF made the largest single donation to the United Way – $175,000, with $90,000 from the EECF and company executives, and $85,000 from the company. The EECF also sent packages of candy and "smoking cheer" to hospitalized veterans. At Christmas time, Eatonians made up and delivered hampers to needy pensioners.

Contacts

I N 1932, EATON'S BEGAN publishing a monthly newsmagazine "for distribution to the Co-workers of the Organization." Like its counterparts in other Canadian cities, Contacts provided information about the company and its employees.

Besides publicizing the achievements of employees, Contacts often recognized the accomplishments of their family members as well. In 1960, 14-year-old pianist Burton Cummings, son of Rhoda Cummings who worked in the wages office, won a trophy in a television competition for amateur entertainers on television station CJAY. The editor wondered "Have we a great Jazz pianist or band leader in the making here?"

Contacts was utilized to inform employees of new merchandise and upcoming sales campaigns, as well as changes in company policies. Consistent with Eaton's emphasis on service to its customers, there were frequent articles on customer relations. One condemned "gum chewing in the faces of our shopping public," calling it "a violation of good manners and the rights of others."

The magazine reported extensively on the numerous social and sporting activities, with write-ups and photographs. Features on Eatonians who achieved milestones of service, retirements, promotions, and transfers were in almost every issue. Some articles kept track of the activities and travels of retired Eatonians. The deaths of active and retired Eatonians and their family members were faithfully reported.

A regular feature titled "And So They Were Married" told of the marriages of Eatonians, often followed by birth announcements. Articles on the achievements of Eatonians and their family members in the community demonstrated the company's recognition that its employees distinguished themselves outside of their work responsibilities. Regular columns from each department in the store and Catalogue helped ensure that Eatonians knew about others, even if they didn't actually work together.

Originally intended as chatty monthly updates that employees would read and probably discard, remaining issues of *Contacts* have become important sources of historical information. Long-time editor W. E. C. (Bill) Hurlburt, who oversaw publication from 1933 until 1952, and his successor Bill Gray may not have foreseen how valuable their publications would become for future researchers.

The employee discount

ONE OF THE MOST appreciated and most utilized benefits enjoyed by Eaton's employees was the discount they received on purchases. For regular staff, the employee discount was ten percent, but a pre-Christmas discount of twenty percent ensured that many employees did all of their gift shopping at Eaton's. For managers, an impressive twenty-five percent discount was a bonus added to often-substantial salaries. Even after retirement, Eatonians continued to be eligible for the employee discount.

As well, employees who were making purchases for themselves or their families were often given special prices even before the discount was applied. Watchmaker Ron Collins, a duck hunter, recalls being able to buy shotgun shells for fifty cents a box. Gary Filmon, who worked as a salesperson in men's clothing while attending university, tells how he often went home with no money in his pocket on payday. His colleagues would point out particularly stylish articles of clothing and offer him such attractive prices that he couldn't resist. He laughs, "I was one of the best-dressed guys at university despite the fact I didn't have any money to speak of."

PARCEL GIRLS AND TRUCK BOYS

MANY FEMALE EATONIANS began their careers as parcel girls. Betty Ashton, who would eventually have a career of 48 years with the company, left school at the age of 17. Like most young people of her era who wanted to find work, she applied for a job at Eaton's. Unfortunately, she found herself in the dilemma of being considered too old to be a parcel girl and too young to be a clerk, so she took her brother's advice and said she was only 16. Her role as a parcel girl was to take merchandise that customers had purchased from sales clerks, wrap it in brown paper, and tie it with string. If a package was to be delivered, she would paste an address label on it and put it into a wheeled wooden "truck". The job of a truck boy (which was an entry-level position for many young males) was to wheel those loads of parcels from the various departments, down the elevators, and through the underground tunnel to the Catalogue, where it would be sorted for delivery. Many truck boys found that the mobility of the job provided countless opportunities to flirt with parcel girls.

Keep this under your hat

LONG AFTER MOST OTHER employers began the practice of issuing payroll cheques, Eaton's employees continued to receive small brown envelopes containing cash on Friday mornings. It wasn't until 1970 that cheques were used, and eventually a direct deposit option was available.

In keeping with the high level of autonomy that was granted to departments, managers were authorized to decide when increases in pay (Timothy preferred the term "rate adjustments") were to be granted. In the absence of any union involvement, a manager's assessment of employee performance was more of a factor than seniority in determining levels of compensation. Notification of a raise in pay was done quietly, as a manager took a fortunate employee aside and gave the good news with the caution "It's a secret. Don't tell anyone," or "Keep this under your hat." The spirit of this practice was understood by employees, and Eatonians report that the code was generally honoured. Even though people in the same departments often became close friends and spent time together socially, they rarely compared their rates of pay.

One persistent criticism of Eaton's was that the company underpaid its employees. At the very least, it can be said that, with the exception of some managers who received relatively high salaries, Eaton's was nowhere near the top of the scale in comparison to other employers. Personal factors were often taken into account in determining the pay rate for a particular employee. In an era where questions about a person's marital status, dependents, and living arrangements were allowed, these factors as much as the job description and performance level were

Even though people in the same departments often became close friends and spent time together socially, they rarely compared their rates of pay.

"I WORK AT EATON'S"

IN THE 1930S, Eaton's staff across Canada totaled more than 36,000 people. In Winnipeg alone in the 1950's, the number of full-time and part-time employees in the store and Mail Order was approximately 27,000. Estimates of the number of people employed by Eaton's across Canada during the 1960s range from 60,000 to 70,000, positioning the company in competition with the Canadian Pacific Railway for the distinction of being Canada's largest private employer. By the time Eaton's closed in 1999, only 13,000 people worked for the company.

PERSONNEL PRACTICES SELECTIVE

often the main determinant of wages. Of course, in the early era, men were paid more than women in similar jobs.

Personnel manager Ken Gibson explains that Eaton's pay rates in the 1950s and 1960s were based to a large extent on comparisons with those of the City of Winnipeg. Based on the premise that Eaton's employees received approximately one-third of their compensation through such benefits as holidays, sick leave, company pension contributions, and the employee discount, their actual wages were then pegged at the seventy-five percent of City wages. Other benefits, such as the extensive social and recreational programs, were also considered to be part of the compensation package.

Holiday time

THE AMOUNT OF PAID HOLIDAY time that Eaton's employees received was adjusted gradually over the years to keep pace with other employers. In general, holiday entitlement was two weeks after one year, and then increased to three weeks after five years, five weeks after fifteen years, and six weeks after twenty years. In the 1990s, regular employees with more than twenty-five years were entitled to eight weeks of holidays, but managers actually received less holiday time as a result of cutbacks. A one-time bonus for all employees was an additional six weeks of holidays in the twenty-fifth anniversary year. One unique touch was that in 1969, the company's hundredth anniversary year, employees were given an extra day off on their birthdays.

ONE OF THE MOST PERSISTENT criticisms of the T. Eaton Company was that it practiced discrimination in its hiring and promotional procedures. From its very beginning, Eaton's was a proudly family-owned company. There was adamant resistance, not only from Timothy but also from some of his descendants, to any efforts to restrict or even influence their ability to hire, promote, or fire at will. Preferential treatment on the basis of ethnic origin, religious affiliation, and gender was clearly practiced by Eaton's (and many other employers) for a number of years and this appears particularly unfair when judged by the standards of later decades.

There are numerous anecdotes that demonstrate Timothy Eaton's preference for hiring employees of Irish descent, with other Anglo-Saxons enjoying some special consideration as well. Listings of employees who achieved managerial or executive positions with the company, even past the middle of the twentieth century, show the dominance of British names. Even ordinary employees were predominantly from that background for several decades, with names of other origins clearly in the minority. Later, when the company itself was utilizing relatively liberal hiring practices, resistance to change among some employee continued to be a problem. Lillian Vadeboncoeur recalls that when she was first hired in the mid 1940s, the fact that she was a woman with a university education and a French-Canadian name made it difficult for her to be accepted by her numerous less-educated male colleagues with Irish names.

In Manitoba, a massive influx of immigrants from eastern European countries in the late nineteenth and early twentieth century dramatically changed the profile of the population. In addition to being some of Eaton's most loyal customers, many new arrivals went to Eaton's in search of employment. While they were pleased to obtain entry-level jobs, many believed (with some justification) that their opportunities to move up in the company ranks were limited. Some Eaton's employees with Slavic names even went to the extent of anglicizing their names to enhance their chances of career advancement.

Religious background also entered into the picture, with Protestants (rather than Catholics) being employed by Eaton's in numbers that were significantly out of proportion with their representation in the community. An especially sensitive area in examining Eaton's staffing practices is the relatively small number of Jewish employees until well into the 20th century.

Women occupied a large number of positions with Eaton's (particularly in sales and clerical positions), but it was only later in the life of the company that they found their way into managerial and executive positions. In Winnipeg, the careers of Lillian Vadeboncoeur, Susan Thompson, and Debra Jonasson-Young illustrate that it did eventually become possible for women to be appointed to positions of significant responsibility within Eaton's.

Paternalism and
UNIONIZATION

ANOTHER TRADITIONAL CRITICISM of Eaton's is that its approach towards its employees was paternalistic. Indications of that attitude can be traced back to Timothy, Margaret, and Sir John, who tended to regard employees as members of their own extended family and were in the habit of referring to them as their "boys and girls." Timothy once wrote a personal cheque for $3,000 to obtain cash to be given to employees in need, and would often hand over money from his own pocket to employees having problems. The availability of social and recreational programs (including inexpensive summer camps for employees), numerous examples of helping employees and their families when problems came up, and free medical and dental care are used as the basis for portraying the company as putting itself in the position of a parent to a large group of dependent workers.

Resentment of this perceived paternalism, concerns over low wages, and objections to the company's personnel practices were some of the reasons for attempts to unionize Eaton's employees. As well, many activists in the union movement labeled Eaton's as an anti-union company and believed that the winning a battle against the family-controlled empire would be a huge victory.

A major campaign began in Toronto in 1948, with the Retail Wholesale and Department Store Union (financially backed by the Steelworkers of America) launching an aggressive effort to certify approximately 10,000 Eaton's employees. It proved to be a lengthy and expensive fight, with some employees strongly in favour of unionization and others (who called themselves "The Loyal Eatonians") reaffirming their allegiance to the company, the Eaton family, and all of the benefits they and their colleagues received. When a vote was finally taken in December, 1951, the union was rejected. A second campaign in the mid-1980s saw the employees of six Ontario stores voting in favour of union certification, and a bitter strike at all of these stores followed. Eventually many of the striking workers crossed the picket lines to return to their jobs.

In Manitoba as well, efforts were made to organize Eaton's employees, and the Brandon store workers went as far as voting in favour of certification. The company vowed it would close that store if the workers gave approval to being represented by a union, and actually began to move merchandise to the main floor in preparation for the closure. The employees then voted to defeat the union.

The often-heated debates among Eatonians in favour of and opposed to union representation took their toll. One Winnipeg Eatonian describes the issue as a wedge that split the "one big family".

Shorter hours of business

ALTHOUGH TIMOTHY EATON devoted most of his time and effort to his business, his family, and his church activities, he did become active in the semi-political Early Closing Movement. This was an effort to deal with the fact that it was common practice for retail businesses to be open from early morning until nine or ten o'clock at night from Monday to Friday, and often until eleven or midnight on Saturdays. It was only on Sundays that stores closed and employees had a day away from work. Members of the movement believed that reduced hours of work would be beneficial to the general health of employees, and would enable them to take educational and training programs to improve their lot in life.

Timothy's concerns over this matter were probably based in part on his own experiences as a thirteen-year-old apprentice to a dry goods merchant in Ireland, where he was required to work six fourteen-hour days each week. His strong religious convictions prodded him to action when he was told that some employees were often too fatigued to attend church on Sundays. As well, Timothy was convinced that there would be no reduction in the amount of business transacted if business hours were shortened. Sir John said in 1919 that his father once expressed the hope that within John's lifetime the day would come when their stores would be closed all day on Saturdays. Timothy predicted that the week's work would be done between Monday morning and Friday evening, leaving Saturday for leisure activities, and Sunday for rest and worship.

Not long after opening his Toronto store, Timothy began to curtail the hours. Earlier closing times were gradually implemented. By 1910, Eaton's employees in Winnipeg and Toronto were working only 43 to 48 hours per week, a significant improvement over the more than 70 hours that employees worked each week when the Toronto store opened in 1869. These changes were achieved with no reductions in employees' pay.

In 1886, Timothy began a campaign to gain public support for earlier closing on Saturdays. Newspaper advertisements appealed to customers to schedule their shopping at other times. The advertisements included ballots for customers to vote for either a 6:00 p.m. closing time or an almost-revolutionary 2:00 p.m. closing. A major theme in the campaign was that earlier closing would be beneficial to the store employees, most of whom were women, and customers were urged to "liberate your fellow-beings." The result of the balloting was that 1,500 were in favour of the 2:00 p.m. closing, and 1,900 preferred that the store stay open until 6:00. As a demonstration of his concern for his employees, Timothy chose to override the apparent public preference and announced that the store would close at 2:00 p.m. on Saturdays during July and August. By 1890, that became 1:00 pm.

As part of the company's Golden Jubilee celebration in 1919, Sir John Eaton announced that the Saturday closing time of 1:00 p.m. would be in effect all year except in July and August, when the store would remain closed all day Saturday. The five-day work week, at least for two months each year, became a reality.

On December 11, 1919, Sir John attended the presentation of the statue of his father in Winnipeg, and an announcement was made that was applauded by the throng of employees who had gathered together for the ceremony. Store manager H. M. Tucker told them that, effective the following month, the store's regular weekday closing time of 5:30 p.m. would become 5:00 p.m..

In later years, as the trend to having stores open evenings became increasingly prevalent, Eaton's continued to resist. In 1956, president John David Eaton reluctantly authorized Eaton's stores to remain open evenings "at least during the month of December," with specific arrangements to be determined by each division of the company. In his message to employees, he reminded them that the company was traditionally opposed to night openings and that Timothy Eaton was a "pioneer in shortening the work day."

Training and promotions

ONE FACTOR THAT contributed to many Eatonians' having careers that spanned their entire working lives was the company's record of providing opportunities for training and promotion.

In the early decades, most training was strictly on-the-job. In a kind of informal mentoring program, new employees were taken under the wings of managers or other experienced workers to learn about the Eaton's way of doing business. Because these employees were typically veterans within their departments and were knowledgeable in all aspects of their work, they had a great deal to offer. Now ninety years old, Evelyn Murray, who began at age seventeen in shoe sales, still respectfully remembers her first manager, Mr. Morris. "He taught me everything he knew about shoes, starting with the animals that produced the leather."

Many of the top managers of Eaton's began their careers with the company in lowly positions, and worked their way up through the ranks. Susan Thompson, who went on to become the mayor of Winnipeg, began as a part-time

As part of the company's Golden Jubilee celebration in 1919, Sir John Eaton announced that the Saturday closing time of 1:00 p.m. would be in effect all year except in July and August, when the store would remain closed all day Saturday.

It was not unusual for people born in the first half of the twentieth century to obtain employment in their teens, and to remain with the same employer until they retired at the age of sixty or sixty-five.

salesperson in the dress shirt department while attending university, and moved on to become a buyer and manager. Steve Kiz began by driving a horse-drawn delivery wagon and became the western region transportation manager. Herbert Mason Tucker's journey to a company vice-presidency began at the age of fourteen as a parcel boy in the shipping room of the Toronto store.

Many Eatonians with no special training were able to upgrade their skills while employed on a full-time basis. A typical illustration of this is the career path of Gordon Bailey. His father worked in the Hargrave Street company garage, and Gordon's explanation of how, after leaving school, he came to be hired by Eaton's is straightforward and far from unusual. "Dad got me the job. It was always the way." Gordon's first assignment was carrying the tools of a refrigeration technician. After some basic on-the-job experience, Gordon attended a number of week-long refrigeration training courses while receiving his regular pay, and became a qualified refrigeration technician. The fees for the courses were paid by the company. Looking back on his 44-year career, Gordon recalls "If you wanted to learn something, as long as you attended and applied yourself, they paid for it. You just took in your receipt and proof you passed." Both Jim Thomson and Ron Collins completed their apprenticeships in the store's watch repair department, and as journeymen watchmakers, each went on to manage that department.

In the later years, more formalized training programs were implemented. Management training programs instituted in the early 1960s

supplemented the previous practice of moving management trainees among various departments to increase their skills, and in the 1990s the company partnered with Ryerson Polytechnic University to create the Eaton School of Retailing.

Susan Thompson describes Eaton's training as "the best you could ever hope for. To this day, paying attention to detail is one of the things that Eaton's taught me that have been so important in my life."

The Eaton Retirement Annuity Plan

IN 1948, COMPANY PRESIDENT John David Eaton announced the creation of a contributory pension plan and put in $50 million of company money to get it started. Employees contributed 5% of their income and the company matched that amount. After twenty-five years of service, pensions were to be paid to female employees at age sixty and to male employees at age sixty-five.

Although there were some improvements over the years, the provisions of the plan in general proved to be far from generous. Because the wages of many employees (especially women) were relatively low, retired Eatonians often found that they had to rely on their savings and government pension plans to maintain their desired standard of living. One silver lining in the cloud of financial difficulties that Eaton's encountered in the late 1990s was that half of a substantial surplus accumulated by the pension

fund was given directly to retirees in lump-sum payments. This unexpected bonus made a big difference to the retirement lifestyles of many Eatonians.

Long service

IT WAS NOT UNUSUAL for people born in the first half of the twentieth century to obtain employment in their teens, and to remain with the same employer until they retired at the age of sixty or sixty-five. The result is that Eatonians with forty or even fifty years of service were not rarities. One factor contributing to this fact is that jobs were not always easy to find. As many Eatonians put it, "you were lucky to have a job, any job." A more important factor, however, is that the ethics of the times valued stability, and moving from one job to another was seen as a sign of irresponsibility.

One of the biggest milestones in the career of an Eatonian was becoming a member of the Quarter Century Club. This distinctive practice began in the company's Golden Jubilee Year when approximately sixty Eatonians with at least twenty-five years of service with the company received numbered certificates admitting them to the Timothy Eaton Quarter Century Club. Certificate Number One was awarded to Sir John Eaton.

In addition to the certificates, members were presented with special gifts from the company, the best-known of which was the Quarter Century watch. Originally these were gold pocket watches for men and wristwatches for women, with the words 1/4 CENTURY CLUB replacing the usual numerals around the dial. What made these watches even more distinctive is that for many years they were manufactured by Rolex, and in place of that manufacturer's prestigious name, the word "Eaton" appeared on the dial. These watches are among the most sought-after of Eaton's collectibles. Most of them have become family heirlooms, so these watches are not often found for sale. When they are put on the market, they generally command very high prices – for example, a Rolex men's wristwatch presented in 1958 sold on Ebay in May 2004 for $2500. In the early 1970s, Rolex was replaced by the less-expensive, but still very collectible, Bulova Accutron.

Over the decades, Eatonians offered an increasingly wider range of choices of Quarter Century Gifts. Both men and women were able to select from engraved watches or diamond

A LEGACY OF
FRIENDSHIP

WHEN WATCH REPAIR MANAGER Jim Thomson retired in 1988, he and another retired Eatonian, Reg Hart, wondered if their fellow retirees would be interested in forming a club that would enable them to get together periodically. This led to the creation of an organizing committee and the development of a constitution.

Jim recalls that they decided to book the Assembly Hall for a first meeting of the retirement club in May 1989 to see how much interest there might be. There were approximately sixteen hundred retirees at the time, and invitation letters were sent to those who might be able to attend. Jim and Reg had a bet, with Jim predicting that they would be lucky to have a hundred people in attendance. As more and more Eatonians flowed in, the volume level of their excited chatting increased and additional chairs needed to be found. Eventually there were more than three hundred retired Eatonians in the room and there was standing room only. Reg clearly won the bet and the Eaton's Retirement Club had begun.

Since the formation of the club, paid memberships have remained in the vicinity of five hundred people (the majority are women) each year. Faced with the reality that several members pass away each year and that others are no longer sufficiently mobile to attend meetings, the membership requirements have been gradually relaxed. When the club began, membership was open to retired Eatonians with a minimum of ten years of service. This was later reduced to five years, and now no minimum length of service is required. The club is currently open to all former Eaton's employees, whether they worked full or part time, as well as to the spouses of members and the spouses of deceased employees. The membership fee is a modest twelve dollars a year.

Members receive a bi-monthly newsletter containing information about the club's social and recreational activities, membership reports, recipes, pension information, and volunteer opportunities. Articles are often contributed by members recalling "the good old days" at Eaton's (and providing useful information for future historians). Get-well wishes are included for ailing members and, increasingly as time passes, in memoriam items recognize members and other former colleagues who have died.

Monthly coffee parties began with the founding of the club, and still attract an average of more than two hundred members to chat, reminisce, and enjoy sandwiches and other goodies. Although most members have active lifestyles, some make the coffee party their main social event of the month. Occasional gourmet luncheons and an annual dinner supplement the coffee parties. Originally held in the Assembly Hall and then the Grill Room, the meetings relocated to a church after the store closed. Meeting locations moved several times, in an effort to find facilities large enough to accommodate the attendees and reasonably priced enough to be handled by the club's limited budget. They are currently held in a retirement residence.

One particularly significant meeting was on January 23rd, 1996. A "Luncheon to Remember" was held in the Grill Room just days before the venerable restaurant closed its doors. Alan Finboggason was the guest speaker and reminisced about the history of the grand old room.

In the earlier years of the club, group charter trips were organized to the British Isles, Las Vegas, the New England states, and Hawaii, as well as a Caribbean cruise. In recent years, travel activities have been limited to bus excursions within Manitoba and to casinos in Minnesota and North Dakota. The annual "Mystery Trip" (with the destination revealed only at the time of departure) continues to be especially popular.

Carrying on the tradition of the social and recreational activities organized through the T. Eaton Company for its employees, the club continues to offer five-pin bowling, curling, golf, and lawn bowling. Social activities within Winnipeg include riverboat cruises and visits to the Assiniboia Downs race track.

The tradition of community service has also continued. Club members have carried on the tradition (begun after World War Two by the Eaton's Employees Charitable Fund) of visiting the Deer Lodge Centre on

Remembrance Day to serve cookies to veterans. Donations by club members to the Christmas Cheer Board have increased over the years, totaling over $1100 in 2002.

While the downtown store was still open, Eaton's held monthly Seniors' Days sales, and club members volunteered their time to serve coffee and cookies to customers.

The closing of the Winnipeg Eaton's stores and the subsequent controversy over the demolition of the Big Store were especially emotional times for these Eatonians. A local television news team paid an unexpected (and unwelcome) visit in 1999 to a club coffee party in an attempt to capture for the six o'clock news the Eatonians' reactions to the company's failure. Understandably, this was not appreciated by members, and as a result, the location and dates of the coffee parties are not generally publicized.

For many Eatonians, the closing of the T. Eaton Company was similar to the death of an old friend, and the process of grieving included the usual steps of denial, anger, and eventual acceptance. At first, many could not believe that an institution that was an integral part of the Canadian way of life for so long would no longer be there. Some still express anger at the Eaton family and are convinced that decisions made "down east" doomed a thriving Winnipeg business. A handful of retired Eatonians are unwilling to discuss the history of Eaton's in Winnipeg and declined offers to be interviewed for this book, saying "That's all over and done with."

Kim Tronrud began as an elevator operator and went on to a successful career in cosmetics sales with Eaton's. Her grandparents and father were Eatonians before her. She recalls that, as she drove by the demolition site at Portage and Hargrave, she couldn't help bursting into tears. It wasn't her job that she was grieving, it was her memories of Eaton's.

The great majority of Eatonians, however, have accepted the fact that Eaton's is gone and prefer to focus on the positive aspects. As they were interviewed, club members frequently praised the company for providing them with rewarding careers. They are justifiably proud of the service that they and the company they represented provided to countless thousands of Manitobans for almost a century. They recall the many social and recreational activities that were available and the benefits they received as employees. As club president Joan Collins observes, "They'll never lose their memories of Eaton's."

A closely-knit group (Eatonians claim they can recognize each other instantly), these former colleagues remain good friends. Although club meetings are held only once a month, Eatonians keep in touch by phone and through their sports and social activities. If a member is ill, others know about it and make a point of visiting and keeping in touch. Groups of Eatonians who worked together in particular departments have created their own informal retirement clubs and get together regularly for coffee or lunch.

A typical attitude among Winnipeg Eatonians is that the Big Store was "just bricks and mortar." They watched with sadness as the landmark was reduced one storey at a time until it became an empty lot. But they recognize that the most important legacy of the T. Eaton Company is one that cannot be removed by jack hammers and bulldozers, and that is the legacy of friendship.

The Eaton's Retirement Club is the product of an era when the loyalty of employees to a company and of a company to its employees were fundamental components of the work ethic. Men and women became sweethearts, and then husbands and wives, because they met at Eaton's (and they often saw their own children go on to work at Eaton's as well). People who at first were only fellow employees have established decades-long friendships that will continue for the remainder of their lives. Many are unmarried or widowed, and in many ways fellow Eatonians have become like family to them.

The T. Eaton Company is gone, but it has left a legacy of friendship that is as cherished and enduring as the bronze and marble statue of its founder.

rings. For a few years, an engraved silver tray was also an option. Women eventually had a choice of several kinds of diamond rings, or dinner rings with various kinds of gems. Because many of the women receiving the rings were unmarried and were so devoted to the company, their colleagues sometimes jokingly told them that they had become "the brides of Eaton."

The official presentations by members of the Eaton family to Quarter Century Club inductees were made for many years at special breakfasts held in the Grill Room. In addition, colleagues honoured recipients with office or house parties and additional gifts. Two other major landmarks that were celebrated were forty years of service, and retirement, with an Eaton in attendance to express the gratitude of the family and the company.

Staying healthy

WHEN THE BIG STORE opened in 1905, it included a small hospital ward with a cot and two stretchers. By 1946, the store hospital on the seventh floor had expanded to six beds, a first-aid room, and a dental clinic. Its counterpart in the Mail Order had five beds and a first-aid room. These facilities provided services primarily to staff members who had accidents or suffered from minor ailments, but they also provided emergency assistance to customers who had mishaps or sudden illnesses. In 1948, almost 15,000 cases were handled. The hospital was staffed by company nurses and, on a part-time basis, a company doctor.

When employees were sick at home, nurses often drove to their homes to visit them. They provided treatment, delivered medication, and even took care of housekeeping and grocery shopping if needed. An added bonus is that they delivered employees' pay envelopes.

The dental clinic went far beyond treating tooth-aches. The company dentist was able to take x-rays, do fillings, and even perform extractions. These, like the medical services,

When employees were sick at home, nurses often drove to their homes to visit them.

were free of charge. Free eye examinations were also available to employees. Another regular service for employees was provided by a chiropodist, since so many employees spent all day on their feet. Many of these services were scaled back or eliminated by the 1970s.

Quiet favours

ABOVE AND BEYOND THE formal programs for the well-being of employees, there are countless instances where Eaton's made extraordinary gestures. It is these unusual and often small acts of kindness that many Eatonians remember best.

In the late 1920s, a man who worked in the Mail Order went missing while duck hunting in the Netley Marsh. Eaton's recruited all available male employees, transported them to the marsh, outfitted them with warm clothing, and arranged for boats and local guides to conduct a search. The missing man was found within a day or so. This was done at company expense and without publicity.

Betty Ralph, a printing plant employee for more than forty years, tells that when her father, also an Eatonian, passed away, two men came to the family home to offer cars for the funeral service. Although the offer was declined, more than fifty years later she still appreciates the thoughtful gesture.

Betty Ashton, a 48-year Eatonian, tells of the time in the mid-1950s when two managers paid a home visit to an employee who had cancer. While they were there, the man's medication was delivered by a drug store, and the managers were astounded at its high price. When they returned to the store, arrangements were made with the personnel department, and the employee's medication bills were quietly taken care of by the company from then on.

After Eatonians Joan and Ron Collins were married in the 1950s, they hoped to buy a home in St. Boniface, but were short $3,000 for the down payment. As much as they wanted to avoid a second mortgage, they saw no other way to come up with the money. One of their managers heard about their situation and told them the company would lend them the money, which they could repay with a $5.00 deduction from each of their pay envelopes each week. The arrangement was based totally on mutual trust, and no documents were signed. As Ron observes, "that's the type of company they were."

Another Eatonian will never forget the kindness shown by the Eaton brothers. The family owned a hunting lodge near St. Ambroise, Manitoba, and knew that the employee's son, who was chronically ill, loved to hunt. Whenever the Eatons came to Manitoba to use the lodge, they would call the employee and arrange for his son to accompany them.

Friends and family

BECAUSE EATON'S WAS such a major employer in Winnipeg, it was very common to find that several members of the same family worked at Eaton's, and that more than one generation of a family included Eatonians. The huge numbers of people who worked for Eaton's plus the number of social and recreational activities available led to the formation of countless friendships, and many of those friendships became marriages.

One of the earliest illustrations of this is recounted by Ann McGregor, who worked in the Catalogue and the Polo Park store. Her husband's mother, Gertrude Hardy, was one of the original staff members who came from Toronto to open the new Winnipeg store in 1905. Only nineteen years old, Gertie was hesitant to leave her family behind, but decided to take her father's advice and "try it out." Living in a boarding home, and being so far from her family made her very homesick, especially during the first year. The company recognized that these feelings were shared by many of the Originals, and that the first

Christmas in a strange prairie city would be especially difficult, so Eaton's hosted a Christmas party for all of them, complete with a full Yuletide dinner, a decorated tree, and presents for all.

Soon she met another Original, young Howard McGregor, a shoe salesman who became a buyer and manager. He courted Gertrude and, in 1908, they travelled back to Toronto, but only long enough to be married. Like almost all of the other Originals, they chose to live the rest of their lives in Winnipeg. Gertrude left Eaton's a year after they were married to raise their family, but Howard's career with the company lasted forty-five years. They had four sons, and three of them became Eatonians with a combined service of more than 120 years.

David McFetridge was born in Ireland about half a mile from the birthplace of Timothy Eaton. In addition to his own career of forty-four years with Eaton's, his father, two uncles, three cousins, brother, sister, wife, and four sons were all Eatonians.

Personnel manager Ken Gibson lists his father, whose career with Eaton's spanned fifty-one years from 1914-1965, his brother, his sister, his wife, and seven members of his wife's family.

Joan Collins, president of the Eaton's Retirement Club, chronicles her own family's involvement: "My dad worked for Eaton's, and he met my mother at Eaton's. I met my husband Ron at Eaton's when we played baseball. My brother

Bruce Meisner and his nephew Austin Smith chat with Punkinhead. This mascot costume was donated, as one of Eaton's final community service gestures, to the Manitoba Children's Museum at The Forks. After the costume was carefully cleaned and refurbished, Punkinhead was reborn (wearing a railroad engineer's denim cap and kerchief) as Choo-Choo, the Museum's official mascot. His new role was to appear at pre-schoolers' birthday parties and to delight the grandchildren and great-grandchildren of Punkinhead's original admirers.

met his wife at Eaton's when they both worked there. Our son also worked for Eaton's."

The managers

MORE OFTEN THAN NOT, people who occupied managerial positions with Eaton's came up through the ranks, and most never lost the common touch. Many Eatonians speak with respect of the people to whom they reported because the managers worked side-by-side with them and were so approachable.

One of the daily routines for many years was a tour of the store by the top executives, including the general manager, the operating manager, and the display manager. Generally, the tours would begin either in the basement or on the top floor, and the procession would cross each floor as it moved from one bank of escalators to the other. The managers would pause frequently to chat with employees, ask questions, or make suggestions. As one department manager comments, "They would make the rounds of the store every morning and they would notice everything that wasn't the way it was supposed to be." While some employees might have regarded this kind of scrutiny as intimidating, most welcomed the interest shown by the executives. The comment of Eatonian Joyce Howe is typical. "When Mr. Tucker or Mr. Palk walked around the store, you knew who they were and you respected them. They were nice men."

Eaton's encouraged their managers to maintain a high profile in the community as well as on the job, and paid for their memberships at Elmhurst and other country clubs, as well as in the Chamber of Commerce, service clubs, and other community organizations.

Dressing to impress

IN KEEPING WITH THE company's goal of presenting a professional and business-like image to its customers, there were clear expectations about employee's appearance. The first dress code, issued not long after the Big Store opened, required female employees to wear black dresses or black skirts and white shirtwaists. In the 1940s, women were expected to wear black in winter and white in summer. If an employee wore a garment that strayed from these requirements, long-sleeved black smocks were on hand to cover the unacceptable clothing. Men were required to wear navy blue suits and conservative ties, although lighter coloured suits were allowed during summer months. Floorwalkers made it part of their mandate to ensure that the appearance of all employees was up to the company's standards.

"Dress Regulations," issued in 1950, applied to salespeople and any other employees who dealt with the public. Women were required to wear dresses or suits (but with skirts, not slacks) in either solid black, navy, or dark grey. As a small concession, pinstripes were allowed in these materials. An alternative was skirts in black, grey, or navy and white blouses – but not short-sleeved. Hosiery and business-like shoes, black, navy, or tan only, were expected. Sandals, "ballet-type" shoes, and "play shoes and such" were forbidden. Hair styles were to be "simple and tidy at all times."

Male employees were required to wear business suits "conservative in material and colour." Suit coats were not to be removed. All office staff and supplementary help were expected to present a similarly conservative image. Other staff members were advised to wear clothing that was appropriate for the kind of work they did, and drivers and many other support workers wore bluish-grey uniforms and hats issued by the company. In fact, wearing a uniform was mandatory when driving a company truck.

Knowing the Eatons

ALTHOUGH MOST EMPLOYEES only occasionally caught a glimpse of a member of the Eaton family, and most would have had direct contact with an Eaton only on special occasions, many Winnipeg Eatonians felt that they knew the Eatons. Partly as a result of the enduring influence of Lady Eaton, the family took on an almost-regal image, and this was enhanced by the charisma that many of them intuitively possessed. Meeting a charming and well-dressed Eaton had an impact on many employees similar to an audience with a member of the Royal Family.

Best known to many older Winnipeg employees was Gilbert McCrea Eaton. One of the four sons of Sir John and Lady Eaton, Gilbert moved to Winnipeg in 1938, serving as a director. Gilbert frequently represented the family at formal events, and this might explain why one Eatonian comments that she always saw him wearing a pin-striped suit. The nautical life was one of his passions. Gilbert was the owner of a yacht that he proudly navigated on Lake Winnipeg and an active supporter of the Navy League of Canada. He was a familiar sight in the store, and his presence reminded employees of the active interest of the Eaton family in the Winnipeg operation. Gilbert retired in 1963 and subsequently lived in the Caribbean and Florida. He died in 1985.

Various members of the family came to Winnipeg on regular cross-country tours of the stores, particularly during the Christmas season. They shook hands with staff members, chatted with customers, and generally familiarized themselves with the local operation.

For many years, president John David Eaton presided at Grill Room breakfasts to honour Eatonians' achievements, and he was succeeded in this duty by his four sons. Very often, this pleasant task was carried out by John Craig Eaton, who frequently impressed Eatonians with his ability to remember a person after only one meeting, and with his charming and easy-going manner.

Although some Winnipeg Eatonians hold the "Eaton boys" at least partly responsible for the downfall of the company, most continue to regard the family with respect. They value the interest that the family showed in the store, and, more importantly, in the employees as individuals. Although the appearances of the Eatons in Winnipeg were only occasional, they appear to have had a significant impact on Winnipeg Eatonians. The employees appreciated the personal touch. ■

The managers would pause frequently to chat with employees, ask questions, or make suggestions.

The big store closes

In 1968, thousands of teenagers swarmed the Big Store for a "Teen Takeover Night" promotion. Thirty years later, the store was deserted by shoppers of all ages.

FOREVER

"This individual is insolvent"

IT SHOULDN'T HAVE COME as a shock, but it did. Media reports left no doubt that Eaton's was in serious trouble, but many Manitobans, like other Canadians from coast to coast, had held out hopes that the problems would be solved. After all, this was Eaton's, as much a Canadian institution as the Stanley Cup and the maple leaf. But efforts to save the company were unsuccessful, and it was finally announced that the T. Eaton Company was out of business.

The terse message on the signs seemed so blunt and personal. "This individual is insolvent" is what shoppers read as they walked through the familiar Portage entrances. Some glanced at the sign, then quickly looked away, as though they were seeing a friend in a casket. They knew there had been a death, but they weren't ready to accept it.

Warning signs in Winnipeg

ALTHOUGH MANY OF THE FACTORS that led to the closing of Eaton's had their roots outside of Manitoba, there were a number of signals to Winnipeggers that the once-mighty empire was in trouble.

One early warning sign was the cancellation of the Winnipeg Santa Claus Parade in 1967. After more than sixty years, this pivotal part of the Christmas season for generations of Manitoba families was suddenly dropped.

Then there was the closing of the Catalogue in 1976. This shocking decision was seen by many Manitobans as the obliteration of an almost-sacred institution, and it was greeted with outbursts of nostalgia, puzzlement, and anger. The impact of the Catalogue closure was felt right across Canada, but for Winnipeggers the Eaton's catalogue was more than a book from which goods could be ordered to be shipped from some faceless and faraway place. To them, Eaton's Catalogue meant that handsome brown brick building on Graham Avenue. Many thought of

The once-mighty empire was in trouble.

Epilogue

By the time the last day arrived, almost all of the counters and fixtures had been removed. When Walter Wright posed for a photograph under the clock which had served as a meeting place for decades, he was surrounded by emptiness.

Eaton's
COLLECTIBLES

AFTER THE CLOSING OF Eaton's, memorabilia of the once-famous business took on added appeal for collectors. Almost anything bearing the name of the company or its branded lines, including catalogues, watches, pill bottles, spice tins, and even the distinctive boxes and bags could be found in antique stores and on Internet auction sites. The coveted Eaton Beauty Dolls prized by children since they first appeared in 1901, gained added collectibility. Nor long after the store was demolished, tin ceiling tiles bearing the trademark diamond "E" were displayed at Winnipeg antique sales.

family members or friends who still worked there and were about to lose their jobs. Others remembered working there part-time when they were younger. When Manitobans got past the shock of the announcement, they felt betrayed.

The introduction of Everyday Value Pricing in 1990 eliminated sales events and was seen by price-savvy Winnipeggers as another affront to treasured memories. An Eaton's sale inspired the thrill of the hunt for bargains and the afterglow of gloating over money that might have been spent but wasn't. Twenty-five-year saleswoman Fran Johnstone assesses Everyday Value Pricing in no uncertain terms: "When they did away with Trans-Canada Sales, that finished Eaton's. It was the biggest mistake they ever made." Eaton's without sales just wasn't the same old Eaton's.

As a matter of fact, there were many ways that Eaton's wasn't the same anymore. The store itself was looking worn-out, almost decrepit. The crowds of excited shoppers that many remembered were long gone. Only a few people wandered through the aisles, and many of them looked like they were there only because their memories made them think this was the place to shop. The selection of merchandise was sparse; malls had much more to offer. The sales clerks (if

they could be found) didn't seem to know very much about what they had for sale, and, even worse, didn't seem to care. The personal service that so many customers had come to value at Eaton's was replaced to a large extent by self-serve displays.

So when the end came, it wasn't the Eaton's of the 1990s that Winnipeggers mourned. It was the vibrant and exciting place they remembered from previous decades that they missed, and many seemed to forget that the Eaton's of their memories hadn't been there for a long time. Some felt guilt, knowing they'd abandoned Eaton's to shop at the malls, the specialty shops, the big box stores, and the discount stores. Most felt sadness because a local institution was dead.

"Right-sizing"

THE OVERWHELMING DOMINANCE of Eaton's in Winnipeg was only a memory by the 1990s. The flagship downtown store achieved $104 million in sales in 1985, but by 1995, sales dwindled to approximately $44 million. Because the store had much more space than it needed, departments on the seventh and eighth floors were moved to lower floors in the

"NOT ENOUGH MONEY IN THE WHOLE WORLD..."

IN 1920, RESPONDING TO rumours that the Eaton family was planning to sell its company, Sir John Eaton proudly declared "There is not enough money in the whole world to buy my father's name." Eaton's was a family-owned business, and the Eatons were determined to keep it that way. The first blow to this determination came in 1998 when the company was listed on the Toronto Stock Exchange and shares in the company were publicly traded. Although the family retained the majority of the shares, they were no longer the sole owners.

mid-1990s and those two levels were closed to the public. Soon after, the sixth floor was also vacated. Only the presence of the restaurants on the fifth floor prevented further floor closures. To avoid the negative connotations of the word "downsizing," the company encouraged employees to call these changes "right-sizing." Keeping in mind that Timothy Eaton determined in 1904 that the initial structure should be limited to five storeys, he probably would have agreed with this Eatonially-correct euphemism.

Debra Jonasson-Young, who was based in the downtown Winnipeg store as general manager for all seven stores in Manitoba and northwestern Ontario, believes that downsizing was essential and that even more floors could have been closed. "With what I know now, there was no way the downtown store could have been saved in its format. It could have been reduced down to three floors and possibly been successful."

Other Eatonians saw this as a further step in making the store less and less of a complete department store. One says "they kept closing everything up. I said they would downsize until they were down to nothing."

Along with the downsizing of the store, the company closed many familiar departments and services and chose to focus on high-end fashion merchandise. Tom Lenton, a 34-year manager and buyer, believes that Eaton's stopped appealing to the masses. "Eighty percent of your business comes from twenty percent of your assortment. They bought expensive merchandise at the expense of basic bread and butter stuff."

An even more dramatic event occurred in October 1999, when Sears Canada purchased the common shares of the T. Eaton Company Limited. Included in the transaction were all of the trademarks and intellectual properties of Eaton's. Despite Sir John's 1920 declaration about his father's name, and in what has to be one of greatest ironies in the history of Canadian business, Eaton's traditional rival bought Timothy Eaton's name. The price was approximately 80 million dollars. Included in the deal were sixteen former Eaton's store locations, including the flagship Eaton Centre in Toronto and the Polo Park store in Winnipeg.

The mall display windows at Polo Park saw changes in signs and ownership as "Eaton's" became "eatons."

In November 2000, Sears reopened seven of the former Eaton's stores it had acquired (including Polo Park) under the name "eatons." These upscale stores with the Internet-hip name were unveiled with much fanfare and the slogan "eatons now." Even the catalogue that had died in 1976 was resurrected.

Winnipegger Betty Ralph worked for more than forty years in the company printing plant. She was a loyal Eatonian not only in her dedication as an employee but also in her choosing to purchase almost everything she owned from Eaton's. When she learned of the opening of eatons, she smiled and quietly said "It's not the real Eaton's."

It was obvious that many other Canadians shared Betty's viewpoint. The new incarnation lacked more than the capital letter and apostrophe of its predecessor. It lacked the ability to attract customers. Within sixteen months, the experiment was found to be a failure and the stores closed. In Winnipeg, the name "eatons" was removed from the Polo Park store, Sears temporarily moved in from the other end of the mall while it expanded and upgraded its own store, and then the Bay became the fourth retailer to occupy the building.

In the meantime, Timothy's statue sat in the mall, its back turned to all of the comings and goings.

James O'Conner

In April 2004, The Governor's statue returned from its temporary home at Polo Park Mall to be hoisted into the new MTS Centre.

His wife, Andrea Lenton, who was a salesperson and buyer, sums it up: "Eaton's lost touch with their customers."

Sears, one of Eaton's major competitors, describes the downfall of Eaton's in its fiftieth anniversary book: "As the decade drew to a close it was becoming clear that an old rival wouldn't survive into the new century. Eaton's tried to adapt to the changing market by dropping most of its hard lines and switching its focus to fashion. In the end, it simply wasn't nimble enough and the end came officially on December 30th, 1999."

Winnipeg loses its clout

WINNIPEG EATONIANS, too, knew that things weren't what they used to be. Those who worked for the company during the fifties, sixties, and seventies had been part of a prosperous local institution with considerable say within the larger company. Greg Purchase,

who left Winnipeg for the Toronto head office, wrote that "the Winnipeg operation had been the most profitable for the company for several decades" and Winnipeg Eatonians, especially those in management, knew that the company's head office showed respect and even deference to this part of their operation.

Debra Jonasson-Young comments "This was a powerhouse within the T. Eaton Company. It was a force to be reckoned with, and when Winnipeg people spoke, the company listened because it drove so much volume at certain times. People who had positions of power in the company came out of Winnipeg."

By the 1990s, the region from Winnipeg to Thunder Bay was generating only about ten percent of the company's total revenue. If Eaton's was to be saved, available money needed to be diverted to regions that had some chance of success. Winnipeg was basically a passive observer as its fate was determined. More and more of the company's decisions were made in Toronto.

The anger of some Winnipeg Eatonians over the centralization of decision-making and the loss of local autonomy can be seen in the comment of 25-year-veteran George Whyte: "They sent all these people from down east to inform us how to operate the business. These geniuses didn't recognize the fact that Eaton's Winnipeg was the one that made more money for the Eaton organization than anybody else."

One aspect of centralization that was particularly resented by Winnipeg Eatonians was the buying of merchandise, and their frustration

was compounded by frequent vacillation by the head office from the 1960s and into the 1980s on whether buying should be regional or central. This one issue rankled local Eatonians beyond most others, and some still focus on it as the major reason for the decline of Eaton's in Winnipeg and the eventual downfall of the company.

To many of the Winnipeg employees, the authority of local managers and buyers to choose the merchandise that would be sold in their stores became a symbol of their independence. Added to this, of course, was the traditional resentment felt by Manitobans of anything that takes place "down east" – and especially in Toronto. This perspective is typified in the comment of one Winnipeg manager who says "When they gave us the autonomy, we did well. When we operated our own buying unit in Winnipeg, we were very successful."

Forty-four-year veteran salesperson Anne Elviss still resents what she sees as a blindness to local preferences: "I used to get in lots of discussions with department managers. We haven't got the same tastes and why are they doing this? The managers sided with those down east." Her comments are echoed by Fran Johnstone: "Toronto didn't really realize they've got people down there that are totally different from people in the west. When the merchandise came in, I looked at it and said 'How the heck do they expect us to sell this stuff?' And they ended up practically giving the stuff away." Gloria Sokalski, who worked as a salesperson over a period of thirty-six years, focuses on the uniqueness of Winnipeg: "They had buyers in Toronto who didn't really know what Eaton's was like in Winnipeg. In the good old days we had buyers who knew what the little old Ukrainian ladies wanted, like wool stockings. It was too bad when they started to bunch us up with other places." Fashion director Lillian Vadeboncoeur says that when the Winnipeg buyers left, it was "the beginning of the end."

Other Winnipeg Eatononians whose careers began later in the history of the company see some centralization in buying as a necessary move. Debra Jonasson-Young believes it was the correct way to go at that time in the company and does not believe centralized buying contributed to the company's demise.

Others point out the price advantages of quantity purchasing and maintain that most kinds of merchandise can be sold right across Canada. Tony LaMantia's perspective, based on his thirty-seven-year career with Eaton's, which included being senior vice-president of merchandising and marketing, is that "ninety-five percent of what you sell is pretty well common and there might be an opportunity for maybe five percent to be selected locally": A similar opinion is expressed by Debra Jonasson-Young: "Eighty to eighty-five percent of what is offered within a store will sell right across Canada. Maybe fifteen or twenty percent can be tweaked locally." And Tom Lenton believes that Winnipeg didn't lose its voice in Toronto: "The Toronto people spent a great deal of time considering input from the people in the west about local market trends."

One aspect of centralization that was particularly resented by Winnipeg Eatonians was the buying of merchandise, and their frustration was compounded by frequent vacillation by the head office from the 1960s and into the 1980s on whether buying should be regional or central.

The competition changes

ONE OF THE MAIN FACTORS in the decline of the T. Eaton Company was some significant changes that took place in the shopping habits of consumers by the 1980s. Although these shifts happened across North America, they were particularly dramatic in Winnipeg.

One of the most important of these was that consumers had much more choice. Debra Jonasson-Young points out that prior to then "we had market share by virtue of not having much competition. It was in the mid-1980s that a ton of competition came into the city." Partly as a result of the North American Free Trade Agreement, a host of new retailers entered the Winnipeg scene. Discount department stores like Woolco, Zellers, K-Mart, and especially Wal-Mart offered bread-and-butter merchandise at attractive prices. Specialty retailers such as Future Shop and Canadian Tire offered lines that Eaton's no longer sold (or stocked in only a very limited selection) and at very attractive prices. Where Eaton's, the Bay, and a handful of local stores had been the places to purchase furniture in the past, Leon's and The Brick moved into that market. A host of specialty clothing stores took over another area which Eaton's used to dominate. Sears, with its emphasis on hardware, its appeal to moderate-income shoppers, and its still-strong catalogue arm, continued to prosper.

Winnipeggers' love affair with their downtown came to an end as suburban malls multiplied. The lure of easy and free parking became more enticing as shoppers increasingly relied on their cars and shunned transit buses. A host of specialty stores in an upbeat atmosphere made malls like Polo Park and St. Vital Centre especially attractive. Urban sprawl saw many Winnipeggers move to the outer parts of the city and conveniently close to the glittering malls, so

there were fewer and fewer reasons to go downtown.

Some previously loyal Eaton's customers still returned to Eaton's when they saw prices that were too good to resist. This might have assuaged some of the guilt they felt for deserting the Big Store, but it did little to help a company that they knew to be hurting. Sales associate Betty Murray reflects on these well-intentioned customers: "I had customers who really believed they were saving Eaton's when they came down and bought things that were seventy-five percent off. They truly believed they were saving the store."

The era of the traditional department store, in many ways, had passed. The concept of a vertical shopping destination that offered a complete range of goods and services under one roof, along with other diversions to keep shoppers within its confines, was replaced by horizontal malls. These, like traditional department stores, provided customers with a wide choice of merchandise, but this was offered by a score of individual retailers. And, for those who had loyalties to Eaton's and the Bay, those companies' mall outlets were more accessible than their downtown stores. The decline in the popularity of the large Eaton's and Hudson's Bay stores in downtown Winnipeg was really a microcosm of a continent-wide development that saw the closing of a number of previously prosperous department stores.

The market was much more competitive than it was in the early days of the T. Eaton Company, and casualties of this could easily be seen at the local level. Gambles, K-Mart, Consumer's Distributing, and Woolco were just some of the names that came and went.

In the meantime, the character and the atmosphere of Winnipeg's downtown changed. The throngs of window-shoppers who used to stroll almost shoulder-to-shoulder along the south Portage Avenue sidewalk between Eaton's

The decline in the popularity of the large Eaton's and Hudson's Bay stores in downtown Winnipeg was really a microcosm of a continent-wide development that saw the closing of a number of previously prosperous department stores.

(Opposite) Winnipeg artist Guy St. Godard depicted one of the final opportunities for Winnipeggers to see the Big Store as part of this busy Portage Avenue scene in Last Four Days.

On top of all of the insecurity they were feeling about their own future job prospects, they were witnessing the closing of a Winnipeg institution.

and the Bay were gone. Many of the people who did choose to shop in the downtown area were hidden in Portage Place and the overpasses, so the sidewalks were virtually empty of pedestrians. At the street level, there appeared to be more empty storefronts than operating businesses. Panhandlers and other down-and-outers on an almost-deserted Portage Avenue introduced an element of fear that was in sharp contrast to malls full of busy and well-dressed shoppers. As fewer people shopped downtown, the image of its being a deserted area was strengthened, the atmosphere became less inviting, and even fewer people shopped downtown.

The liquidation sale

DURING THE FINAL WEEKS of the Big Store, liquidators arranged for the final sale of merchandise at clearance prices. Virtually anything and everything was up for grabs, including odds and ends of out-of-date items that had not sold when they were first put into inventory.

Even the fixtures of the store were for sale, including the mirrors from the clothing departments, the mannequins that once proudly wore the latest fashions, and the furnishings from the luxurious executive offices. Some retired Eatonians visited for a last nostalgic look at the once-proud store and winced as they saw what they considered callous insensitivity to the greatness that once was Eaton's. To them, this disrespect was salt on the emotional wounds they were already feeling.

For the staff of Eaton's of Winnipeg that remained, it was a very difficult period. On top of all of the insecurity they were feeling about their own future job prospects, they were witnessing the closing of a Winnipeg institution. Cosmetics salesperson Kim Tronrud was at the Polo Park Store during the final months and remembers the tears and hugging that took place among staff members and customers as they dealt with feelings of grief and uncertainty. Yet the spirits of some remained remarkably high. Secretary Hazel Workman's recollection is more positive: "The employees didn't feel angry, we just bonded together. We knew it was the end, but it wasn't doom and gloom. It was sad but we were not bitter." Her point of view is echoed by 18-year saleswoman Sylvia Coulombe: "People's spirits were still good. I enjoyed it right up until the last day. Even if I knew that I wasn't going to have a job. I figured 'Hey, there's always another job somewhere'."

The building comes down

AFTER THE DOORS CLOSED FOR the final time on the store at 320 Portage Avenue in October 1999, the fate of the building became a major political issue. Fact, opinion, and emotion blended in a protracted series of debates and events that were as heated as the controversy that took place over the loss of the Winnipeg Jets NHL team. Nothing happened quickly.

The Big Store was methodically "deconstructed" one storey at a time.

Many components of the building were donated for recycling and a thousand souvenir red bricks were salvaged to be used as a fundraiser by Habitat for Humanity.

While the debate dragged on, the building, denuded of its fixtures, sat locked and deserted. Winnipeggers who wanted to pass from Portage Place to Eaton Place or the Somerset Building were allowed to walk though a desolate portion of the once-grand store, watched over by a solitary security guard sitting at a desk. Orange plastic snow-fencing confined them to parquet-floored aisles. In the chilly semi-darkness beyond the fence, carpeting and mirrored pillars were the only clues that this was once a busy retail area. The only time that another part of the building was opened to the public was the use of three areas as venues for the 2001 Winnipeg Fringe Festival.

Speculation abounded that there were alternative uses for the huge building. After all, the former Catalogue building had survived and become Eaton Place, a combination of a shopping mall and office space. Rumours suggested that residential use was a possibility, leading some Eatonians and former Eaton's shoppers to wonder what it would be like to live in the Big Store. Others saw the site as a potential location for a new arena. The Jets were gone, but many maintained that the Winnipeg Arena, built in 1955, needed to be replaced. Underlying much of the discussion was the hope for downtown revitalization.

The fundamental issue was whether the building should be saved or destroyed. The idea of a new arena on the site of the store came to the forefront, championed by a newly-formed group of local business leaders operating under the name of True North Sports & Entertainment Ltd. By June 2001, a citizens' group that called itself the Save the Eaton's Building Coalition was formed.

What followed was a very lengthy series of political and legal maneuvers. True North argued for the demolition of the former store and the building of a downtown sports and entertainment complex. The SEBC took their cause to the public through the media – there was even a "group hug" of the building in June 2001 to dramatize the issue – and lobbied unsuccessfully for heritage designation. Alternative uses for the building were proposed and explored. Court challenges as high as the Supreme Court of Canada and political appeals at various levels stalled any final decisions.

Finally, in the fall of 2002, the concept of a downtown entertainment complex was successful and floor-by-floor dismantling of the old store began. Many components of the building were donated for recycling and a thousand souvenir red bricks were salvaged to be used as a fundraiser by Habitat for Humanity.

By mid-2003, construction began on the sports and entertainment complex that was later named the MTS Centre. As a concession to the historically minded, the design was adjusted somewhat to incorporate more red brick. But this tip of the hat to a previous era did little to console those citizens who considered Eaton's of Winnipeg "a store like no other." ∎

Charles Shilliday

EATON'S
OUND

ⓘ EATONS

WESTBOUND

MEETING AND WISHING

Many Manitobans would agree that the most memorable attraction within the Big Store was the bronze statue of Timothy Eaton. For eighty years, this effigy of the company's founder served as a rendezvous for countless thousands of people. "I'll meet you at the statue" was what friends, husbands and wives, girlfriends and boyfriends, and parents and children told each other for eight decades. In fact, people who came to downtown Winnipeg for any reason (even if that didn't include shopping at Eaton's) often chose the familiar landmark as their place to get together.

Besides serving as a convenient meeting place, the statue achieved the status of a good luck charm, befitting the Irish heritage of the Eaton family. Rubbing the left toe of The Governor was believed by several generations to be a way to achieve good fortune, and as a result the toe of one bronze boot was always a shiny gold colour that contrasted with the darker bronze tone of the rest of the statue. One reason that has been given for the origin of this practice is that Timothy's left foot bothered him in damp weather.

The statue had its own mystique. The regal portrayal of the founder of the Company was almost shrine-like in its ability to attract throngs of people each day. Located in subdued lighting in a main floor alcove and flanked by memorials to the Eatonians who did not return from two World Wars, Timothy's statue seemed to represent the dominance and dignity of the T. Eaton Company.

Whether it was fact or urban legend, many Winnipeggers retold the story that for years a mysterious uniformed man would stop in front of the statue each morning, salute the bronze Timothy, and then stride away to blend in with the throngs of shoppers.

CREATING THE STATUES

To commemorate the fiftieth anniversary of the T. Eaton Co Ltd. in 1919, employees in both Toronto and Winnipeg decided to present the Eaton family with a special gift in each location. The gifts would be identical bronze statues of Timothy Eaton (who had died in 1907), to be placed in the company's two stores as a tribute to The Governor and in appreciation of the many considerations shown to their employees by the Eaton family.

To create these Golden Jubilee gifts, the employee groups turned to Ivor Lewis, who at the time was in the Toronto advertising department. A graduate of the Ontario College of Art, Lewis undertook with a handful of colleagues to immortalize the company's founder. One wore a double-breasted suit coat and sat in a wooden chair to serve as the model for the statue. Beginning with small plaster versions, Lewis created a stern and paternal representation of The Governor, seated in a throne-like chair and holding a pen and a scroll of paper. The two ten-ton bronze statues were cast in New Jersey because no plant in Canada could be found to handle a project of that size.

THE OFFICIAL UNVEILING

Each statue was unveiled at a ceremony witnessed by loyal Eatonians. The Toronto event took place on December 8, 1919, in the presence of an estimated ten thousand employees. A similar ceremony took place in the Winnipeg store at 8:00 a.m. on Thursday, December 11th. Thousands of Winnipeg Eatonians looked on as Harry McGee, company secretary J. J. Vaughan, and store manager H. M. Tucker announced that the "Boys and Girls of Winnipeg" would enjoy shortened hours of work. Sir John was in attendance, but a severe cold prevented him from personally thanking the employees for their gift.

THE FAREWELLS

When the decision was made to close the store in 1999, the statue became a gathering place for those who came to mourn. Flowers, wreaths, and cards of condolence were laid nearby. A guest book placed on the pedestal by an employee was quickly filled with the messages of sympathy and the signatures of grieving (and sometimes angry) customers and Eatonians. Additional books were soon needed. Timothy's statue, even more than before, became a symbol of the greatness that was Eaton's and of all that the company once represented to Winnipeg.

On the last day of business, October 20, 1999, hundreds gathered for the day in a kind of wake for Eaton's. At closing time an unidentified man sadly sang a solo version of *Auld Lang Syne*.

THE CUSTODY DISPUTES

Because the store was to be closed and possibly demolished, a new location needed to be found for the statue. An extensive lobbying effort to keep it in Winnipeg was begun by members of the Eaton's Retirement Club and loyal former customers.

The Eaton family agreed that the statue would be moved to the Polo Park Shopping Centre, the location of Eaton's first suburban store in Winnipeg and, in the earlier part of the century, the site of the sports grounds of Eatonians. The former Eaton's store, now owned by Sears Canada, was in the process of becoming the only Winnipeg location of the Sears-owned "eatons" stores.

As a final farewell before the statue was moved, a "Farewell to Timothy" luncheon was held at the familiar alcove on November 16, 2000. Eaton's Retirement Club members were honoured guests, and Manitoba Lieutenant Governor Peter Liba spoke nostalgically of his own memories of Eaton's.

Then the 3,500 pound statue was moved to Polo Park and placed outside of the mall entrance to eatons. It could be seen as significant that The Governor appeared to be looking down the mall of the busy shopping centre, once again observing thousands of bustling customers. It might also be symbolic that his back was turned to the new incarnation of the store his family once proudly owned.

But the controversy was not yet over. The Sears attempt, begun in November 2000, to create a new and vibrant version of Eaton's proved to be short-lived. On May 24, 2002, Sears Canada announced that all of its eatons stores were to be closed. It appeared that the statue of Timothy Eaton would soon be on a shopping mall with a former Eaton's store, now also a former eatons store, behind him. To make the situation even more dramatic, there were strong rumours (which later proved to be accurate) that the same store would soon become a temporary Sears outlet and eventually a new location for Eaton's traditional Winnipeg rival, the Hudson's Bay Company.

Fred Eaton, aware that the statue of his great-grandfather had been a gift to the Eaton family, wanted the statue to be in a more appropriate location. He began making arrangements to have it shipped by Sears to St. Marys, Ontario, the location of Timothy Eaton's second store before he moved the business to Toronto in 1869.

Once again, the Eaton's Retirement Club and many other Winnipeggers implored the Eaton family to recognize the

historical and sentimental importance of the statue to Winnipeg. The Eatons were in an awkward position. They appreciated the significance of the statue to Winnipeg, but at the same time a commitment had already been made by the family to the elected officials and residents of St. Marys.

PROTECTED AND ENJOYED

Intervention by the Government of Manitoba resolved the dilemma. On October 22, 2002, it was announced by Eric Robinson, Minister of Culture, Heritage and Tourism, that the statue of Timothy Eaton had been designated a protected provincial heritage object. With the co-operation of the Eaton family, ownership of the statue was transferred to the province and the designation ensured that it would be "preserved for the enjoyment and edification of all Manitobans." It was agreed that it would be reunited with the two war memorial plaques and placed on permanent public display at the new sports and entertainment complex that was being built on the site of the demolished downtown Eaton's store.

The statue remained on the mall until the Bay took occupancy of the previous Eaton's/eatons/Sears store in the fall of 2003. Because the Bay was unwilling to have this reminder of its former competitor located nearby, the statue was moved into storage in late October 2003, and then, in April 2004, it was taken to the atrium of the new MTS Centre to wait to be reunited with the two war memorial plaques and placed on public display.

At last, the statue would return to 320 Portage Avenue, and future generations would have an opportunity to seek to share in the good fortune of The Governor by touching Timothy's toe.

THE DECLINE OF EATON'S

THE DIFFICULTIES BEING EXPERIENCED by The T. Eaton Company, especially during the late 1980s and through the 1990s were the subject of considerable media attention and much discussion. Although most people had stopped making Eaton's a major shopping destination, there seemed to be an assumption that the company should continue to prosper, and the fact that this once-mighty business had fallen upon hard time appears to have come as a surprise to many.

The obvious lightning rods for those difficulties were the four Eaton brothers, John, Fredrik, Thor, and George. The most comprehensive critique of the family is *The Eatons: The Rise and Fall of Canada's Royal Family* by Rod McQueen. In many ways, that book holds the Eaton brothers responsible for the downfall of their great grandfather's business, documenting their alleged lack of interest and involvement, and it concludes with the sentence, "They didn't mind the store." The downfall of the T. Eaton Company, however, had its beginnings several decades before the "Eaton boys" (a title that endured despite the fact that their birth years range from 1937 to 1945) were in positions to influence developments. Many of the contributing factors had as much to do with changes in the retail market as they had to do with the company, its policies, or its executives. Winnipeg Eatonian Debra Jonasson-Young is in the camp of a large number of those who see a range of issues that led to the end of Eaton's and refuses to point a finger at the brothers: "I would challenge anybody to have put themselves in the shoes of the Eaton brothers and to have done it any better. I'm not saying these were perfect people, but I think it's very simplistic to say the brothers weren't minding the store."

Eaton's once-impressive share of department store sales showed progressive deterioration. In 1929, Eaton's had 58% of department store sales across Canada. Although the company's share of the Canadian retail market gradually eroded over the next few decades, Eaton's continued to be a major retailing force from coast to coast. By the 1980s, despite growing competition, Eaton's held a healthy relatively 35% share of department store sales. But the competition became more formidable, and during the 1990s, Eaton's was left behind. By 1997, Eaton's was around 11% (less than half of Wal-Mart's share) and in fifth place behind Wal-Mart, Zellers,

Sears, and the Bay. And, from 1991 to 1996, Eaton's sales across Canada dropped by an estimated $500 million each year.

Paradoxically, some of the factors that weakened the T. Eaton Company were the same ones that gave it strength. The loyalty of Eatonians produced service to the company and its customers that was the envy of other businesses. To earn that loyalty, the company (which was essentially the Eaton family) showed a level of generosity to its employees which, in retrospect, it might not have been in a position to afford. One example of this is the payment of wage subsidies to employees involved in the armed services during both world wars. These alone cost the company more than six million dollars. The contributory pension plan introduced by John David Eaton in the 1940s was kick-started with an astounding fifty million dollars of company money. Benefits to employees, including social and recreational activities, medical services, and countless favours cost the company considerably.

The most famous policy of the T. Eaton Company earned scores of appreciative customers but had a high price tag attached. The Eaton Guarantee of "goods satisfactory or money refunded" continued to be honoured with consistent generosity whether the company was prospering or hurting. Eaton's was convinced that the guarantee created faithful customers, but it also resulted in considerable financial losses.

In retrospect, the introduction of a concept known as "Everyday Value Pricing" in 1990 can be seen one of the worst decisions ever made by the T. Eaton Company. When it was announced by president George Eaton that Eaton's would no longer have sales events or offer reduced prices on merchandise, the plan was greeted with almost universal disappointment by customers. The theory was that Eaton's would simply offer the lowest possible prices all of the time. Customers, used to the sales that were so closely identified with Eaton's, found this new approach to be confusing, and many found other places to shop where they felt they were getting bargains. The policy was dropped in 1995, but the damage was done. As John Craig Eaton observes "we tried to come back to sales, but by that time I think our base was so eroded that we couldn't catch up."

As sales across Canada plummeted for Eaton's, the company experienced red ink in ways that Timothy, Sir John, and John David would never have

James O'Conner

visualized outside of their nightmares. The company's debt load was increasing at a staggering rate. In 1995 and 1996, the Eaton family sold many of their real estate holdings (including their interest in Winnipeg's St. Vital Centre) to raise some of funds needed to pay down the company's debts.

In February 1997, it became dramatically clear just how serious the problems of Eaton's had become. The company sought and was granted protection from its creditors under the Companies' Creditors Arrangement Act. It was given only a few months to develop a restructuring plan. At that point, Eaton's owed approximately $330 million to its suppliers and banks and was in no position to pay off those debts. George Eaton resigned from his position as Eaton's Chief Executive Officer and was replaced by George Kosich, the former president of the Hudson's Bay Company and the mastermind of a massive downsizing that had breathed new life into the Bay and Zellers.

In April 1998, the family announced a dramatic step in the history of the family-owned company. The T. Eaton Company was to be listed on the Toronto Stock Exchange. An eleven-member board of directors was named, which included active and retired executives from several corporations as well as George, Fred, and Thor Eaton. The 11.7 million

common shares were listed at $15 each, and the Eaton family retained control by holding approximately 51% of the shares. This meant that anyone who chose to purchase a share could now own a part of the company.

The restructuring plan overseen by George Kosich closed twenty-one stores, including Winnipeg's never-productive Garden City outlet. More than 2,000 employees across Canada were laid off. In an effort to attract more (and younger) shoppers, Eaton's focused on offering high-end merchandise, especially designer clothing, and declared itself not to be "your grandmother's store." These moves did little to keep the loyalty of the stores' most loyal shoppers (older people who, in many cases, were indeed grandmothers) and failed to persuade young fashion-conscious consumers to abandon the specialty outlets in the malls.

The magic of Eaton's, like many of its stores and much of the basic merchandise that kept everyday people shopping there, was gone. A last-ditch effort to sell some stores to Federated Department Stores, the parent company of Macy's, failed. Eaton's was no longer seriously ill. Eaton's was dead.

Termination notices, effective November 30, 1999, were given to the 13,000 employees who remained with the company, and liquidation began.

C
Top
19⁰⁰

D
Top
15⁰⁰
Shorts
10⁰⁰

Fashion favour:
velvety velours

Popularly priced for your sportive living

A to **D** By Regent: for today's woman, a cle
collection of super-soft separates! T
trendsetting casuals take to your active life w
ease and utmost comfort. They're fashion-
shaped from a machine-washable blend of p
ester and cotton knit terry velour, that looks a
feels like velvet.

A) Make your summer livin' easy with this d
ing trio. 41-blue; 13-peach; 70-white.
Wrap jacket: sports the look you love with it
tie belt, roomy patch pockets.
46-K 6005BM—Misses' 10 to 18 3
Stripey halter: elasticized at back and under
to self ties, for extra good fit.
46-K 6006CM—One size fits all 1
Pull-on pants: so comfy, with elasticized wa
loose straight leg. About 32" inseam.
46-K 6002BM—Misses' 10 to 18 2
B) A duo of leisure-time lovelies that look gr
anywhere. 41-blue; 13-peach.
Versatile top: has cross-over V-neck insert,
knit at waist and sleeve bands.
46-K 6008BM—Misses' S(10-12), M(14-
L(18). Each 1
A-line skirt: flippy little pull-on style has neat
fitting elasticized waist.
46-K 6003BM—Misses' 10 to 18 2
C) **Blouson pullover top:** casual and oh, so
fortable. Plain knit at the cuffs and waistban
13-peach; 41-blue.
46-K 6004BM—Misses' S(10-12), M(14-
L(18). Each 1
D) Get this terrific team to help you keep yo
cool. 13-peach; 41-blue; 70-white.
Striped-up topper: young and lively pullover
plain knit at round neck, waist, arm band.
46-K 6007BM—Misses' S(10-12), M(14-
L(18). Each 1
Short shorts: great hot weather fare in pull-c
style with elasticized waist. Smart stitching
accent on the legs.
46-K 6001BM—Misses' 10 to 18 1

Regent sizes may differ from your usual Eatc
size. Before ordering, measure and select yc
size from chart below.

Sizes	10	12	14	16
Bust	35	36½	38	39½
Waist	26½	28	29½	31
Hips	36	37½	39	40½

THE T. EATON COMPANY WAS OWNED AND CONTROLLED by members of the Eaton family for a century after Timothy Eaton opened his first store in 1869. It was only in the last thirty years of the business that non-family members were permitted to be in charge, and even then, majority ownership remained in the hands of Eatons.

Timothy Eaton (*president 1869 to 1907*)

Born in 1834, Timothy Eaton emigrated from Ireland to seek his fortune. A deeply-religious man, he was sometimes abrupt and arbitrary in his dealings with people, but was generally regarded by his employees as caring and fair. Although his first business ventures met with limited success, Timothy persisted and eventually operated a thriving retail enterprise, with two large department stores (in Toronto and Winnipeg) and a successful mail order business. He is generally credited with innovating a number of revolutionary business practices, but most of these were borrowed and then adapted, rather than created, by Timothy. Some reasons for his amazing success as a businessman were his determination and strong work ethic, his willingness to take calculated risks, and the fact that a number of developments in Canadian society were fortunate for the type of business he chose to establish.

John Craig (Sir John) Eaton (*president 1907 to 1922*)

When Timothy died in 1907, his youngest son, John Craig, succeeded him as president and served in this position until his death in 1922. Outgoing and charming, Jack became immensely popular with his employees as he made major improvements in their working conditions. Although there was some expansion of the company during his term as president, he devoted much of his time to enjoying his life of luxury.

Robert Young Eaton (*president 1922 to 1942*)

After the death of Sir John in 1922, his cousin Robert Young Eaton became president. The terms of Sir John's will stipulated that one of his four sons should succeed him, but this could not take place until the youngest son reached the age of 27. The shy R. Y. was seen by many family members as a caretaker leader, and Sir John's widow, the outgoing and sometimes-outspoken Lady Eaton, carefully watched developments as a company director during his term. Although he didn't possess the outgoing personality or the physical presence of his predecessor, Robert Young Eaton expanded the Eaton empire dramatically by opening fifty new stores. An interesting Manitoba connection is that R. Y. met and married Hazel Margaret Ireland of Carberry, and their wedding took place in that town.

John David Eaton (*president 1942 to 1969*)

It was decided in 1942 that John David was the best-qualified of Sir John's four sons to take over the leadership of the family dynasty. He had served a lengthy apprenticeship with the company, working as a salesclerk, truck driver, manager and director. Although much of this experience was in Toronto, he did spend some time in Winnipeg, where his duties included the uninspiring task of helping the Research Bureau conduct comparison tests on grapefruit. A much more momentous result of his stay in Winnipeg was that he met and married Signy Hildur Stefansson, a charming and talented woman who grew up on Victor Street. They had four sons. Although initially reluctant to take over the leadership of the family business, John David served in the position for 27 years. The company appeared in many ways to be growing and prospering, but the some of the seeds of its demise had already been sown.

The family steps aside (*1969 to 1977*)

When John David Eaton left the presidency in 1969, none of his sons felt prepared to succeed him. For the first time in the history of the company, the presidency was not occupied by an Eaton. From 1969 to 1975, Robert (Bob) Butler held the position. A long-time Eaton's employee, he had become a vice-president in 1968. His successor as president in 1975 was Earl Orser, who carried out the difficult task of shutting down Eaton's Catalogue.

Fredrik Stefan Eaton (*president 1977 to 1988*)

When Fredrik Eaton's appointment to the presidency saw a family member return to the position, much of the decision-making was actually carried out in concert with his three brothers. During his term, the company's financial difficulties continued to grow.

George Ross Eaton (*president 1988 to 1997*)

The company's declining sales and escalating monetary problems were further complicated by George Eaton's introduction in 1990 of Everyday Value Pricing. Eaton's debts reached massive proportions.

George Kosich (*president 1997-1998*)

The company had been granted court protection from its creditors. The former president of the Hudson's Bay Company, George Kosich was given the mandate of replicating with Eaton's the successful turnaround he had engineered with the Bay. Stores were closed, staff was reduced, and Eaton's shares were publicly sold. These (and other) efforts were not enough to save the company.

Bibliography

ARCHIVES

Archives of Ontario: T. Eaton Co. fonds
Archives of Manitoba
City of Winnipeg Archives

NEWSPAPERS AND PERIODICALS

Contacts and other periodicals published by the T. Eaton Company for its
    employees in Manitoba and western Canada
Eaton's Retirement Club Newsletter (Winnipeg)
Winnipeg Free Press
Winnipeg Sun
Winnipeg Telegram
Winnipeg Tribune

BOOKS

Artibise, Alan, *Winnipeg: An Illustrated History, James Lorimer and Company and National Museums of
    Canada*, Toronto, 1977.

_____, *Winnipeg: A Social History of Urban Growth 1874 - 1914*, McGill – Queen's University Press,
    Montreal, 1975.

Barnes, Carolyn, *Timothy Eaton*, Canadian Library Association, Ottawa, 1981.

Bassett, John M., *Timothy Eaton*, Fitzhenry and Whiteside, Don Mills, 1975.

Bellan, Ruben, *Winnipeg – First Century: An Economic History*, Queenston House Publishing,
    Winnipeg, 1978.

Bumsted, J. M., *The Manitoba Flood of 1950: An Illustrated History*, Watson and Dwyer Publishers,
    Winnipeg, 1993.

Coates, Ken and McGuinness, Fred, *Manitoba: The Province and the People*, Hurtig Publishers,
    Edmonton, 1987.

Dafoe, Christopher, *Winnipeg: Heart of the Continent*, Great Plains Publications Ltd., Winnipeg, 1998.

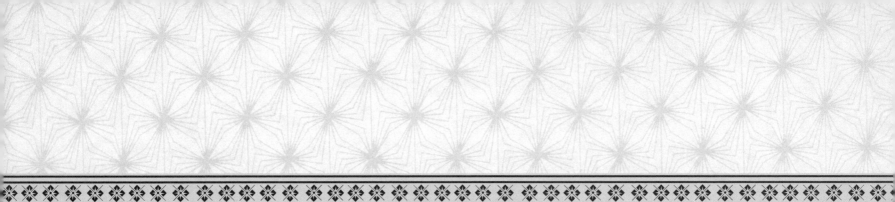

Eaton, Flora McCrea, *Memory's Wall: The Autobiography of Flora McCrea Eaton*, Clarke, Irwin and Company, Toronto, 1956.

Friesen, Gerald, *The Canadian Prairies: A History*, University of Toronto Press, Toronto, 1987.

Hamilton, John David and Dickie, Bonnie, *A Winnipeg Album: Glimpses of the Way We Were*, Hounslow Press, Toronto, 1998.

Henry, Les, *Catalogue Houses: Eatons' and Others*, Henry Perspectives, Saskatoon, 2000.

Macpherson, Mary-Etta, *Shopkeepers to a Nation: The Eatons*, McClelland and Stewart Limited, Toronto, 1963.

McQueen, Rod, *The Eatons: The Rise and Fall of Canada's Royal Family*, Stoddart Publishing Co. Ltd., Toronto, 1998.

McWilliams, Margaret, *Manitoba Milestones*, J. M. Dent and Sons Ltd., Toronto, 1928.

Morrissette, George, *Finding Mom at Eaton's*, Turnstone Press, Winnipeg, 1981.

Morton, W. L., *Manitoba: A History (Second Edition)*, University of Toronto Press, Toronto, 1967.

Nasmith, George G., *Timothy Eaton*, McClelland and Stewart Ltd., Toronto, 1923.

Phenix, Patricia, *Eatonians: The Story of the Family Behind the Family*, McClelland and Stewart Ltd., Toronto, 2002.

Purchase, Gregory, *Hard Rock Retailing*, published privately, Toronto, 1996.

Santink, Joy L., *Timothy Eaton and the Rise of His Department Store*, University of Toronto Press, Toronto, 1990.

Sears Canada, *Sears Canada: A Legacy of Quality, Value, Service & Trust*, Sears Canada Inc., Toronto, 2001.

Shilliday, Gregg (editor), *Manitoba 125: A History*, Great Plains Publications Ltd., Winnipeg, 1994.

Stephenson, William, *The Store That Timothy Built*, McClelland and Stewart, Toronto, 1969.

Sufrin, Eileen Tallman, *The Eaton Drive: The Campaign to Organize Canada's Largest Department Store 1948 to 1952*, Fitzhenry & Whiteside, Toronto, 1982.

The Scribe, *Golden Jubilee 1869 – 1919: A Book to Commemorate the Fiftieth Anniversary of the T. Eaton Co. Ltd.*, T. Eaton Co. Ltd., Toronto and Winnipeg, 1919.

Walz, Gene, *Cartoon Charlie: The Life and Art of Animation Pioneer Charles Thorson*, Great Plains Publications Ltd, Winnipeg, 1998.

Index

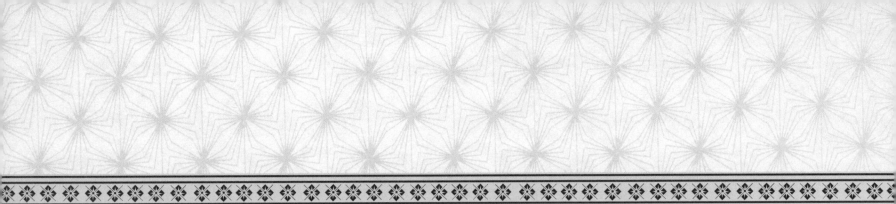

Photo Credits

NOTE: *Many of the images included in this book were obtained from the Eaton Archives in the Archives of Ontario and are listed as "EA Archives of Ontario". These are used with permission of Sears Canada Inc.*

Cover

The images on the front and back covers are used within the book and are listed below.

Introductory pages (pages 1 to 13)

Page 1: Eaton's Winnipeg Catalogue No. 1 (Fall and Winter 1905-1906) page 106. Used with permission of Sears Canada Inc.

Page 2: Eaton's Winnipeg Catalogue No. 1 (Fall and Winter 1905-1906), page 110. Used with permission of Sears Canada Inc.

Page 8: Eaton's downtown store on Portage Avenue, May 1940. (EA Archives of Ontario F 229-308-0-203, AO 6602).

Page 9: Eaton's downtown store on Portage Avenue, May 1940. (EA Archives of Ontario F 229-308-0-203, AO 6602).

Page 9 (inset): Four-year old twins Diane and Wendy looking at Buckingham Palace Display at Eaton's Bonspiel Week, 1954. (EA Archives of Ontario F 229-308-0-1121, AO 6665).

Page 10: Eaton's doorman holding open car door for customer, Winnipeg, 1951. (Phillips-Gutkin and Associates Ltd., Winnipeg). (EA Archives of Ontario F 229-308-0-957, AO 6663).

Prologue: A Store and a City (pages 14 to 25)

Page 14: Eaton's store interior, main floor with coronation decorations, Winnipeg, 1953. (EA Archives of Ontario F 229-308-0-713, AO 6667).

Page 15: Eaton's Tourist Rest Room in Emerson, Manitoba, exterior, November, 1939. (EA Archives of Ontario F 229-308-0-175, AO 6591).

Page 16: Bird's eye view of Winnipeg buildings from drawing, June, 1926. (EA Archives of Ontario F 229-308-0- 182, AO 6593).

Page 17: Winnipeg bus station, 1940. (EA Archives of Ontario F 229-308-0-208, AO 6624).

Page 18: Eaton's store interior, post office, Winnipeg 1940. (EA Archives of Ontario F 229-308-0-206, AO 6604).

Page 19: Gary Filmon as a Junior Executive. *Contacts* (T. Eaton Co. Ltd, Winnipeg, September, 1960), page 8. Used with permission of Sears Canada Inc.

Page 20 (top): Garry Peterson. *Contacts* (T. Eaton Co. Ltd, Winnipeg, May, 1950), page 4. Used with permission of Sears Canada Inc.

Page 20 (bottom): Good Deed Club felt crest. Used with permission of Sears Canada Inc.

Page 21: Doorman Ed Logan shovelling snow at Hargrave Street entrance on the morning of December 5, 1961. Courtesy Tim Eaton.

Page 22: Eaton's store exterior with coronation decorations, Winnipeg, 1953. (EA Archives of Ontario F 229-308-0-1713, AO 6668).

Page 23: Home Service League advertisement, Winnipeg, 1944. Used with permission of Sears Canada Inc.

Page 24: *Contacts* (T. Eaton Co. Ltd, Winnipeg, May, 1956), page 12. Used with permission of Sears Canada Inc.

Page 25: Early escalators in the Winnipeg store. The Scribe, *Golden Jubilee 1869 – 1919: A Book to Commemorate the Fiftieth Anniversary of the T. Eaton Co. Ltd.* (T. Eaton Co. Ltd., Toronto and Winnipeg, 1919), page 229.

Chapter 1: Building the Big Store (pages 26 to 45)

Page 26: Eaton's store under construction, April 11, 1905. (EA Archives of Ontario F 229-305-0-184, AO 6595).

Page 27: John Craig and Flora Eaton on board the *Lusitania* on its maiden voyage from New York, 1907. Flora McCrea Eaton, *Memory's Wall: The Autobiography of Flora McCrea Eaton* (Clarke, Irwin & Company Limited, Toronto, 1956), photo opposite page 101.

Page 28: Men and horses excavating the basement at the store site, 1905. (EA Archives of Ontario F 229-308-0-187, AO 6639, #9).

Page 29: Bricklayers on last lap, 1905. (EA Archives of Ontario F 229-308-187, AO 6640, #35).

Page 29 (inset): Northwest corner of Eaton block, August 2, 1904. (EA Archives of Ontario F 229-308-0-187, AO 6636, #1).

Page 30: Construction gang of new store, 1905. (EA Archives of Ontario F 229-308-0-187, AO 6638, #7).

Page 31: Timothy Eaton. From various publications of the T. Eaton Co. Ltd, Toronto. Courtesy Giles Bugailiskis. Used with permission of Sears Canada Inc.

Page 32: Home of Eatonian Club - Strevel House, 1905. (EA Archives of Ontario F 229-308-0-187, AO 6637, #2).

Page 33: Laying last stone of Eaton's store in Winnipeg, May 18, 1905. (EA Archives of Ontario F 229-308-0-194, AO 6598).

Page 34: Winnipeg garage, 1927 (Power House in background). (EA Archives of Ontario F 229-308-0-213, AO 6612).

Page 37: Two power house generators. The Scribe, *Golden Jubilee 1869 – 1919: A Book to Commemorate the Fiftieth Anniversary of the T. Eaton Co. Ltd.* (T. Eaton Co. Ltd., Toronto and Winnipeg, 1919), page 192. Used with permission of Sears Canada Inc.

Page 38: Mr. T. Eaton's luncheon on the opening day of the Winnipeg store, July 15, 1905. (EA Archives of Ontario F 229-308-0-201, AO 6599).

Page 41: A corner of the drapery department, Winnipeg. The Scribe, *Golden Jubilee 1869 – 1919: A Book to Commemorate the Fiftieth Anniversary of the T. Eaton Co. Ltd.* (T. Eaton Co. Ltd., Toronto and Winnipeg, 1919), page 181. Used with permission of Sears Canada Inc.

Page 42: Official opening Jubilee Year (Gilroy and Tucker), 1919. (EA Archives of Ontario F 229-308-0-21 AO 6641).

Page 43: Millinery department, Winnipeg. The Scribe, *Golden Jubilee 1869 – 1919: A Book to Commemorate the Fiftieth Anniversary of the T. Eaton Co. Ltd.* (T. Eaton Co. Ltd., Toronto and Winnipeg, 1919), page 179. Used with permission of Sears Canada Inc.

Page 45: "With their growing family at the beginning of the year 1910. Timothy was then seven, John David a few months old." Flora McCrea Eaton, *Memory's Wall: The Autobiography of Flora McCrea Eaton* (Clarke, Irwin & Company Limited, Toronto, 1956), photo opposite page 84.

Chapter 2: The Wishing Book (pages 44 to 61)

Page 46: Eaton's Winnipeg Catalogue No. 1 (Fall and Winter 1905 - 1906), front cover. Used with permission of Sears Canada Inc.

Page 48: Eaton's Mail Order Building under construction in Winnipeg, May 5, 1916. (EA Archives of Ontario F 229-308-0-221, AO 6621).

Page 49: Eaton's Winnipeg Catalogue No. 1 (Fall and Winter 1905-1906), page 106. Used with permission of Sears Canada Inc.

Page 51: Eaton's catalogue, Summer, 1946, front cover. Used with permission of Sears Canada Inc.

Page 51 (inset): Eaton's Catalogue, Summer, 1946, page 53. Used with permission of Sears Canada Inc.

Page 52: Eaton's catalogue, Spring and Summer 1976, front cover. Used with permission of Sears Canada Inc.

Page 52 (inset): Eaton's catalogue, Spring and Summer, 1976, page 207. Used with permission of Sears Canada Inc.

Page 53: Eaton's catalogue, Spring and Summer, 1976, page 338. Used with permission of Sears Canada Inc.

Page 54: Eaton's Winnipeg Catalogue No. 1 (Fall and Winter 1905-1906), page 50. Used with permission of Sears Canada Inc.

Page 55: Eaton's Winnipeg Catalogue No. 1 (Fall and Winter 1905-1906), page 90. Used with permission of Sears Canada Inc.

Page 57: *Contacts* (T. Eaton Co. Ltd, Winnipeg, May, 1956), page 12. Used with permission of Sears Canada Inc.

Page 59: Eaton's catalogue, Spring and Summer 1976, page 648. Used with permission of Sears Canada Inc.

Page 60: Eaton's horses at Portage la Prairie Fair, 1947 (EA Archives of Ontario F 229-308-0-1001, AO 6628).

Page 61: Eaton's catalogue, Spring and Summer, 1976, page 163. Used with permission of Sears Canada Inc.

Page 61: Jack Barrow quotation. *Sears Canada, Sears Canada: A Legacy of Quality, Value Service & Trust* (Sears Canada Inc, Toronto, 2001), page 50. Used with permission of Sears Canada Inc.

Page 62 (upper): Eaton's catalogue, Spring and Summer, 1976, page 649. Used with permission of Sears Canada Inc.

Page 62 (lower): Eaton's catalogue, Spring and Summer, 1976, page 33. Used with permission of Sears Canada Inc.

Page 63: Eaton's catalogue, Spring and Summer, 1976, page 76. Used with permission of Sears Canada Inc.

Chapter 3: The Friendliest Thing on Wheels (pages 64 to 77)

Page 64: Shipping and Delivery horse lineup, 1942. (EA Archives of Ontario F 229-308-1005, AO 6631).

Page 65: *Contacts* (T. Eaton Co. Ltd, Winnipeg, August , 1945), page 12. Used with permission of Sears Canada Inc.

Page 66: "Old Brit". *Contacts* (T. Eaton Co. Ltd, Winnipeg, July, 1935), page 6. Used with permission of Sears Canada Inc.

Page 67: First time out for Birthday Sale, 1942. (EA Archives of Ontario F 229-308-0-1006, AO 6632).

Page 68: Drivers, horses, wagons at Winnipeg Shipping and Delivery department, 1913. (EA Archives of Ontario F 229-308-0-995, AO 6625).

Page 69 (top): *Hoofbeats* (T. Eaton Co. Ltd., Winnipeg, 1943), cover . Used with permission of Sears Canada Inc.

Page 69 (bottom): Eaton's delivery rig, Winnipeg, 1911. (EA Archives of Ontario F 229-308-0-1000, AO 6626).

Page 70: Agricultural Fair, Regina, 1946. (EA Archives of Ontario F 229-308-0-1001, AO 6629).

Page 71 (top): Eaton's stables on Pembina Highway, July, 1943. (EA Archives of Ontario F 229-308-0-1007, AO 6633).

Page 71 (bottom right): Peacock and driver Alf Goodall. Hoofbeats (T. Eaton Co. Ltd., Winnipeg, 1943), inside front cover. Used with permission of Sears Canada Inc.

Page 72: Hoofbeats (T. Eaton Co. Ltd., Winnipeg, 1943), page 1. Used with permission of Sears Canada Inc.

Page 73: Eaton's delivery horse show at the Agricultural Fair, Winnipeg, 1943. (EA Archives of Ontario F 229-308-0-1001, AO 6627).

Page 74: Eaton's delivery rig. *Contacts* (T. Eaton Co. Ltd, Winnipeg, December , 1943), page 7. Used with permission of Sears Canada Inc.

Page 74 (top right): Restored White truck. Courtesy Steve Kiz.

Page 75: Mercedes-Benz truck. *Contacts* (T. Eaton Co. Ltd., Winnipeg, September, 1960), page 22. Used with permission of Sears Canada Inc.

Page 76: Eaton's semi-trailer unit. Courtesy Steve Kiz.

Page 77: *Hoofbeats* (T. Eaton Co. Ltd., Winnipeg, 1943), page 9. Used with permission of Sears Canada Inc.

Chapter 4: In Times of War (pages 78 to 87)

Page 78: Eaton Machine Gun Battery Officers at Exhibition Grounds Art Gallery in Toronto, 1915. (EA Archives of Ontario F 229-308-0-2161, AO 6658).

Page 79: *Florence* yacht owned by J.C. Eaton, 1910. (EA Archives of Ontario F 229-308-0-2419, AO 4234).

Page 80: Drivers' Victory Garden, Winnipeg, 1940. (EA Archives of Ontario F 229-308-0-1003, AO 6630).

Page 82 (inset): J. D. Eaton with veteran Jim Maltby at veterans' banquet, Winnipeg, 1946. (EA Archives of Ontario F 229-308-0-1293, AO 6635).

Pages 82 and 83: Veterans' banquet at Fort Garry Hotel, Winnipeg, 1946. (EA Archives of Ontario F-229-308-0-1293, AO 5913).

Page 83 (inset): Eaton family group photo at veterans' banquet, Winnipeg, 1946. (EA Archives of Ontario F 229-308-0-1293, AO 6634).

Page 84: United Services Centre in Donald Annex, Winnipeg, in early to mid-1940's. (EA Arvhives of Ontario F 229-308-0-227, AO 6623).

Page 85: Remembrance Day window display, Winnipeg, 1938. (EA Archives of Ontario F 229-308-0-1128, AO 6666).

Page 87: V.E. Day decorations, Winnipeg, in 1945. Postcard printed and distributed by the T. Eaton Co. Ltd., 1945. Used with permission of Sears Canada Inc.

Page 87 (bottom right): Eaton Machine Gun Battery armoured car, 1915. (EA Archives of Ontario F 229-308-0-2160, AO 6659).

Chapter 5: Winnipeg's Christmas Store (pages 88 to 99)

Page 88: Eaton's Santa Claus Parade, Winnipeg, 1934. (EA Archives of Ontario F 229-308-0-908, AO 6662).

Page 90: Eaton's Santa Claus Parade on the outskirts of Winnipeg, November 14, 1914. (EA Archives of Ontario F 229-308-0-900, AO 1800).

Page 91 (top): Men's clothing display. Courtesy Bruce Meisner.

Page 91 (bottom): Eaton's Santa Claus Parade passing All Saints' Church, Winnipeg, 1932. (EA Archives of Ontario F-229-308-0-906, AO 6661).

Page 92: Eaton's store interior, Winnipeg, approximately 1950. (EA Archives of Ontario F 229-307-2-46, AO 6652).

Page 93: Eaton's Santa Claus Parade, Winnipeg, November 15, 1929. (EA Archives of Canada F 229-308-0-903, AO 6660).

Page 94: Cover of *Punkinhead the Sad Little Bear*. Published in 1948 by the T. Eaton Co. Ltd. Used with permission of Sears Canada Inc.

Page 95: Punkinhead drawing. Used with permission of Sears Canada Inc.

Page 96: Breakfast with Santa at the downtown store, Winnipeg, mid-1990's. Courtesy Bruce Meisner.

Page 97: Bruce Meisner on his first visit with Santa at the downtown store, early 1960's. Courtesy Ruth Meisner.

Page 98: Christmas family scene window display at the downtown store, 1970's. Courtesy Bruce Meisner.

Page 99: Eaton family Christmas cards. Courtesy Anne Elviss.

Chapter 6: Goods Well Displayed (pages 100 to 111)

Page 100: Four-year old twins Diane and Wendy looking at Buckingham Palace Display at Eaton's Bonspiel Week, 1954. (EA Archives of Ontario F 229-308-0-1121, AO 6665).

Page 102: Exterior decorations welcoming the Duke of Connaught (Canada's Governor General), possibly 1912. Archives of Manitoba.

Page 103: Display of automatic ironing machine at Eaton's Bonspiel Fair, Winnipeg, 1951. (EA Archives of Ontario F 229-308-0-1166, AO 6664).

Page 104: Eaton's store interior, floral display on main floor, Winnipeg, approximately 1950. (EA Archives of Ontario F 229-307-2-31, AO 6642).

Page 107: Pierre Cardin fashion show at the Centennial Concert Hall, Winnipeg, 1969. Courtesy Lillian Vadeboncoeur.

Page 108: Eaton's store interior, women's clothing, Winnipeg, approximately 1950. (EA Archives of Ontario F 229-307-2-39, AO 6648).

Page 109: "Uncrate the Sun" event in reconstructed aircraft interior. Courtesy Bruce Meisner.

Page 110 (top): Chad Allan and the Expressions. Courtesy Lillian Vadeboncoeur.

Page 110 (bottom): Ray St. Germain and Wayne Finucan. Courtesy Lillian Vadeboncoeur.

Page 111: Window display in Eaton's downtown store, 1980's. Courtesy Bruce Meisner.

Chapter 7: The Tastes of Eaton's (pages 112 to 123)

Page 112: Eaton's store interior, Grill Room Products, Winnipeg, approximately 1950. (EA Archives of Ontario F 229-307-2-37, AO 6647).

Page 114: Fashion show in the Grill Room. Courtesy Lillian Vadeboncoeur.

Page 115: Eaton's store interior, coffee bar, Winnipeg, approximately 1950. (EA Archives of Ontario F 229-307-2-35, AO 6645).

Page 116: Eaton's store interior, meat counter, Winnipeg, approximately 1950. (EA Archives of Ontario F 229-307-2-35, AO 6646).

Page 117: Valley Room cafeteria, third floor, downtown store, 1980's. Courtesy Bruce Meisner.

Page 121: Eaton's Winter Folder, November 10, 1941 to March 14, 1942, Courtesy Anne Elviss. Used with permission of Sears Canada Inc.

Page 122: Eaton's store interior, Foodateria, Winnipeg, approximately 1950. (EA Archives of Ontario F 229-307-2-40, AO 6649).

Chapter 8: When Disaster Strikes (pages 124 to 139)

Page 124: Flooded Winnipeg homes, 1950. Archives of Manitoba. .

Page 126: Tribune front page. Winnipeg Tribune Collection, University of Manitoba.

Page 127 (top): Shea's Brewery truck unloading flood relief supplies, 1950. Archives of Manitoba.

Page 127: Eaton's trucks unloading flood relief supplies. *Contacts* (T. Eaton Co. Ltd., Winnipeg, July, 1950), page 2. Used with permission of Sears Canada Inc.

Page 128: The flood of 1950. Winnipeg Tribune Collection, University of Manitoba.

Page 129: Time Building and Dismorr Building ablaze. Archives of Manitoba.

Page 130: Eaton's volunteers fighting the fire from the roof of the Eaton's store, 1954. (EA Archives of Ontario F 229-308-0-3, AO 6657).

Page 132: "Black Tuesday" editorial script used with permission of radio station CJOB, Winnipeg.

Pages 133: Cars and transit buses paralyzed by the March 1966 blizzard. *Contacts* (T. Eaton Co. Ltd., Winnipeg, March, 1966), front cover. Used with permission of Sears Canada Inc.

Page 134: Three women sharing a bed during the March 1966 blizzard. *Contacts* (T. Eaton Co. Ltd., Winnipeg, March, 1966), page 6. Used with permission of Sears Canada Inc.

Page 136: Men pushing car during the March 1966 blizzard. *Contacts* (T. Eaton Co. Ltd., Winnipeg, March, 1966), page 1. Used with permission of Sears Canada Inc.

Page 137: Eaton's employee writing messages on a blackboard during the March 1966 blizzard. *Contacts* (T. Eaton Co. Ltd., Winnipeg, March, 1966), page 6. Used with permission of Sears Canada Inc.

Page 139: Women in bunk beds during the March 1966 blizzard. *Contacts* (T. Eaton Co. Ltd., Winnipeg, March, 1966), page 6. Used with permission of Sears Canada Inc.

Chapter 9: Canada's Greatest Store (pages 140 to 159)

Page 140: Eaton's Groceteria in Transcona on opening date, September 14, 1927. (EA Archives of Ontario F 229-308-0-180, AO 6592).

Page 142: *The Guide for Eaton Advertising*. Published by the T. Eaton Co. Ltd., 1950's. Used with permission of Sears Canada Ltd.

Page 143: Hargrave annex and store, July, 1951. (EA Archives of Ontario F 229-308-0-203, AO 6601).

Page 144: Eaton's parking building on Hargrave Street, 1958. (EA Archives of Ontario F 229-308-0-218, AO 6616).

Page 145: Eaton's Hargrave Street parking lot, 1955. (EA Archives of Ontario F 229-308-0-218, AO 6617).

Page 146: Eaton's credit cards. Courtesy Bruce Meisner. Used with permission of Sears Canada Inc.

Page 147: *RMS Titanic* signed menu card. (EA Archives of Ontario F 229-308-0-2, AO 6654).

Page 149: Eaton Groceteria on north Main Street (exterior), Winnipeg, 1929. (EA Archives of Ontario F 229-308-0-216, AO 6614).

Page 150 (left): Polo Park Shopping Centre exterior before opening, Winnipeg, May, 1968. (EA Archives of Ontario F 229-308-0-207, AO 6606).

Page 150 (top right): Mrs. J. D. Eaton, W. Weir, S. Juba at Polo Park store opening May 2, 1968. (EA Archives of Ontario F 229-308-0-208, AO 6607).

Page 151: Eaton's store St. Vital Centre exterior, October 17, 1979. (EA Archives of Ontario F 229-308-0-211, AO 6610).

Page 152 (top left): Eaton's Heavy Goods Store in Portage la Prairie, Manitoba, January, 1960. (EA Archives of Ontario F 229-308-0-168, AO 65781).

Page 152 (top right): Eaton's Order Office in Brandon, Manitoba, Store (interior), 1953. (EA Archives of Ontario F 229-308-0-168, AO 6580).

Page 152 (second from top on right): Eaton's Groceteria and TECO store in Brandon, Manitoba, 1928. (R.M. Coleman, freelance photographer, Brandon) (EA Archives of Ontario F 229-308-0-170, AO 6586).

Page 152 (second from bottom on right): Brandon, Manitoba, TECO store, 1928. (EA Archives of Ontario F 229-308-0-1708, AO 6590).

Page 152 (bottom right): Eaton's store exterior in Brandon, Manitoba, 1950. (EA Archives of Ontario F 229-308-0-172, AO 6589).

Page 152 (bottom left): Eaton's Order Office in Virden, Manitoba, January 20, 1956. (EA Archives of Ontario F 229-308-0-168, AO 6579).

Page 153: Eaton's refund cheque. Courtesy Bruce Meisner. Used with permission of Sears Canada Inc.

Page 154: Eaton's Research Bureau lab, Winnipeg, late 1940's. Courtesy Lillian Vadeboncoeur.

Page 155: Eaton's brand labels. *Contacts* (T. Eaton Co. Ltd., Winnipeg, July, 1960), page 14. Used with permission of Sears Canada Inc.

Page 156: Timothy Days event badge. Courtesy Bruce Meisner. Used with permission of Sears Canada Inc.

Page 157: Eaton's Service Building, Winnipeg, October, 1963. (Glen Robinson, photographer, Winnipeg) (EA Archives of Ontario F 229-308-0-219, AO 6620).

Page 158: (upper): Design from Eaton's box used with permission of Sears Canada Inc.

Page 158: (lower): Trans-Canada Sale logo used with permission of Sears Canada Inc.

Page 159: Timothy Days event badge. Courtesy Bruce Meisner. Used with permission of Sears Canada Inc.

Chapter 10: You'd Never Find a Better Place to Work (pages 160 to 177)

Page 160: Eaton family Christmas card. Courtesy Anne Elviss.

Page 162: Exterior of Eaton's Winnipeg store on the opening day – July 15, 1905. (EA Archives of Ontario F 229-308-0-201, AO 6600).

Page 163 (left): Eaton's employees curling. *Contacts* (T. Eaton Co. Ltd, Winnipeg, November 1967), page 11. Used with permission of Sears Canada Inc.

Page 163 (right): Eaton's employees bowling. *Contacts* (T. Eaton Co. Ltd, Winnipeg, issue date unknown). Used with permission of Sears Canada Inc.

Page 164: Burton Cummings. *Contacts* (T. Eaton Co. Ltd, Winnipeg, March, 1962), page 9. Used with permission of Sears Canada Inc.

Page 165: Delivery trucks. *Contacts* (T. Eaton Co. Ltd, Winnipeg, August, 1967), page 6. Used with permission of Sears Canada Inc.

Page 168: Customer information pamphlet published by the T. Eaton Co. Ltd., Winnipeg. Date unknown (probably 1940's). Courtesy Lillian Vadeboncoeur. Used with permission of Sears Canada Inc.

Page 169: Bruce Meisner was one of many Eatonians who wore period costumes to celebrate Timothy Days. Courtesy Bruce Meisner.

Page 170: Quarter-century watch. Courtesy Rita Valliquette.

Page 171: Quarter Century Club certificate presented to Betty Ralph on May 21, 1966. Courtesy Betty Ralph.

Page 175: Bruce Meisner and his nephew Austin Smith chat with Punkinhead. Courtesy Bruce Meisner.

Epilogue: The Big Store Closes Forever (pages 178 to 189)

Page 178: Teen Takeover Night, 1968. Courtesy Lillian Vadeboncoeur.

Page 180: Walter Wright standing under main floor clock, downtown store, October, 1999. Courtesy Walter L. Wright.

Page 181: Mall entrance to Polo Park store with the (upper) Eaton's (1999) and (lower) eatons (2000) signs. Courtesy Bruce Meisner. Used with permission of Sears Canada Inc.

Page 182: Moving the statue of Timothy Eaton to the True North Centre, April 2004. Courtesy James O'Connor, Private Eye Studios, Winnipeg.

Page 182: Quotation from Sears Canada, *Sears Canada: A Legacy of Quality, Value Service & Trust* (Sears Canada Inc, Toronto, 2001), page 96. Used with permission of Sears Canada Inc.

Page 184: *Last Four Days*. Winnipeg artist Guy St. Godard's depiction of one of the final opportunities for Winnipeggers to see the Big Store as part of the busy Portage Avenue scene. It was reproduced in 500 full-colour numbered prints

(approximately 23" by 16"). Courtesy Guy St. Godard, Guy St. Godard Art Studio, Winnipeg.

Page 186: Moving of Timothy Eaton statue. Courtesy James O'Connor, Private Eye Studios, Winnipeg.

Page 187: Demolition of the downtown store. Courtesy James O'Connor, Private Eye Studios, Winnipeg.

Page 189: Winnipeg Transit signs are a reminder of Eaton's as the MTS Centre nears completion. Courtesy Charles Shilliday (Image Management).

Appendices (pages 190 to 196)

Page 191: Statue of Timothy Eaton during the final days of the downtown store. Courtesy Walter L. Wright.

Page 193: Demolition of the downtown store. Courtesy James O'Connor, Private Eye Studios, Winnipeg.

Page 194: Eaton's catalogue, Spring and Summer, 1976, page 5. Used with permission of Sears Canada Inc.

Page 195 (upper): Timothy Eaton. From various publications of the T. Eaton Co. Ltd, Toronto. Courtesy Giles Bugailiskis. Used with permission of Sears Canada Inc.

Page 195 (lower): Sir John Eaton. From various publications of the T. Eaton Co. Ltd, Toronto. Courtesy Giles Bugailiskis. Used with permission of Sears Canada Inc.

Page 196 (upper): Robert Young Eaton. From various publications of the T. Eaton Co. Ltd, Toronto. Courtesy Giles Bugailiskis. Used with permission of Sears Canada Inc.

Page 196 (lower): John David Eaton. From various publications of the T. Eaton Co. Ltd, Toronto. Courtesy Giles Bugailiskis. Used with permission of Sears Canada Inc.

Page 197: Time Building fire. A curtain of water from hoses manned by Eaton's volunteer firefighters cascades down the walls of the store. (EA Archives of Ontario F 229-308-0-3, AO 6556).